THE OLDER HOUSE

TIME LIFE BOOKS ®

Other Publications:

AMERICAN COUNTRY

VOYAGE THROUGH THE UNIVERSE

THE THIRD REICH

THE TIME-LIFE GARDENER'S GUIDE

MYSTERIES OF THE UNKNOWN

TIME FRAME

FIX IT YOURSELF

FITNESS, HEALTH & NUTRITION

SUCCESSFUL PARENTING

HEALTHY HOME COOKING

UNDERSTANDING COMPUTERS

LIBRARY OF NATIONS

THE ENCHANTED WORLD

THE KODAK LIBRARY OF CREATIVE PHOTOGRAPHY

GREAT MEALS IN MINUTES

THE CIVIL WAR

PLANET EARTH

COLLECTOR'S LIBRARY OF THE CIVIL WAR

THE EPIC OF FLIGHT

THE GOOD COOK

WORLD WAR II

HOME REPAIR AND IMPROVEMENT

THE OLD WEST

THE OLDER HOUSE

TIME-LIFE BOOKS
ALEXANDRIA, VIRGINIA

Fix It Yourself was produced by
ST. REMY PRESS

MANAGING EDITOR	Kenneth Winchester
MANAGING ART DIRECTOR	Pierre Léveillé

Staff for *The Older House*

Series Editor	Brian Parsons
Editor	Marc Cassini
Series Art Director	Diane Denoncourt
Art Director	Francine Lemieux
Research Editors	Naomi Fukuyama, Donald Harman
Designers	Luc Germain, Julie Léger
Contributing Writers	Andrea Johnston, Randy Lake, Patricia Ryffranck, Frances Slingerland
Contributing Illustrators	Gérard Mariscalchi, Jacques Proulx
Cover	Robert Monté
Index	Christine M. Jacobs
Administrator	Natalie Watanabe
Production Manager	Michelle Turbide
Coordinator	Dominique Gagné
Systems Coordinator	Jean-Luc Roy
Photographer	Robert Chartier

Time-Life Books Inc. is a wholly owned subsidiary of
THE TIME INC. BOOK COMPANY

President and Chief Executive Officer	Kelso F. Sutton
President, Time Inc. Books Direct	Christopher T. Linen

TIME-LIFE BOOKS INC.

Managing Editor	Thomas H. Flaherty
Director of Editorial Resources	Elise D. Ritter-Clough
Director of Photography and Research	John Conrad Weiser
Editorial Board	Dale Brown, Roberta Conlan, Laura Foreman, Lee Hassig, Jim Hicks, Blaine Marshall, Rita Mullin, Henry Woodhead
PUBLISHER	Joseph J. Ward
Associate Publisher	Trevor Lunn
Editorial Director	Donia Steele
Marketing Director	Regina Hall
Director of Design	Louis Klein
Production Manager	Marlene Zack
Supervisor of Quality Control	James King

Editorial Operations

Production	Celia Beattie
Library	Louise D. Forstall
Correspondents	Elisabeth Kraemer-Singh (Bonn); Christina Lieberman (New York); Maria Vincenza Aloisi (Paris); Ann Natanson (Rome).

THE CONSULTANTS

Consulting editor **David L. Harrison** served as an editor for several Time-Life Books do-it-yourself series, including *Home Repair and Improvement*, *The Encyclopedia of Gardening* and *The Art of Sewing*.

Richard Day, a do-it-yourself writer for over a quarter of a century, is a founder of the National Association of Home and Workshop writers and is the author of several home repair books.

James S. Facinelli, C.S.R., a specialist in the restoration of old houses, offers consulting, design, custom millwork and contracting services through the company Restorations Unlimited, Inc. in Elizabethville, PA.

John Leeke has restored historic homes for the past 20 years as tradesman and contractor, as well as consulted on historic preservation projects. He is an editor for *The Old House Journal* and publishes *Practical Restoration Reports*, a technical series on preservation topics.

Mark M. Steele, a professional home inspector and construction consultant in the Washington, D.C. area, is an editor of home improvement articles and books.

William J. Warren is the president of Colorado Front Range Building Inspection Service, a company that routinely performs inspection, hazardous materials assessment and consulting work throughout the western United States. He has also written articles on various topics, including the inspection of older homes.

Library of Congress Cataloging-in-Publication Data
The Older House
     p. cm. – (Fix it yourself)
Includes index.
ISBN 0-8094-6288-5 (trade).
ISBN 0-8094-6289-3 (lib. bdg.).
1. Dwellings—Maintenance and repair—Amateurs' manuals.
I. Time-Life Books. II. Series.
TH4817.3.O44 1991
643'. 7—dc20   90-21497
                         CIP

For information about any Time-Life book, please write:
Reader Information
Time-Life Customer Service
P.O. Box C-32068
Richmond, Virginia
23261-2068

CONTENTS

HOW TO USE THIS BOOK

The Older House is divided into three sections. The Emergency Guide on pages 8 to 13 provides you with information that can be indispensable, even lifesaving, in the event of a household emergency. Take the time to study this section *before* you need the important advice it contains.

The Repairs section—the heart of the book—is a comprehensive approach to troubleshooting and repairing problems with an older home. Shown below are four sample pages from the chapter entitled Doors, with captions describing the various features of the book and how they work.

For example, if one of your top-hung pocket doors does not open or close freely, the Troubleshooting Guide on page 42 will suggest a number of possible causes and direct you, for instance, to page 48 for detailed, step-by-step instructions on how to adjust the roller assemblies. Each job has been rated by degree of difficulty and by the average time it will take for a do-it-yourselfer to complete. Keep in mind that this rating is only a suggestion. Before deciding on whether you should attempt a repair, read all the instructions carefully. Then, be guided by your own confidence, and the tools and time available to you. To remove a door

Introductory text
Describes a typical feature of an older house, its most common problems, and basic repair approaches.

Anatomy diagrams
Locate and describe a feature of an older house and its construction.

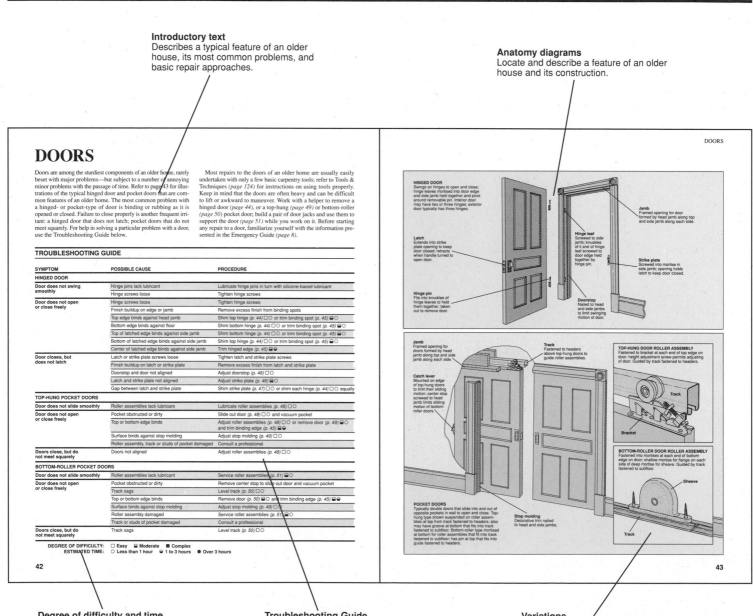

Degree of difficulty and time
Rate the complexity of each repair and how much time the job should take for a homeowner with average do-it-yourself skills.

Troubleshooting Guide
To use this chart, locate the symptom that most closely resembles the problem with your older house in column 1, review the possible causes in column 2, then follow the recommended procedure in column 3. Simple fixes may be explained on the chart; in most cases, you will be directed to an illustrated, step-by-step repair sequence.

Variations
Differences in the construction of an older house feature are described throughout the book, particularly if a repair procedure varies from one type or situation to another.

and trim an edge, for example, you may wish to call for professional help. You will still have saved time and money by diagnosing the problem yourself.

Most of the repairs in *The Older House* can be made with standard household tools and equipment. Any special tool required is indicated in the Troubleshooting Guide. Basic tools—and the proper way to use them—along with information on fasteners, electrical safety and finishes is presented in the Tools & Techniques section starting on page 124. If you are a novice at home repair, read this chapter in preparation for a job.

Making repairs to an older house can be simple and worry-free if you work logically and systematically, following all safety tips and precautions. Always use the proper tool for the job—and use it correctly. Wear the recommended safety gear for the job: safety goggles when there is a risk of eye injury; work gloves with sharp or rough materials; rubber gloves with chemicals or electrical equipment that may shock; respiratory protection against dust or hazardous vapors. Concentrate on the job and take periodic breaks to inspect your work; do not rush or take short cuts. Keep children and pets away from the work area.

Name of repair
You will be referred by the Troubleshooting Guide to the first page of a specific repair.

Tools and techniques
General information on carpentry techniques and working safely with electricity is covered in the Tools & Techniques chapter *(page 124)*. When a specific tool or method is required for a job, it is described within the step-by-step repair.

Insets
Provide close-up views of specific steps and illustrate variations in techniques or situations.

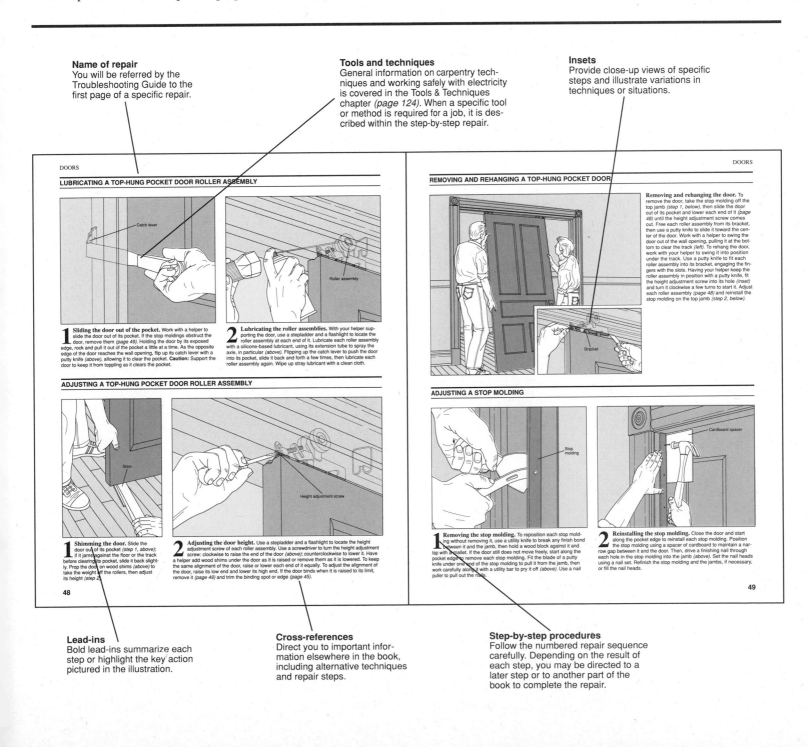

Lead-ins
Bold lead-ins summarize each step or highlight the key action pictured in the illustration.

Cross-references
Direct you to important information elsewhere in the book, including alternative techniques and repair steps.

Step-by-step procedures
Follow the numbered repair sequence carefully. Depending on the result of each step, you may be directed to a later step or to another part of the book to complete the repair.

EMERGENCY GUIDE

Preventing problems in older house repair. Making repairs to your older home need not be any more dangerous than working on a newer house. Most accidents arise from carelessness: the improper use of tools, unsafe work habits at heights and the mishandling of hazardous materials. The list of safety tips at right covers basic guidelines for any older house repair. Take the time to set up properly for a repair, gathering together the tools, equipment and materials you need; always use any safety gear recommended. Work methodically; never hurry through a job.

Accidents, however, can befall even the most careful worker. Sharp tools can cut skin. Wood can cause splinters. Many finishing products contain chemicals that can emit toxic fumes, causing dizziness, faintness or nausea. Prepare yourself to handle emergencies before they occur by reading the Troubleshooting Guide on page 9; it places emergency procedures at your fingertips, providing quick-action steps to take and referring you to pages 10 to 13 for detailed instructions. Also review the chapter entitled Tools & Techniques *(page 124)*; it provides valuable information on repair procedures and the safe use of tools.

Be prepared to act quickly in any emergency requiring you to shut off electricity *(page 10)*; know how to treat a victim of electrical shock *(page 12)*. Fire is a life-threatening emergency that can be deprived of its element of surprise by installing smoke detectors throughout your home. Have the correct fire extinguisher ready to snuff out a blaze before it gains the upper hand; learn how to use it before you need it *(page 11)*. Do not move the victim of a fall if you suspect he has suffered a spinal injury; call an ambulance immediately, then cover him with a blanket to regulate body temperature in case of shock *(page 12)* until medical help arrives.

Keep in mind the potential hazards of any tool or material you use. Store a well-stocked first-aid kit in a convenient, accessible location of your home; in the event of a medical emergency, you will want anyone to be able to find it quickly to administer first aid *(page 13)*. Keep people away from any repair area and keep an adequate stock of clean-up supplies on hand: cat litter or fuller's earth and absorbent cloths for mopping up spills of chemicals. If you act quickly to clean up spills *(page 11)*, harm and damage can be prevented. Put your tools and materials safely away as soon as you finish using them—well out of the reach of children and pets.

If you are ever in doubt about your ability to handle an emergency, do not hesitate to call for help. Post the telephone numbers for your local fire department, poison control center, hospital emergency room, ambulance service as well as your physician near the telephone; in most areas, dial 911 in the event of a life-threatening emergency. Also seek technical help when you need it; even in a situation that is not an emergency, a qualified building professional can answer questions about the condition of your older home.

SAFETY TIPS

1. Before beginning any repair in this book, read the entire procedure; familiarize yourself with the safety information.

2. Choose the right tool for the job and use it correctly. Refer to Tools & Techniques *(page 124)* for instructions on the use and maintenance of tools.

3. Wear the proper safety gear for the job: safety goggles with power tools or hammers and for work overhead; work gloves with sharp or rough materials; rubber gloves with chemical materials; respiratory protection with tools that create dust; hearing protection with noisy tools.

4. Concentrate on the job; do not rush or take short cuts. Take periodic breaks to rest and inspect your work.

5. Keep children and pets away from your job site.

6. Use only power tools and extension cords that bear a recognized seal of approval: the UL (Underwriters Laboratories) or CSA (Canadian Standards Association) stamp. Outdoors, use extension cords rated for outdoors—marked W or WP.

7. Work with power tools only in dry conditions. Plug a power tool only into an outlet protected by a GFCI (ground-fault circuit interrupter). Never cut off or bypass the third (grounding) prong of a plug on a power cord.

8. Never force a tool to work beyond its capability. Do not leave a tool on the ground where it can be tripped over. When working with a cutting tool, stand to one side and never cut directly toward yourself.

9. Store chemical products in airtight containers away from sources of heat. Store cloths soaked with chemicals for disposal in airtight metal or glass containers—preferably outdoors, out of direct sunlight.

10. Follow basic safety rules for working on ladders and on the roof *(page 124)*. Work with a helper or within earshot of someone else and only in good weather conditions—never when it is wet or windy. Do not attempt any repair on a roof if it is wet or laden with snow or ice.

11. Work outdoors only in good weather conditions, never when it is wet or windy; wear a hat if it is hot and sunny.

12. Keep a first-aid kit on hand; stock it with mild antiseptic, sterile gauze dressings and bandages, adhesive tape and bandages, scissors, tweezers and a packet of needles.

13. Have a portable ABC-rated fire extinguisher on hand and know how to use it *(page 11)*.

14. Ensure that your home is equipped with a judicious number of smoke detectors.

15. Post the telephone numbers for your local emergency services near the telephone: the fire department, the hospital emergency room, the ambulance service, the poison control center and your physician.

TROUBLESHOOTING GUIDE

PROBLEM	PROCEDURE
Electrical fire: flames or smoke from power tool, extension cord or outlet	Have someone call fire department immediately
	If fire large or not contained or if flames come from inside ceiling or wall, evacuate house and call fire department from home of neighbor
	Control fire using ABC fire extinguisher (p. 11)
	Shut off electricity (p. 10)
Electrical shock	If victim immobilized by live current, knock him free of source using dry wooden tool (p. 12)
	Have someone call for medical help immediately
	If victim not breathing, administer artificial respiration
	If victim has no pulse, administer cardiopulmonary resuscitation (CPR) only if qualified
	If victim breathing, has pulse and has no back or neck injury, place him in recovery position (p. 12)
Electrical fixture, tool or appliance sparks, shocks or hot to touch	Shut off electricity (p. 10)
	Locate and repair cause of electrical problem before using fixture, tool or appliance
Chemical fire: flames or smoke from paint or other chemical product	Have someone call fire department immediately
	If fire large or not contained, evacuate house and call fire department from home of neighbor
	Control fire using ABC fire extinguisher (p. 11)
Exposure to toxic chemical vapors: headache, dizziness, faintness, fatigue or nausea	Treat exposure to toxic chemical vapors (p. 13)
Chemical or other poison ingested	Do not give victim anything to eat or drink or induce vomiting unless advised by physician
	Immediately call local poison control center, hospital emergency room or physician for instructions; provide information on victim's age and weight, and type and amount of poison ingested
	If medical treatment necessary, bring product container with you
Chemical splashed in eye	Flush chemical from eye (p. 13)
	Cover eyes with sterile gauze and seek medical help immediately
Chemical spilled on skin	Immediately brush off dry product or wipe off liquid product
	Wash skin thoroughly with soap and water
	If skin irritation develops, seek medical attention
Chemical spilled in work area	For spill of more than 1 quart of flammable chemical, evacuate house and call fire department from home of neighbor
	Otherwise, clean up spilled chemical (p. 11)
Fall from roof or ladder	Do not move victim if spinal injury suspected
	Have someone call for medical help immediately
	Treat victim of fall (p. 12)
Object embedded in skin	Do not attempt to remove embedded object
	Immobilize embedded object and seek medical help immediately
Splinter	Pull out splinter (p. 13)
	If splinter cannot be removed or wound becomes infected, seek medical attention
Cut	Treat cut (p. 13)
	If bleeding persists, cut deep or gaping, or wound becomes infected, seek medical attention
Bruise	Apply ice pack to reduce swelling
	If pain does not diminish or swelling persists, seek medical attention
Particle in eye	If particle on cornea, embedded or adhered, or cannot be seen, cover eyes with sterile gauze and seek medical help immediately
	Otherwise, remove particle from eye using moistened tip of clean cloth or tissue
	If particle cannot be removed, cover eyes with sterile gauze and seek medical help immediately

SHUTTING OFF THE ELECTRICITY

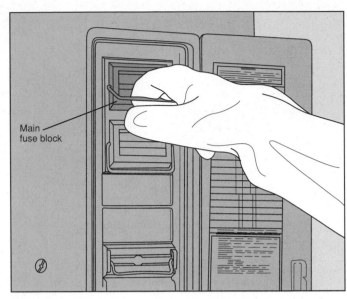

Shutting off the system at a main fuse block. Caution: Work only in dry conditions; if the area at the service panel is damp, stand on a dry board and wear rubber boots. Wear rubber gloves, work only with one hand and avoid touching any metal. Locate the main fuse block, a large pull-out block usually at the top of a fuse-type service panel. Grip the handle of the main fuse block and pull it out *(above)*, shutting off the system; if there is more than one main fuse block, pull out each one. To restore electricity, push the main fuse block back in until it snaps into place.

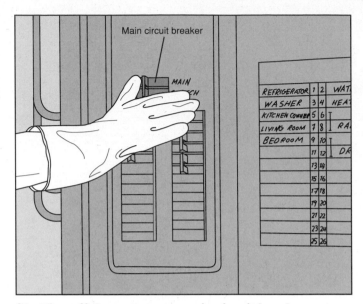

Shutting off the system at a main circuit breaker. Caution: Work only in dry conditions; if the area at the service panel is damp, stand on a dry board and wear rubber boots. Wear rubber gloves, work only with one hand and avoid touching any metal. Locate the main circuit breaker, typically a linked, double breaker of a breaker-type service panel isolated above or at the top of the other circuit breakers and marked MAIN. Flip the main circuit breaker to OFF *(above)*, shutting off the system. To restore electricity, flip the main circuit breaker fully to OFF, then to ON.

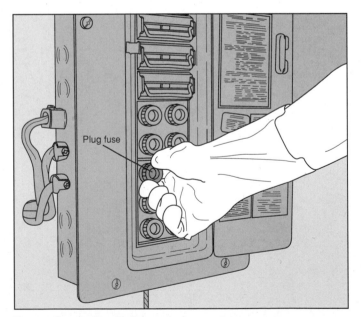

Removing a circuit fuse. Caution: Work only in dry conditions; if the area at the service panel is damp, stand on a dry board and wear rubber boots. Wear rubber gloves, work only with one hand and avoid touching any metal. Locate the plug fuse for the circuit; if the circuits are not labeled, shut off the system *(step above)*. Otherwise, remove the fuse for the circuit, shutting off electricity to it; grasp the fuse only by the insulated rim and unscrew it *(above)*. To restore electricity to the circuit, screw the fuse back in.

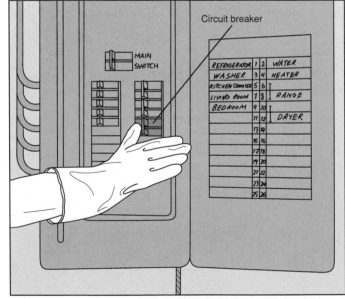

Shutting off a circuit breaker. Caution: Work only in dry conditions; if the area at the service panel is damp, stand on a dry board and wear rubber boots. Wear rubber gloves, work only with one hand and avoid touching any metal. Locate the circuit breaker for the circuit; if the circuits are not labeled, shut off the system *(step above)*. Otherwise, flip the circuit breaker for the circuit to OFF *(above)*, shutting off electricity to it. To restore electricity to the circuit, flip the circuit breaker fully to OFF, then to ON.

CONTROLLING A FIRE

Using a fire extinguisher. Call the fire department immediately; if flames or smoke come from inside the chimney, a wall or a ceiling, evacuate the house and call from the home of a neighbor. To extinguish a small chemical, electrical or other fire, use a dry-chemical fire extinguisher rated ABC. Position yourself 6 to 10 feet from the fire with your back to the nearest exit. Holding the extinguisher upright, pull the lock pin out of the handle and aim the nozzle at the base of the flames. Squeeze the handle and spray in a quick side-to-side motion *(left)* until the fire is out. Watch for "flash-back," or rekindling, and be prepared to spray again. If the fire spreads, leave the house. Dispose of burned waste following the advice of the fire department. Have the extinguisher recharged after every use; replace it if it is non-rechargeable.

HANDLING A CHEMICAL SPILL

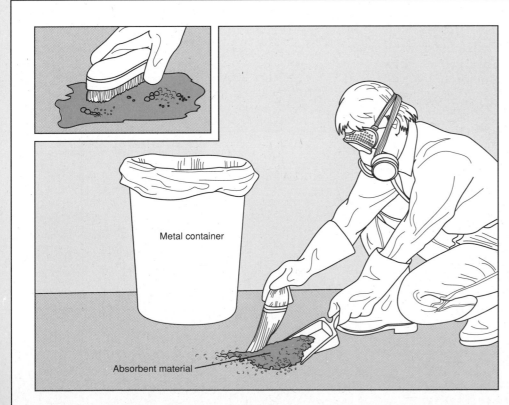

Cleaning up spilled chemicals.
For a spill of more than 1 quart of a product labeled EXTREMELY FLAMMABLE, call the fire department immediately; otherwise, ventilate the site, turn off nearby sources of heat and electrical units, and keep others away. Clean up the spill wearing rubber boots, rubber gloves and safety goggles; also a respirator if the spill is of a product labeled with POISON vapor or ventilation warnings. Soak up a small spill with cloths or paper towels, disposing of them in a metal container double-lined with heavy-duty plastic trash bags. Soak up a large spill by covering it with an absorbent material such as fuller's earth or cat litter. When the absorbent material soaks up the spill, sweep it up into a dustpan *(left)*, disposing of it the same way. Clean up remaining residue using an appropriate solvent, rinsing the site thoroughly with water; scrub using a stiff-bristled fiber brush *(inset)* or wipe with a cloth. Seal the waste materials for safe disposal following the environmental regulations of your community.

TREATING A VICTIM OF ELECTRICAL SHOCK

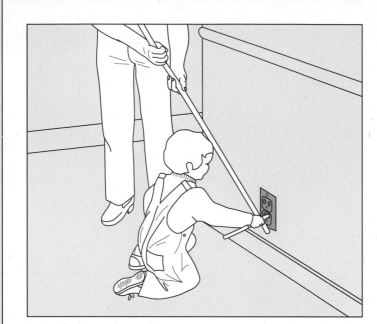

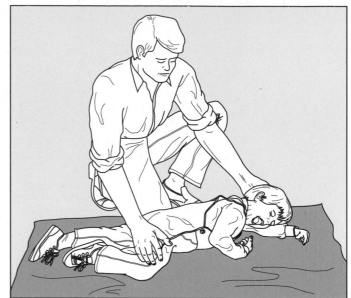

Freeing a victim from a live current. Usually a person who contacts a live current is thrown back from the electrical source; sometimes, however, his muscles contract involuntarily around it. **Caution:** Do not touch the victim or the electrical source. Immediately stop the flow of current, shutting off electricity to the system or circuit *(page 10)*. If the electricity cannot be shut off immediately, use a wooden broom handle or other dry wooden tool to knock the victim free of the electrical source *(above)*.

Handling a victim of electrical shock. Call for medical help immediately, then check the victim's breathing and pulse. If there is no breathing, give mouth-to-mouth resuscitation; if there is no pulse, give cardiopulmonary resuscitation (CPR) only if you are qualified. If the victim is breathing and has no neck or back injury, place him in the recovery position *(above)*. Tilt the head back with the face to one side and the tongue forward to maintain an open airway. Keep the victim calm until help arrives.

TREATING A VICTIM OF A FALL

Handling a victim of a fall. Call for medical help immediately. Reassure the victim that help is on the way, then cover him with a blanket *(left)*, helping regulate his body temperature in case of shock. **Caution:** Do not move the victim if a spinal injury is suspected: severe pain in the back, neck or head; loss of feeling or tingling in the limbs; loss of bladder or bowel control; blood or other fluid flowing from the ears or nose; or, loss of consciousness. Until medical help arrives, help the victim to stay calm and keep others from crowding around him. Do not give the victim anything to eat or drink.

PROVIDING MINOR FIRST AID

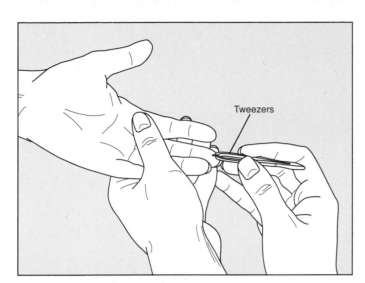

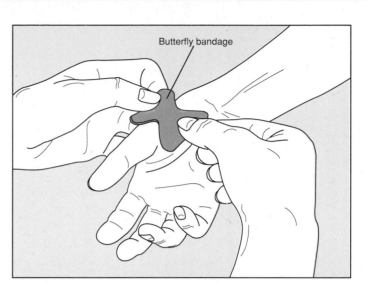

Butterfly bandage

Tweezers

Pulling out a splinter. Wash the skin around the splinter using soap and water. A metal splinter may require treatment for tetanus; seek medical help. Otherwise, sterilize a needle and tweezers with rubbing alcohol or a match flame. Ease the splinter from the skin using the needle, then pull it out with the tweezers *(above)* and wash the wound with soap and water. If the splinter cannot be removed or the wound becomes infected, seek medical attention.

Treating a cut. Wrap the wound in a clean cloth and apply direct pressure with your hand to stop any bleeding; keep the wound elevated. If the cloth becomes blood-soaked, wrap another cloth over it. If bleeding persists or the wound is deep or gaping, seek medical help. Otherwise, wash the wound with soap and water, then bandage it; for a narrow, shallow wound, draw its edges closed with a butterfly bandage *(above)*. If the wound becomes infected, seek medical attention.

HANDLING EXPOSURE TO CHEMICALS

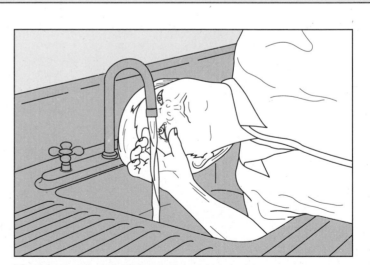

Treating exposure to chemicals vapors. Exposure to toxic vapors can cause headache, dizziness, faintness, fatigue or nausea; at the first sign of a symptom, leave the work area to get fresh air. Loosen your clothing at the neck, chest and waist; remove any clothing splashed by a chemical. If you feel faint, sit with your head lowered between your knees *(above)*. Have someone ventilate the work area and close all chemical containers. If any symptom persists, seek medical attention.

Flushing a chemical from the eye. Holding the eyelids apart with the forefinger and thumb of one hand, flush the eye thoroughly for at least 15 minutes under a gentle flow of cool water from a faucet *(above)* or pitcher; tilt the head to one side to prevent the chemical from being washed into the uninjured eye. If you are outdoors, flush the eye the same way using a garden hose. Gently cover both eyes with sterile gauze dressings and seek medical help immediately.

YOUR OLDER HOUSE

The classic older home was constructed during a bygone period of relatively low costs for materials and labor, contributing to its usual uniqueness and superior craftsmanship. Glinting leaded-glass windows, sliding pocket doors, detailed plaster cornices, elaborate wood trim, solid hardwood flooring, polished brass light fixtures and other hallmarks of an older home are irresistible allures—but charms that can be easily obscured when eventual problems inevitably arise. For, however incomparable or well-built, an older home is still nonetheless vulnerable to the deteriorating forces of time, weather and routine daily life.

Shown at right is an illustration of a typical older home, with its usual features and their common problems highlighted in brief captions on chapters of this book. Refer to the specific chapters for more details on the construction of features particular to an older home, as well for information on the repairs that can be undertaken to remedy their problems—and preserve the distinctive character of an older home. Handling a minor irritant of an older home as promptly as possible can help prevent it from mushrooming into a major aggravation.

Repairing your older home can be as individual a challenge as the structure itself; many of its features are likely to predate the building standards and codes of today. Yet, the satisfaction of a repair that respects and maintains the authenticity of your older home is usually more than ample reward for the effort or patience the repair may entail. Carefully evaluate a problem and plan a strategy before carrying out a repair, gathering together all the tools and the supplies needed. Confirm the availability of replacement materials, a hunt that can be time-consuming and wearying; for information and ideas on sources, refer to page 127.

Before undertaking a repair to your older home, identify and remedy any underlying cause of the problem to prevent it from recurring. For example, patching or replacing a section of the roofing or an exterior wall is a repair that, however much needed or worthwhile, does not correct a damaged gutter or downspout, a perforated water pipe or other cause of the problem—and is a repair that is likely to be needed again prematurely unless the cause of the problem is located and fixed.

When performing a repair to your older home, be prepared for the possibility of encountering unexpected problems. For example, patching a section of an interior wall may prompt the discovery of deteriorated studs, damaged electrical wiring or leaky plumbing pipes behind it. Or, replacing a section of hardwood flooring may lead to the uncovering of a weakened or rotted subfloor under it. Arrange for a professional evaluation before proceeding with a repair to your older home that exposes hidden or unanticipated damage. Also seek a professional assessment if a structural problem is suspected: extreme bulging of the interior walls or ceilings or sagging of the flooring, or extensive damage to the foundation, exterior walls or roofing.

EXTERIOR WALLS AND TRIM *(page 16)*
Repair or replace damaged clapboards, shingles and trim. Patch cracks and holes in stucco. Repoint deteriorated mortar joints and replace damaged bricks.

FAUCETS AND PIPES *(page 92)*
Replace the seat washer or stem packing or dress the seat of a leaky or drippy faucet. Plug pinholes, repair joints and replace corroded sections of leaky pipes.

WINDOWS *(page 52)*
Unjam windows that cannot be opened. Replace broken sash cords or chains and adjust or trim sashes of windows that bind or otherwise do not open and close properly. Replace deteriorated glazing compound, reinforce bowed sashes and replace broken panes of leaded-glass windows. Replace broken panes of skylights.

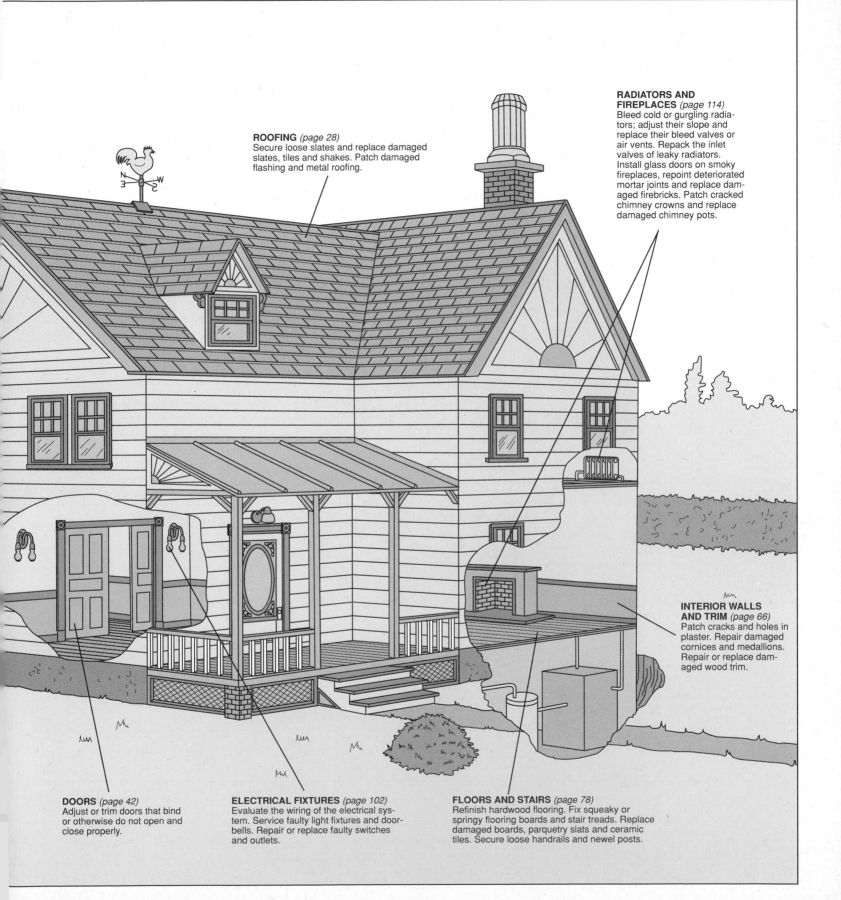

ROOFING *(page 28)*
Secure loose slates and replace damaged slates, tiles and shakes. Patch damaged flashing and metal roofing.

RADIATORS AND FIREPLACES *(page 114)*
Bleed cold or gurgling radiators; adjust their slope and replace their bleed valves or air vents. Repack the inlet valves of leaky radiators. Install glass doors on smoky fireplaces, repoint deteriorated mortar joints and replace damaged firebricks. Patch cracked chimney crowns and replace damaged chimney pots.

INTERIOR WALLS AND TRIM *(page 66)*
Patch cracks and holes in plaster. Repair damaged cornices and medallions. Repair or replace damaged wood trim.

DOORS *(page 42)*
Adjust or trim doors that bind or otherwise do not open and close properly.

ELECTRICAL FIXTURES *(page 102)*
Evaluate the wiring of the electrical system. Service faulty light fixtures and doorbells. Repair or replace faulty switches and outlets.

FLOORS AND STAIRS *(page 78)*
Refinish hardwood flooring. Fix squeaky or springy flooring boards and stair treads. Replace damaged boards, parquetry slats and ceramic tiles. Secure loose handrails and newel posts.

EXTERIOR WALLS AND TRIM

An older home typically boasts exterior walls of clapboards, wood shingles, bricks or stucco, traditional materials that usually weather gracefully over the years; for details on their common construction, refer to the illustrations on page 17. With proper maintenance, many problems with the exterior walls and trim can be prevented. Keep gutters and downspouts clear of debris. Thwart mildew and rot by pruning back vegetation to provide sunlight exposure and air circulation. Refinish wood surfaces routinely every 2 to 5 years. Thoroughly inspect the exterior walls and trim each spring and fall to detect minor problems early; for help in undertaking a repair, consult the Troubleshooting Guide below.

Most repairs to the exterior walls and trim of an older home can be undertaken with only a few basic carpentry tools; the materials needed are usually readily available at a building supply center. Refer to Tools & Techniques *(page 124)* for instructions on using tools properly, as well as for information on working safely from a ladder, mixing stucco, matching mortar color and replicating textured surfaces. When undertaking a repair, keep in mind that the cause of a problem may be damage elsewhere—the roofing, a gutter or downspout, or the caulk along a window or door, for example. Consult a professional for help in locating the cause of a problem, especially of one that recurs.

TROUBLESHOOTING GUIDE

SYMPTOM	POSSIBLE CAUSE	PROCEDURE
CLAPBOARDS		
Board loose	Fastener popped	Secure clapboard *(p. 18)* □ ○
Board split, cracked, dented or gouged	Normal settlement; temperature and humidity changes; accidental blow or impact	Patch clapboard *(p. 18)* □ ○ or replace section of clapboard *(p. 19)* ▬ ○
Board finish peeling or lifting; wood spongy, pitted or crumbling	Wood damaged by rot	Patch clapboard *(p. 18)* □ ○ or replace section of clapboard *(p. 19)* ▬ ○
	Wood damaged by insects	Consult a professional
WOOD SHINGLES		
Shingle loose	Fastener popped	Secure shingle with galvanized nails
Shingle split, cracked, dented or gouged	Normal settlement; temperature and humidity changes; accidental blow or impact	Replace wood shingle *(p. 20)* □ ○ or replace section of wood shingles *(p. 21)* ▬ ●
Shingle finish peeling or lifting; wood spongy, pitted or crumbling	Wood damaged by rot	Replace wood shingle *(p. 20)* □ ○ or replace section of wood shingles *(p. 21)* ▬ ●
	Wood damaged by insects	Consult a professional
STUCCO		
Crack: damaged surface up to 1 inch wide	Normal settlement; temperature and humidity changes; accidental blow or impact	Patch stucco *(p. 22)* □ ○
Hole: damaged section up to 2 square feet	Normal settlement; temperature and humidity changes; accidental blow or impact	Replace section of stucco *(p. 22)* ▬ ●
Crack wider than 1 inch or hole more than 2 feet square	Uneven settlement; structural damage	Consult a professional
BRICKS		
Mortar joint loose, cracked or crumbling	Normal settlement; temperature and humidity changes; accidental blow or impact	Repoint bricks *(p. 24)* □ ○
Brick loose	Mortar joints or brick damaged	Replace brick *(p. 25)* ▬ ◕
Brick cracked or crumbling	Normal settlement; temperature and humidity changes; accidental blow or impact	Replace brick *(p. 25)* ▬ ◕
Brick efflorescing (white, powdery deposits)	Temperature and humidity changes	Clean brick using scrub brush and water
WOOD TRIM		
Trim loose	Fastener popped	Secure trim with galvanized nails or screws
Trim split, cracked, dented or gouged	Normal settlement; temperature and humidity changes; accidental blow or impact	Patch wood trim *(p. 27)* ▬ ◕
Trim finish peeling or lifting; wood spongy, pitted or crumbling	Wood damaged by rot	Patch wood trim *(p. 27)* ▬ ◕
	Wood damaged by insects	Consult a professional

DEGREE OF DIFFICULTY: □ Easy ▬ Moderate ■ Complex
ESTIMATED TIME: ○ Less than 1 hour ◕ 1 to 3 hours ● Over 3 hours

CLAPBOARDS

Overlapping, horizontal rows or courses of boards nailed to studs or to sheathing installed on studs; butt joints between ends of boards offset each course to prevent water penetration.

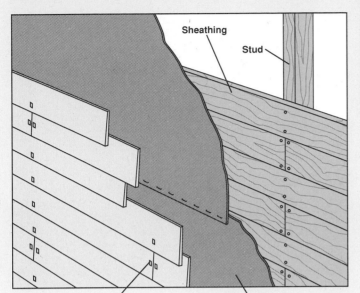

Nail
Usually rectangular, wrought-iron or galvanized box type; boards of each course commonly face-nailed about 1 inch from bottom edge to clear overlapped top edge of boards of course below.

Building paper
Overlapping, horizontal rows of red rosin or tar paper usually installed on sheathing.

WOOD SHINGLES

Overlapping, horizontal rows or courses of shingles nailed to studs or to sheathing installed on studs; 1/4-inch spaces or keyways between shingles offset by 1 1/2 inches each course to prevent water penetration. Doubled-course shingles shown have overcourse about 1/2 inch below undercourse.

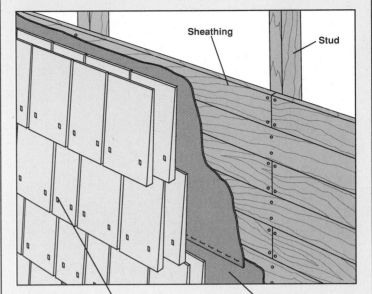

Nail
Usually rectangular, wrought-iron or galvanized box type; shingles of each course commonly face-nailed about 2 inches from bottom edge to clear overlapped top edge of shingles of course below.

Building paper
Overlapping, horizontal rows of red rosin or tar paper usually installed on sheathing.

STUCCO

Mixes of portland cement, lime, sand and water applied in successive coats to metal lath held by self-furring nails to sheathing installed on studs.

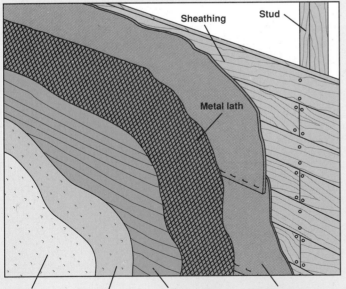

Finish coat
Surface layer at least 1/8 inch thick; typically textured.

Brown coat
Intermediate layer about 1/2 inch thick.

Scratch coat
Base layer about 1/2 inch thick; forms keys in spaces of lath.

Building paper
Overlapping, horizontal rows of red rosin or tar paper usually installed on sheathing.

BRICKS

Horizontal rows or courses of bricks held together with mortar; 3/8-inch joints between bricks offset each course. Single-tiered bricks shown held by wall ties to studs or to sheathing installed on studs.

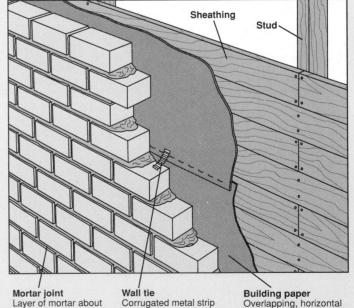

Mortar joint
Layer of mortar about 3/8 inch thick bonds adjacent bricks, providing watertight barrier.

Wall tie
Corrugated metal strip set in mortar of single-tiered bricks and nailed to sheathing or studs every 16 inches vertically and 24 inches horizontally.

Building paper
Overlapping, horizontal rows of red rosin or tar paper usually installed on sheathing.

PATCHING A CLAPBOARD

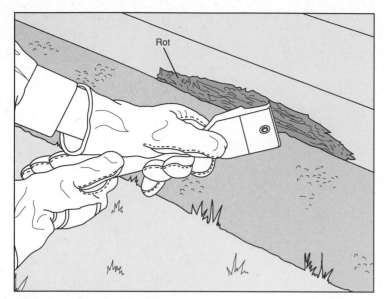

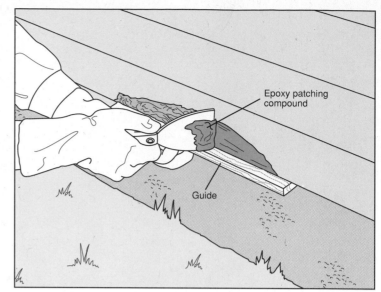

1 Preparing the damaged surface. Test the damaged surface for rot if it is spongy, pitted or crumbling, gray or darkly discolored, or its finish is peeling or lifting. Press an awl into the damaged surface and pry up the fibers; if the wood is soft and gives way, crumbling instead of splintering, it is weakened by rot. If rot penetrates the board, replace the damaged section *(page 19)*; if rot is extensive, consult a siding professional. Otherwise, wear work gloves and safety goggles to remove the damaged fibers with a paint scraper *(above)*, continuing until firm, healthy wood is reached.

2 Patching the damaged surface. Buy epoxy patching compound at a building supply center and apply it following the manufacturer's instructions. Wearing rubber gloves, use a putty knife to work compound into the damaged surface, overfilling it slightly. Scrape off excess compound with the putty knife, using a wood block as a guide along an edge, if necessary *(above)*. To texture the patch to match the surrounding surface, lightly score it with the blade of the putty knife or rake it using a wire brush. Let the compound cure, then sand the patch and finish it to match the surrounding surface.

SECURING A CLAPBOARD

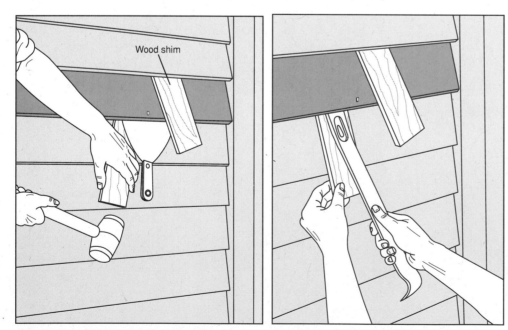

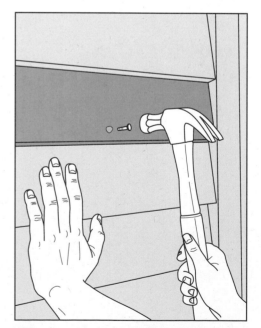

1 Removing old nails. If the nails of a board are rusty, replace them. To reposition a board or replace its nails, work the blade of a wide putty knife far enough along its top edge to fit in a wood shim. Fit in a wood shim along the bottom edge of the board the same way, tapping it with a mallet *(above, left)*. Raise the nail heads by pulling out the bottom edge of the board with a pry bar, using the shim to protect the adjacent surface *(above, right)*. Remove the shims and use the pry bar to pull out the nails. Clean the nail holes using a wire brush or paint scraper and fill them with glazing compound.

2 Installing new nails. Position the board and secure it with hot-dipped galvanized box nails or salvaged wrought-iron nails 1 inch longer than its thickness. Use an electric drill to bore pilot holes near the old nail holes, then drive in the nails *(above)*. Sand and refinish any damaged surface.

REPLACING A SECTION OF A CLAPBOARD

Wood shim

1 Removing the damaged section. Score along the edges of the damaged section with a utility knife to break any finish bond. If the damaged section is large, take out the entire board by removing its nails *(page 18)* and install a replacement board *(step 2)*. Otherwise, mark a cutting line at each end of the damaged section with a carpenter's square and a pencil, using the nailing or board-end pattern of the siding to locate the nearest stud; if there is no pattern, it is nailed to sheathing and can be marked for cutting at any point. To cut each end of the damaged section, work the blade of a wide putty knife far enough along its top edge to fit in a wood shim on one side of the cutting line. Fit in a wood shim along the bottom edge of the damaged section the same way, centering it with the cutting line. Cut the end of the damaged section as far as possible with a backsaw *(above, left)*, carefully making only downstrokes to avoid damaging adjacent surfaces. Using a wood block and mallet, fit in a wood shim along the top edge of the damaged section on the side of the cut opposite the first shim *(inset)*, then complete the cut with a keyhole saw *(above, right)*. Pull any nails out of the damaged section, then take it out.

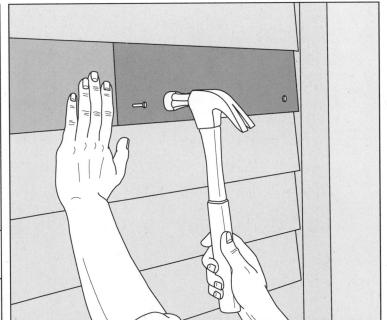

2 Installing the replacement section. Buy a board for a replacement section at a building supply center and cut it to length. Apply a preservative or finish to the back and end grain of the replacement section, then let it dry. To install the replacement section, mark the location of studs for nailing it; if there is sheathing, it can be nailed at any point. Fit the top edge of the replacement section into position *(above, left)* and slide it into place; if necessary, use a wood block and mallet to tap its bottom edge. Secure the replacement section with hot-dipped galvanized box nails or salvaged wrought-iron nails 1 inch longer than its thickness. Following the nailing pattern of the siding, use an electric drill to bore pilot holes into the replacement section, then drive in the nails *(above, right)*; secure any unnailed end adjacent to the replacement section the same way. Sand the replacement section and finish it to match the surrounding surface.

REPLACING A WOOD SHINGLE

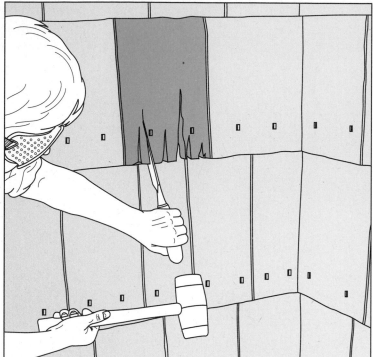

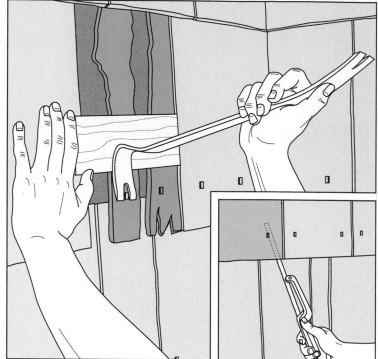

1 **Removing the damaged shingle.** Wearing safety goggles, use a mallet to drive a wood chisel into the bottom edge of the damaged shingle *(above, left)*, splitting it into pieces. Wear work gloves to remove each piece of the damaged shingle, pulling it downward and working it from side to side as necessary to free it. Pull out the exposed nails of the damaged shingle with a pry bar, using a wood block for greatest leverage *(above, right)*. For a stubborn piece of the damaged shingle, use old locking pliers to grip the bottom edge of it and tap the jaws with a ball-peen hammer. Use a mini-hacksaw to cut off any hidden nail securing the damaged shingle *(inset)*—usually a nail of a shingle above it located near its top corner.

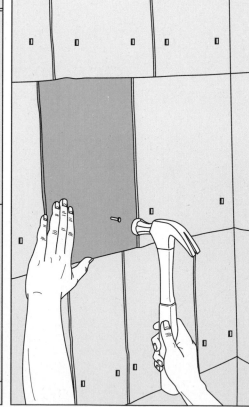

2 **Installing the replacement shingle.** Buy a replacement shingle at a building supply center and trim it to size using a utility knife and a straightedge, allowing for a 1/4-inch key along each side of it; cut excess length off its tapered end, matching the thickness of its bottom edge with the other shingles. Apply a preservative or finish to the replacement shingle, then let it dry. Fit the top edge of the replacement shingle into position and slide it into place, using a wood block and mallet to tap its bottom edge into line with the shingle on each side of it *(far left)*. Secure the replacement shingle with hot-dipped galvanized box nails or salvaged wrought-iron nails 1 inch longer than its thickness. Following the nailing pattern of the other shingles, drive the nails into the replacement shingle *(near left)*; also replace any nail cut off from the shingle above it. If necessary, finish the replacement shingle to match the other shingles.

REPLACING A SECTION OF WOOD SHINGLES

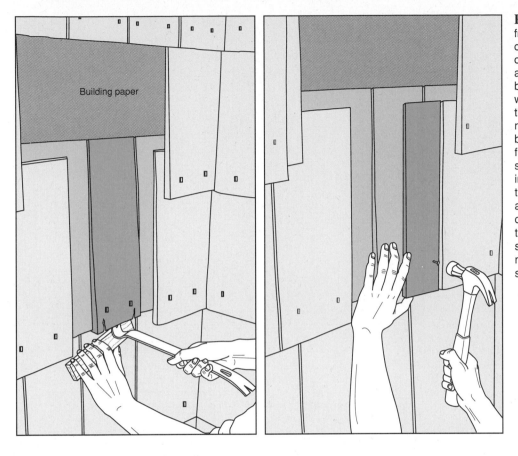

Building paper

Removing and installing shingles. Work from the top to the bottom along each course of the damaged section to remove the shingles one at a time *(page 20)*. For the undercourse of a damaged doubled-course section, use a pry bar to remove each shingle in turn. Using a wood block for greatest leverage, work along the bottom edge of the shingle to pry it out and raise the heads of its nails *(far left)*, then push it back into place and pull out the nails; work carefully to avoid damaging any building paper. Buy shingles for the replacement section at a building supply center and work from the bottom to the top along each course to install them one at a time *(page 20)*. For a replacement doubled-course section, first install the shingles of the undercourse, then position and nail each shingle of the overcourse in turn *(near left)*. If necessary, finish the replacement section of shingles to match the other shingles.

PREPARING STUCCO

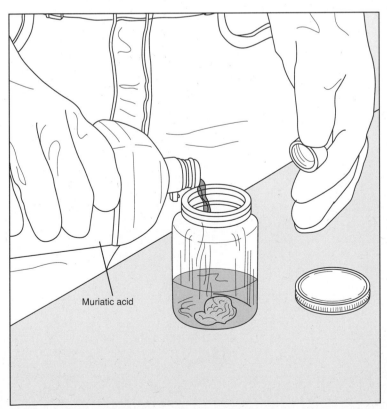

Muriatic acid

STUCCO RECIPES

SAMPLE COAT	SAMPLE CONTENT	COMPATIBLE MIX DRY INGREDIENTS
Scratch or brown	High in lime	1 part portland cement, 1 part lime, 3 parts sand
Scratch or brown	High in portland cement	1 part portland cement, 1/2 part lime, 3 parts sand
Finish	High in lime	1 part portland cement, 1 1/2 parts lime, 3 parts sand
Finish	High in portland cement	1 part portland cement, 1 part lime, 3 parts sand

Choosing a stucco mix. Take a sample of original stucco to use in choosing a stucco mix that is compatible, testing its scratch, brown and finish coats in turn as necessary; a different stucco mix may be needed for each coat. Wearing rubber gloves and safety goggles, place the stucco sample in a glass jar, then submerse it in a solution of equal parts water and 10% muriatic acid. **Caution:** Add the acid to the water *(left)*; never add water to acid. Close the jar and shake it vigorously. If the stucco sample crumbles and dissolves, leaving only sand, it has a high content of lime. If the stucco sample remains intact as a solid or dissolves only slightly, it has a high content of portland cement. To prepare a stucco mix that is compatible with the stucco sample, refer to the chart *(above)* for the proportions of dry ingredients needed.

PATCHING STUCCO

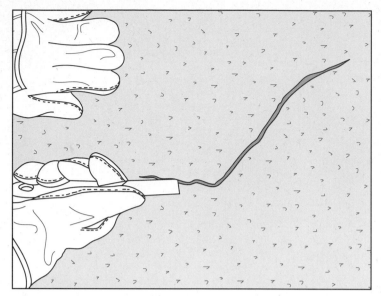

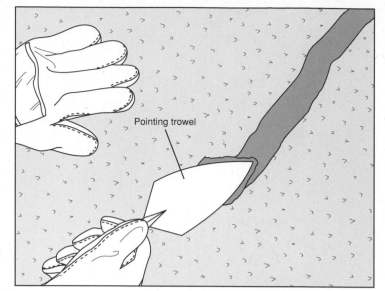

Pointing trowel

1 Preparing the damaged surface. Scratch the brown coat of the damaged surface with the blade of a putty knife; if it is soft or crumbles and falls off, replace the damaged section *(steps below)*. Otherwise, use the putty knife to enlarge the damaged surface slightly, widening it to about 1 inch *(above)*; avoid deepening it beyond the finish coat. Brush loose particles and dust off the damaged surface with a scrub brush or an old paintbrush.

2 Patching the damaged surface. To help the bonding of a patch, coat the damaged surface with a commercial bonding agent—available at a building supply center. Prepare stucco for a patch *(page 21)* and apply it with a pointing trowel or putty knife. Work stucco into the damaged surface, overfilling it slightly *(above)*. Then, texture the patch to match the surrounding surface. Keep the patch moist until it cures, misting it every 12 hours with water from a spray bottle. When the patch cures, apply a primer and paint.

REPLACING A SECTION OF STUCCO

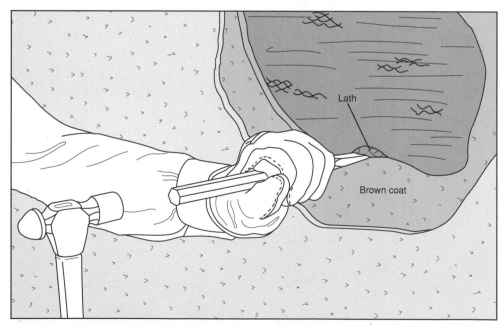

Lath

Brown coat

Building paper

1 Removing the damaged stucco. If the damaged section is larger than 4 square feet, consult a stucco professional. Otherwise, wear work gloves and safety goggles to cut back the edges of the damaged section as far as necessary to reach a solid surface. Use a cold chisel and ball-peen hammer to chip out pieces of stucco, working carefully to avoid damaging the metal lath. Cut the edges of the damaged section clean using a utility knife, then brush off loose particles and dust with a scrub brush or an old paintbrush. If a section of metal lath is rusty or otherwise damaged, remove it *(step 2)*. Otherwise, secure any loose metal lath with self-furring nails, then apply a scratch coat *(step 4)*.

2 Removing the damaged lath. Wearing work gloves and safety goggles, pull out the nails holding the damaged section in place. Cut out the damaged section using tin snips, pulling it slightly out from the surface *(above)* and working carefully along its edges to avoid damaging any building paper.

REPLACING A SECTION OF STUCCO (continued)

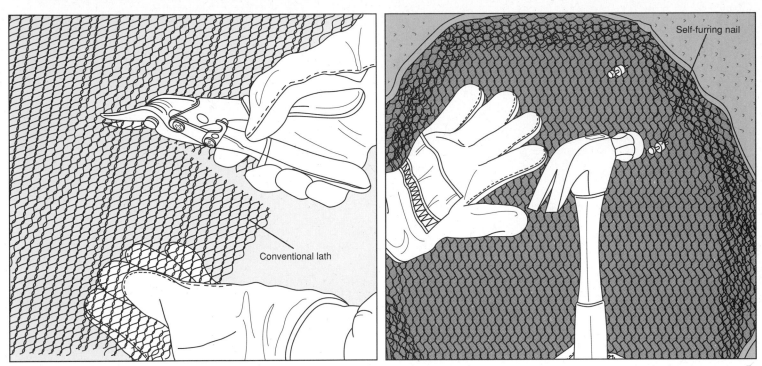

Conventional lath

Self-furring nail

3 **Installing the replacement lath.** Buy hot-dipped galvanized metal lath and fasteners for a replacement section at a building supply center; use conventional metal lath and self-furring nails or self-furring metal lath and conventional nails. Wearing work gloves and safety goggles, use tin snips to cut the replacement section to size *(above, left)*, allowing for an overlap of about 2 inches along its edges. Position the replacement section and hold it taut, then secure it in place by driving in a nail every 4 to 6 inches along its edges *(above, right)*.

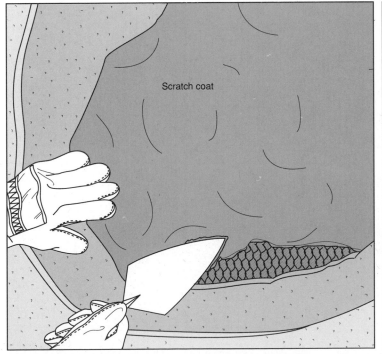

Scratch coat

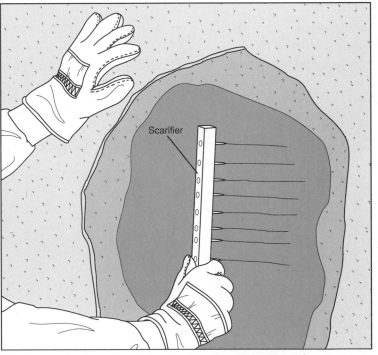

Scarifier

4 **Applying the scratch coat.** To help the bonding of a scratch coat, apply a commercial bonding agent—available at a building supply center. Prepare stucco for a scratch coat *(page 21)* and apply it with a pointing trowel. Work stucco into the damaged section, pressing it through the metal lath *(above, left)* to form keys. Continue applying stucco the same way, providing the damaged section with a scratch coat equal in thickness to the surrounding surface. Level the scratch coat with a wooden float, then scarify it to help the bonding of a brown coat. Make a scarifier by driving 3-inch nails through a 1-by-2 at 1-inch intervals and draw it lightly across the scratch coat, creating horizontal grooves about 1/4 inch deep *(above, right)*. Let the scratch coat set for 24 hours.

REPLACING A SECTION OF STUCCO (continued)

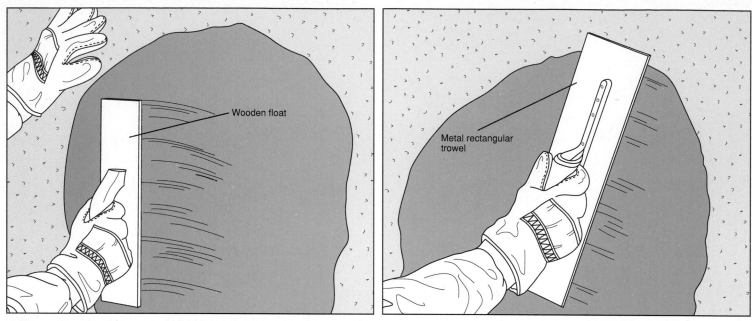

Wooden float

Metal rectangular trowel

5 **Applying the brown and finish coats.** Clean the scratch coat using a scrub brush, then prepare stucco for a brown coat *(page 21)*. Moisten the scratch coat by misting it with water from a spray bottle and apply the stucco using a pointing trowel, providing the damaged section with a brown coat equal in thickness to the surrounding surface. Level the brown coat with a wooden float, drawing it smoothly in broad, sweeping passes *(above, left)*. Scarify the brown

coat to a depth of 1/16 inch and let it set for 24 hours. Prepare stucco for a finish coat and moisten the brown coat with water, then apply the stucco using a metal rectangular trowel *(above, right)*. Texture the finish coat to match the surrounding surface. Keep the finish coat moist until it cures, misting it every 12 hours with water. When the patch cures, apply a primer and paint.

REPOINTING BRICKS

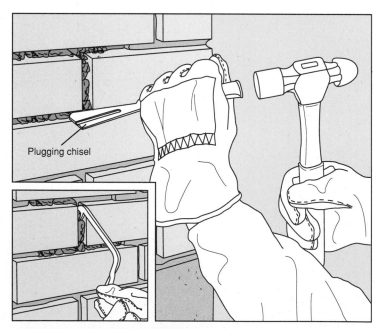

Plugging chisel

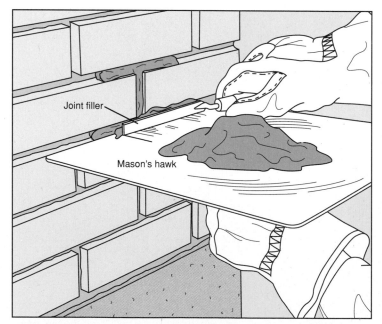

Joint filler

Mason's hawk

1 **Removing the damaged mortar.** Wearing work gloves and safety goggles, use a plugging or cold chisel and ball-peen hammer to cut back each damaged joint as far as necessary to reach sound mortar *(above)*—usually about 3/4 inch deep. Work carefully to avoid damaging the bricks. Use a mortar hook to rake loose mortar pieces out of the joint *(inset)*, then brush out particles and dust with a scrub brush or flush them out using a garden hose.

2 **Filling the joints.** Buy premixed mortar at a building supply center and follow the manufacturer's instructions to prepare it. Wearing work gloves, hold the mortar on a mason's hawk and press it into each joint using a joint filler, packing first any vertical joint, then any horizontal joint *(above)*. Overfill each joint slightly with mortar, then wipe the joint filler clean and draw it along the surface of the bricks to scrape off the excess.

REPOINTING BRICKS (continued)

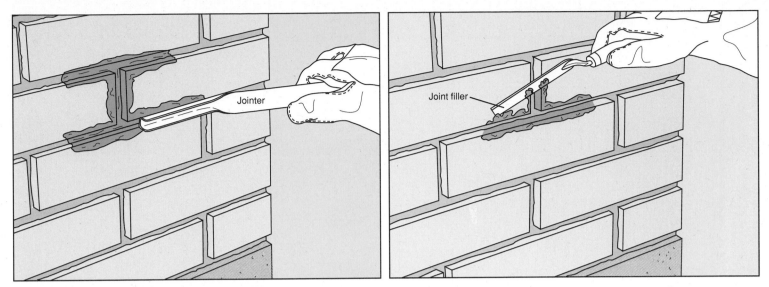

Jointer

Joint filler

3 **Striking the joints.** Let the mortar set until it is just hard enough to hold a thumbprint—usually about 30 minutes. Then, strike the joints in the same sequence used to fill them with a jointer that matches the shape and depth of the undamaged joints. Wet the jointer with water and apply firm, steady pressure to draw it along each joint *(above, left)*, creating a watertight seal. Draw a joint filler along the bricks to scrape off mortar forced out of the joint by the jointer *(above, right)*. Use a wet scrub brush and a cloth to clean mortar residue off the bricks. Keep the mortar moist until it cures for 3 days, misting it every 12 hours with water from a spray bottle.

REPLACING A BRICK

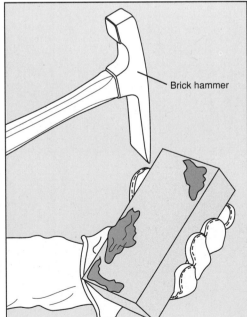

Brick hammer

1 **Removing the brick.** If the brick is loose but not damaged, remove the mortar from its joints *(page 24)* and try to remove it intact. Wear work gloves and safety goggles to pry the brick free, working along its edges with a pry bar. If the brick is damaged or cannot be pried free, break it into pieces using a cold chisel and small sledgehammer *(above, left)*; work carefully to avoid damaging adjacent bricks. Chip out the entire brick if it is a stretcher (long face exposed); chip it out to a depth of 4 inches if it is a header (short face exposed). If the brick can be removed intact, chip adhered mortar off it using a brick hammer *(above, right)* ; otherwise, buy a replacement brick at a building supply center or brick distributor.

REPLACING A BRICK (continued)

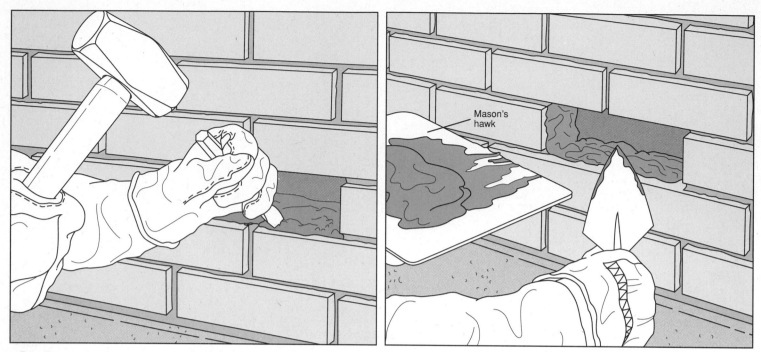

2 **Preparing the wall cavity.** Wearing work gloves and safety goggles, use a cold chisel and small sledgehammer to chip adhered mortar out of the wall cavity *(above, left)*; work carefully to avoid damaging adjacent bricks or dislodging any wall tie. Brush particles and dust out of the wall cavity with a scrub brush, then flush it using a garden hose and wait 30 minutes. Buy premixed mortar at a building supply center and follow the manufacturer's instructions to prepare it. Wearing work gloves, hold the mortar on a mason's hawk and use a pointing trowel to apply a 3/4-inch layer to the sides and bottom of the wall cavity *(above, right)*.

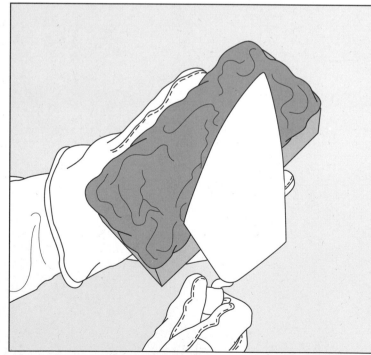

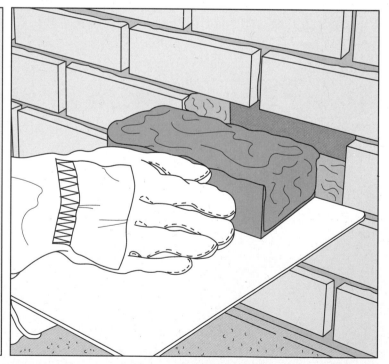

3 **Installing the replacement brick.** To cut the replacement brick to fit the wall cavity, wear work gloves and safety goggles to score a cutting line along each face with a brick chisel and small sledgehammer, then position the chisel along a scored line and strike it sharply with the hammer. Using a pointing trowel, apply a 3/4-inch layer of mortar to the top *(above, left)* and sides of the replacement brick.

Place the replacement brick on a mason's hawk and align it with the wall cavity, then slide it into place *(above, right)*; tap it flush with the adjacent bricks using the trowel handle. If mortar is not forced out of the joints, they are too thin; remove the brick to add mortar. Draw the trowel along the joints to scrape off excess mortar, then strike them *(page 25)*.

PATCHING WOOD TRIM

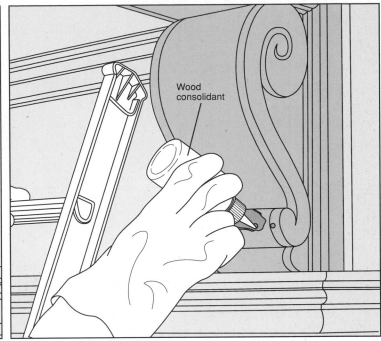

1 **Preparing the damaged surface.** Work when 24 hours of dry weather under 80° F. is expected. To test the damaged surface for rot, press an awl into it and pry up the fibers; if the wood is soft and gives way, crumbling instead of splintering, it is weakened by rot. If rot penetrates the trim, consult a professional to replace it. Otherwise, remove crumbling fibers with a wood chisel and mallet *(above, left)*. To reinforce spongy or pitted fibers, buy an epoxy wood consolidant at a woodworking or marine supply center and follow the manufacturer's instructions to prepare it. Sand end grain using medium sandpaper on a sanding block, then bore a hole 1/4 inch in diameter as far as possible into it every 1 inch along it. Wearing rubber gloves, use an applicator to apply consolidant, coating end grain and filling holes or cracks *(above, right)*. Continue applying consolidant until the wood cannot absorb it, then let it cure.

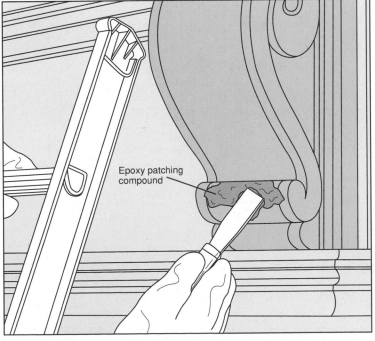

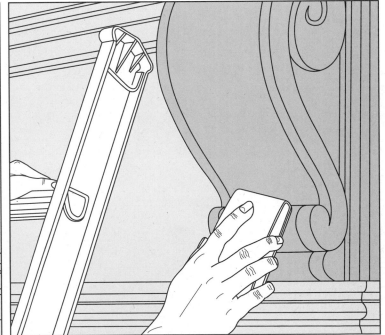

2 **Patching the damaged surface.** Buy epoxy patching compound at a building supply center and apply it following the manufacturer's instructions. Wearing rubber gloves, use a putty knife to work compound into the damaged surface, overfilling it slightly *(above, left)*. Scrape off excess compound with the putty knife, leveling the patch with the surrounding surface; use a wood block as a guide along an edge, if necessary. Shape the patch to match the surrounding surface using sticks, toothpicks, sharp knives or other tools, working with photographs or sketches of original trim elsewhere on the house to match details. Let the compound cure, then sand the patch using medium sandpaper on a sanding block *(above, right)*; wrap sandpaper around a dowel or other tool for contours and indentations. Brush or wipe off particles, then finish the patch to match the surrounding surface.

ROOFING

An older home need not provoke literal worry about the roof over your head. Traditional roofing materials such as metal, slates, interlocking, S-shaped or cap and pan tiles, or wood shakes can usually shrug off the vagaries of the elements unscathed for decades; for details on their common construction, refer to the illustrations below and on page 29. With proper maintenance of the roofing, many problems with it can be prevented. Keep gutters and downspouts clear of debris. Have trees overhanging the roofing pruned back to avoid damage from falling branches, stains from leaves, as well as mildew and rot.

Thoroughly inspect the roofing each spring and fall to detect minor problems early, correcting them before they become major problems. Begin the inspection indoors in the attic or on the top story, checking the wood structure and insulation of the roofing as well as the ceiling and walls below it for moisture, stains and other signs of leakage or a problem. Continue the inspection outdoors, using binoculars or working from a ladder to pinpoint a problem with the roofing—including the flashing. Undertake a repair to the roofing only in good weather conditions; for help, consult the Troubleshooting Guide on page 30.

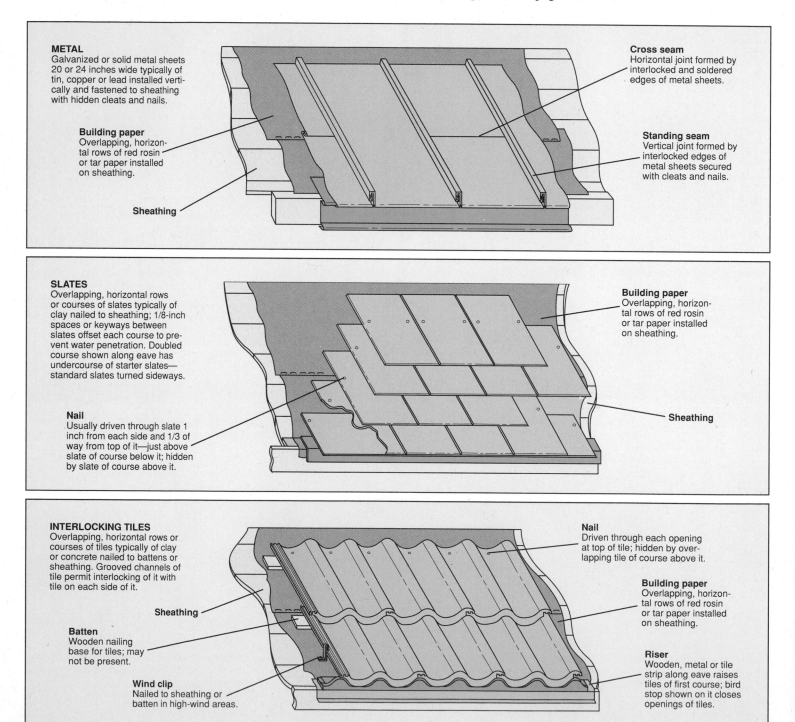

METAL
Galvanized or solid metal sheets 20 or 24 inches wide typically of tin, copper or lead installed vertically and fastened to sheathing with hidden cleats and nails.

Building paper
Overlapping, horizontal rows of red rosin or tar paper installed on sheathing.

Sheathing

Cross seam
Horizontal joint formed by interlocked and soldered edges of metal sheets.

Standing seam
Vertical joint formed by interlocked edges of metal sheets secured with cleats and nails.

SLATES
Overlapping, horizontal rows or courses of slates typically of clay nailed to sheathing; 1/8-inch spaces or keyways between slates offset each course to prevent water penetration. Doubled course shown along eave has undercourse of starter slates—standard slates turned sideways.

Nail
Usually driven through slate 1 inch from each side and 1/3 of way from top of it—just above slate of course below it; hidden by slate of course above it.

Building paper
Overlapping, horizontal rows of red rosin or tar paper installed on sheathing.

Sheathing

INTERLOCKING TILES
Overlapping, horizontal rows or courses of tiles typically of clay or concrete nailed to battens or sheathing. Grooved channels of tile permit interlocking of it with tile on each side of it.

Sheathing

Batten
Wooden nailing base for tiles; may not be present.

Wind clip
Nailed to sheathing or batten in high-wind areas.

Nail
Driven through each opening at top of tile; hidden by overlapping tile of course above it.

Building paper
Overlapping, horizontal rows of red rosin or tar paper installed on sheathing.

Riser
Wooden, metal or tile strip along eave raises tiles of first course; bird stop shown on it closes openings of tiles.

Most repairs to the roofing of an older home typically can be performed with only a few basic carpentry tools; a slate ripper for use when replacing slates or shakes usually can be rented. Refer to Tools & Techniques *(page 124)* for instructions on using tools properly, as well as for information on working safely from a ladder or on the roof. The materials and supplies needed for repairs to the roofing are in most instances readily available at a building or roofing supply center; on occasion, finding the replacement materials to match the original roofing may require a special visit to an architectural salvage yard.

To undertake some repairs to the roofing, you should consult a professional. For example, the homeowner is advised to stay off roofing with a pitch of more than 6 in 12—a slope of more than 6 inches vertically every 12 inches horizontally. Likewise, the homeowner is advised to undertake repairs to roofing of slates or tiles only if he can work safely and comfortably from a ladder or scaffold at the eave; these materials break easily under pressure and should not be walked on. For help in locating the cause of a problem with the roofing, especially of one that recurs, you should also consult a professional.

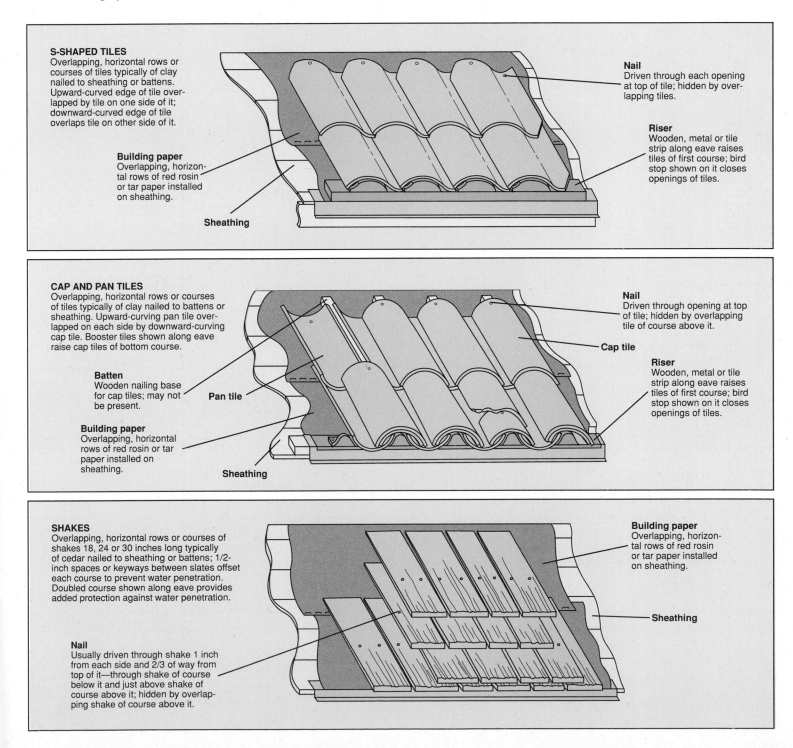

S-SHAPED TILES
Overlapping, horizontal rows or courses of tiles typically of clay nailed to sheathing or battens. Upward-curved edge of tile overlapped by tile on one side of it; downward-curved edge of tile overlaps tile on other side of it.

Building paper
Overlapping, horizontal rows of red rosin or tar paper installed on sheathing.

Sheathing

Nail
Driven through each opening at top of tile; hidden by overlapping tiles.

Riser
Wooden, metal or tile strip along eave raises tiles of first course; bird stop shown on it closes openings of tiles.

CAP AND PAN TILES
Overlapping, horizontal rows or courses of tiles typically of clay nailed to battens or sheathing. Upward-curving pan tile overlapped on each side by downward-curving cap tile. Booster tiles shown along eave raise cap tiles of bottom course.

Batten
Wooden nailing base for cap tiles; may not be present.

Building paper
Overlapping, horizontal rows of red rosin or tar paper installed on sheathing.

Pan tile

Sheathing

Nail
Driven through opening at top of tile; hidden by overlapping tile of course above it.

Cap tile

Riser
Wooden, metal or tile strip along eave raises tiles of first course; bird stop shown on it closes openings of tiles.

SHAKES
Overlapping, horizontal rows or courses of shakes 18, 24 or 30 inches long typically of cedar nailed to sheathing or battens; 1/2-inch spaces or keyways between slates offset each course to prevent water penetration. Doubled course shown along eave provides added protection against water penetration.

Building paper
Overlapping, horizontal rows of red rosin or tar paper installed on sheathing.

Sheathing

Nail
Usually driven through shake 1 inch from each side and 2/3 of way from top of it—through shake of course below it and just above shake of course above it; hidden by overlapping shake of course above it.

TROUBLESHOOTING GUIDE

SYMPTOM	POSSIBLE CAUSE	PROCEDURE
METAL		
Pinholes; pitting or rust up to 3 inches square	Normal aging due to weather stress; accidental blow or impact	For roofing of copper or lead, consult a professional; otherwise, repair metal pinholes (p. 31) □○
Crack; seam open	Normal aging due to weather stress; accidental blow or impact	For roofing of copper or lead or for standing seam, consult a professional; otherwise, repair metal cross seam or crack (p. 31) □○
Hole from 3 inches to 12 inches square	Extreme aging due to weather stress; accidental blow or impact	For roofing of copper or lead, consult a professional; otherwise, repair metal hole (p. 32) ◨◕
SLATES		
Slate loose; out of position	Fastener popped	Secure slate (p. 34) □○
Slate cracked or broken	Normal aging due to weather stress; accidental blow or impact	Replace slate (p. 34) □○▲
Section of slates cracked or broken	Extreme aging due to weather stress; accidental blow or impact	Replace section of slates (p. 35) ◨●▲
INTERLOCKING TILES		
Tile loose; out of position	Fastener popped	Secure interlocking tile as you would to replace it (p. 36) □○
Tile cracked or broken	Normal aging due to weather stress; accidental blow or impact	Replace interlocking tile (p. 36) □○
Section of tiles cracked or broken	Extreme aging due to weather stress; accidental blow or impact	Replace section of interlocking tiles (p. 37) ◨●
S-SHAPED TILES		
Tile loose; out of position	Fastener popped	Secure S-shaped tile as you would to replace it (p. 37) □○
Tile cracked or broken	Normal aging due to weather stress; accidental blow or impact	Replace S-shaped tile (p. 37) □○
Section of tiles cracked or broken	Extreme aging due to weather stress; accidental blow or impact	Replace section of S-shaped tiles (p. 38) ◨●
CAP AND PAN TILES		
Tile loose; out of position	Fastener popped	Secure cap or pan tile as you would to replace it (p. 38) □○
Tile cracked or broken	Normal aging due to weather stress; accidental blow or impact	Replace cap or pan tile (p. 38) □○
Section of tiles cracked or broken	Extreme aging due to weather stress; accidental blow or impact	Replace section of cap and pan tiles (p. 40) ◨●
SHAKES		
Shake loose; out of position	Fastener popped	Secure shake as you would to replace it (p. 41) □○
Shake split, cracked, dented or gouged	Normal aging due to weather stress; accidental blow or impact	Replace shake (p. 40) □○▲ or replace section of shakes (p. 41) ◨●▲
Shake spongy, pitted or crumbling	Wood damaged by rot	Replace shake (p. 40) □○▲ or replace section of shakes (p. 41) ◨●▲
	Wood damaged by insects	Consult a professional
FLASHING		
Pinholes; pitting or rust up to 3 inches square	Normal aging due to weather stress; accidental blow or impact	Repair metal pinholes (p. 31) □○
Crack; seam open	Normal aging due to weather stress; accidental blow or impact	Repair metal cross seam or crack (p. 31) □○
Hole from 3 inches to 12 inches square	Extreme aging due to weather stress; accidental blow or impact	Repair metal hole (p. 32) ◨◕

DEGREE OF DIFFICULTY: □ Easy ◨ Moderate ■ Complex
ESTIMATED TIME: ○ Less than 1 hour ◕ 1 to 3 hours ● Over 3 hours

▲ Special tool required

REPAIRING METAL PINHOLES

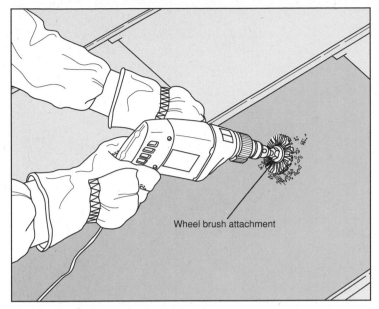

Wheel brush attachment

Roofing cement

1 Preparing the surface. Work safely on the roof *(page 128)* when 24 hours of dry weather below 70° F. is expected. Wearing work gloves, safety goggles and a dust mask, use a paint scraper to clean flakes of paint and debris from the surface. Use an electric drill fitted with a wheel brush attachment to remove rust and paint from the surface *(above)*, working out about 2 inches beyond its edges. Apply a metal primer to the surface and let it dry.

2 Patching the surface. Buy plastic roofing cement at a building supply center. Wearing work gloves, use a putty knife to work cement into the surface, overfilling it slightly *(above)*. Draw the putty knife along the surface to level the cement and scrape off excess, then let it cure. Apply a thin, even layer of cement on the surface the same way, drawing the putty knife outward from the center of the patch to feather its edges and disguise the repair. Let the patch cure, then sand and paint it.

REPAIRING A METAL CROSS SEAM OR CRACK

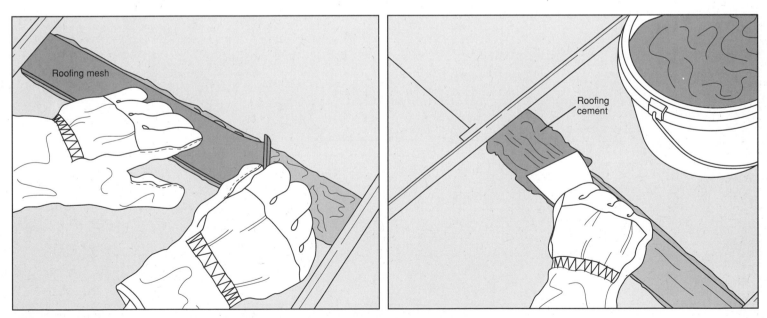

Roofing mesh

Roofing cement

Patching a cross seam or crack. Prepare the seam or crack as you would for pinholes *(step 1, above)*. Buy plastic roofing cement and polyester roofing mesh at a building supply center. Wearing work gloves, use a putty knife to work cement into the seam or crack, overfilling it slightly. Draw the putty knife along the surface to level the cement and scrape off excess, then let it cure. Cut a strip of mesh about 2 inches wider than the seam or crack and apply a thin, even layer of cement as a bed for it, then press it firmly into place *(above, left)*. Cover the mesh with a thin, even layer of cement, drawing it smoothly along the surface with the putty knife *(above, right)* and feathering its edges to disguise the repair. Let the patch cure, then sand and paint it.

REPAIRING A METAL HOLE

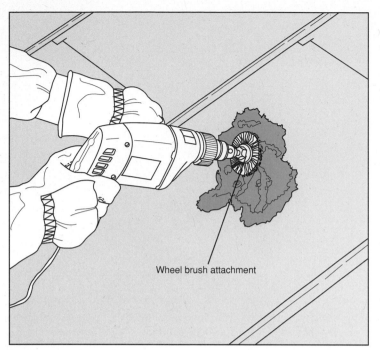

Wheel brush attachment

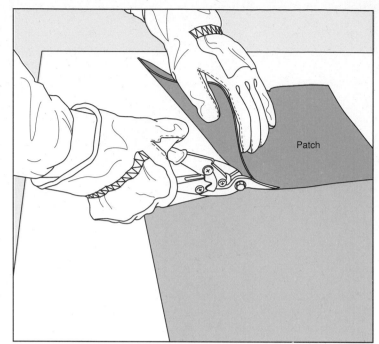

Patch

1 Preparing the surface. Work safely on the roof *(page 128)* when 24 hours of dry weather below 70° F. is expected. Wearing work gloves, safety goggles and a dust mask, use a paint scraper to clean flakes of paint and debris from the hole; cut off any jagged edge with tin snips. Use an electric drill fitted with a wheel brush attachment to remove rust and paint within 4 inches of the hole *(above)*, then apply a metal primer to the surface and let it dry.

2 Preparing the patch. Buy 26-gauge galvanized sheet metal for a patch at a building supply center. Measure the dimensions of the prepared surface and mark the outline of a square-edged patch equal to the length and width of it on the sheet metal. Wearing work gloves and safety goggles, use tin snips to cut the sheet metal along each marked line of the patch *(above)*. Use a file to deburr each cut edge of the patch.

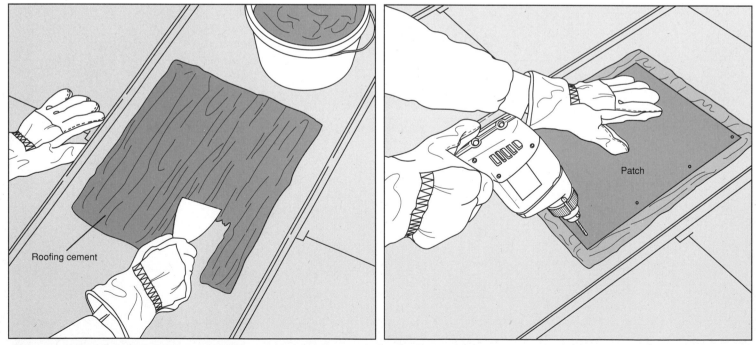

Roofing cement

Patch

3 Installing the patch. Buy plastic roofing cement at a building supply center. Wearing work gloves, use a putty knife to apply an even layer of cement about 1/2 inch thick as a bed for the patch on the prepared surface *(above, left)*, then press the patch firmly into place, centered on the bed of cement. Using an electric drill fitted with a 1/8-inch twist bit, drill a hole through the patch every 4 inches along its edges into the roofing *(above, right)*; avoid drilling into the building paper or sheathing. Stop drilling periodically to let the bit cool and wipe it clean using a cloth dampened with mineral spirits.

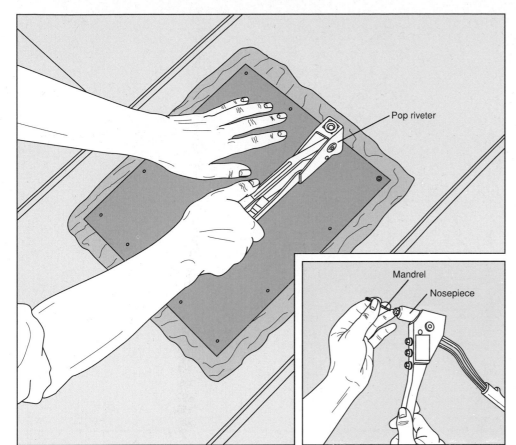

4 **Securing the patch.** Buy 1/8-inch pop rivets just long enough to penetrate through the patch and the roofing at a building supply center. Wearing safety goggles, install the pop rivets with a pop riveter following the manufacturer's instructions. To load the pop riveter, push the mandrel of a pop rivet into its nosepiece *(inset)* until the flange of the pop rivet rests against it. Pressing down firmly on the patch to keep it in position, fasten it to the roofing with a pop rivet at each hole drilled through them *(left)*.

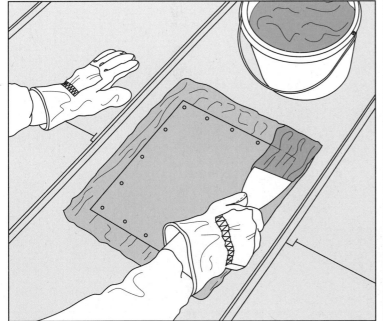

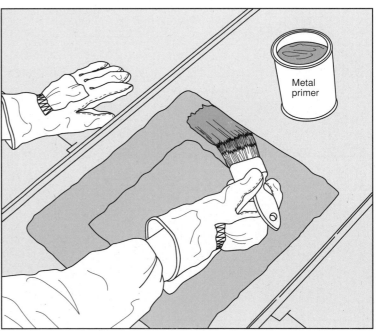

5 **Sealing the patch.** Buy polyester roofing mesh at a building supply center and use it to seal the edges of the patch. Wearing work gloves, use a putty knife to apply a thin, even layer of plastic roofing cement 4 to 6 inches wide along each edge of the patch as a bed for the mesh *(above, left)*. Cut a strip of mesh for each edge of the patch 2 to 4 inches wide and press it firmly into place, centered on the bed of cement. Cover the mesh with a thin, even layer of cement, drawing it smoothly along the surface with the putty knife and feathering its edges to disguise the repair. Let the patch cure, then sand it using medium sandpaper on a sanding block. Brush particles and dust off the surface, then apply a metal primer *(above, right)* and paint.

SECURING A SLATE

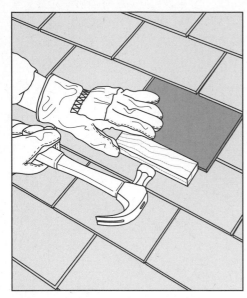

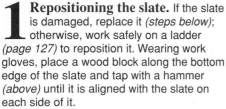

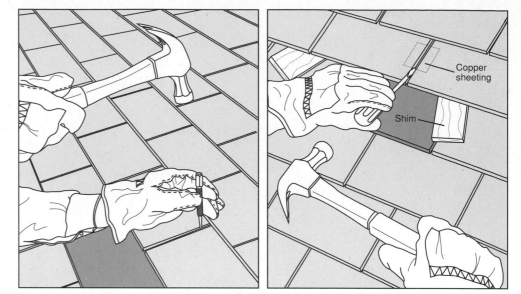

Copper
sheeting

Shim

1 **Repositioning the slate.** If the slate is damaged, replace it *(steps below)*; otherwise, work safely on a ladder *(page 127)* to reposition it. Wearing work gloves, place a wood block along the bottom edge of the slate and tap with a hammer *(above)* until it is aligned with the slate on each side of it.

2 **Securing the slate.** Secure the slate with a copper wire nail near the top edge of it in the gap between the slate on each side of it. Wearing work gloves and safety goggles, drill holes for countersinking a nail 1 inch longer than twice the thickness of the slate; use an electric drill fitted first with a 1/8-inch masonry bit, then with a 1/4-inch masonry bit. Drive in the nail and use a nail set to set its head *(above, left)*. Apply a dab of plastic roofing cement to the nail head and cover it with a piece of 26-gauge copper sheeting. Use a wood shim to slightly raise the bottom edge of the slate on each side of the nail head and slide the sheeting into place with an old screwdriver *(above, right)*.

REPLACING A SLATE

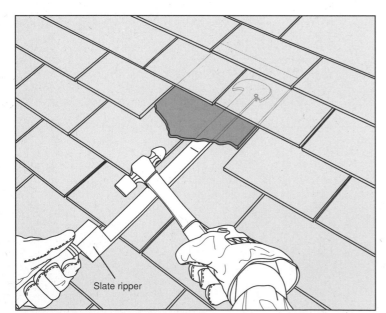

Slate ripper

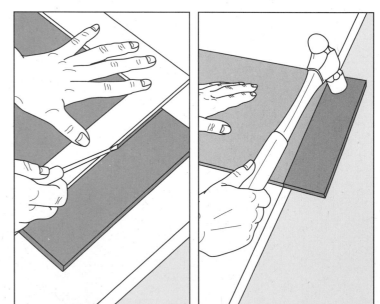

1 **Removing the damaged slate.** Work safely on a ladder *(page 127)* to remove the damaged slate using a slate ripper—available at a roofing supply center. Wearing work gloves and safety goggles, slide the tip of the slate ripper under the damaged slate and around a nail securing it. To help prepare a replacement slate *(step 2)*, mark the location of the bottom edge of the slate on each side of the damaged slate onto the shaft of the slate ripper. To cut the nail, strike the handle of the slate ripper sharply with a ball-peen hammer *(above)*. Cut off each nail of the damaged slate the same way, then pull it out.

2 **Preparing the replacement slate.** Buy a matching replacement slate at a slate dealer and mark it to size: adding 3 inches to the distance between the tip and the mark on the shaft of the slate ripper for its length; subtracting 1/4 inch from the opening in the roofing for its width. Score cutting lines on the replacement slate with a straightedge and an awl *(above, left)*, then wear safety goggles to break it along each scored line. Position the replacement slate with the scored line aligned along an edge of a work table and strike the waste side of it with a ball-peen hammer *(above, right)*.

REPLACING A SLATE (continued)

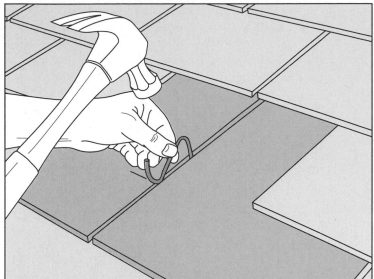

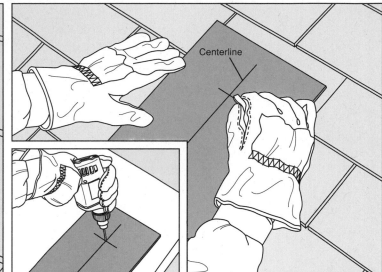

3 **Installing the replacement slate.** Install the replacement slate using a slate hook or with a copper wire nail 1 inch longer than twice its thickness. For a slate hook, position the slate and mark its bottom edge on the roofing, then remove it and drive the slate hook into the gap between slates a little above the marked line *(above, left)*. Slide the slate into place and seat it securely on the slate hook. For a nail, position the slate and mark a hole at the center of it a little below the bottom edge of the slates above it *(above, right)*. Remove

the slate and wear safety goggles to drill holes for countersinking the nail; drill first with a 1/8-inch masonry bit *(inset)*, then with a 1/4-inch masonry bit. Slide the slate into place, then drive in the nail and use a nail set to set its head. Apply a dab of plastic roofing cement to the nail head and cover it with a piece of 26-gauge copper sheeting. Use a wood shim to slightly raise the bottom edge of the slate on each side of the nail head, then slide the sheeting into place using an old screwdriver, tapping gently with a hammer.

REPLACING A SECTION OF SLATES

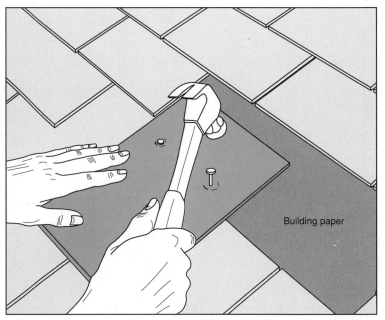

Removing and installing slates. Work from the top to the bottom along each course of the damaged section to remove the slates one at a time. Remove each slate of the first course *(page 34)*, then use a pry bar to take off each slate of the other courses. Using a wood block for leverage, work along the bottom of the slate to pry it up and raise its nail heads *(above, left)*, then push it back down and pull out the nails. Buy slates for the replacement section at a slate dealer and work from the bottom to the top along each course to install them. Prepare

each slate *(page 34)*, allowing for a gap of 1/8 inch along each side of it. Install each slate of other than the last course with copper wire nails 1 inch longer than twice its thickness. Wearing safety goggles, drill holes for countersinking a nail into the slate 1 inch from each side and 1/3 of the way from the top of it; drill first with a 1/8-inch masonry bit, then with a 1/4-inch mason-ry bit. Position the slate and drive in the nails *(above, right)*, using a nail set to set the heads. Prepare and install *(step 3, above)* each slate of the last course.

REPLACING AN INTERLOCKING TILE

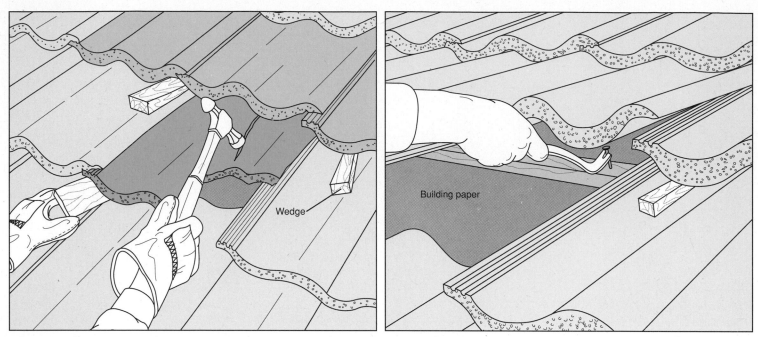

Wedge

Building paper

1 **Removing the damaged tile.** Work safely on a ladder *(page 127)* to prop up each tile overlapping the damaged tile: two tiles of the course above it; one tile beside it. Wearing work gloves, raise the tile enough to slip a wedge under it; consult a professional if the tiles are wired and cannot be raised. To remove the damaged tile, lift it slightly to raise its nail heads, then push it back down and pull out the nails with a pry bar. If the nails are not accessible, prop up the damaged tile and wear safety goggles to break it into pieces using a ball-peen hammer *(above, left)*, striking it at a 45° angle. Pull out each piece of the damaged tile, then remove its nails with the pry bar *(above, right)*.

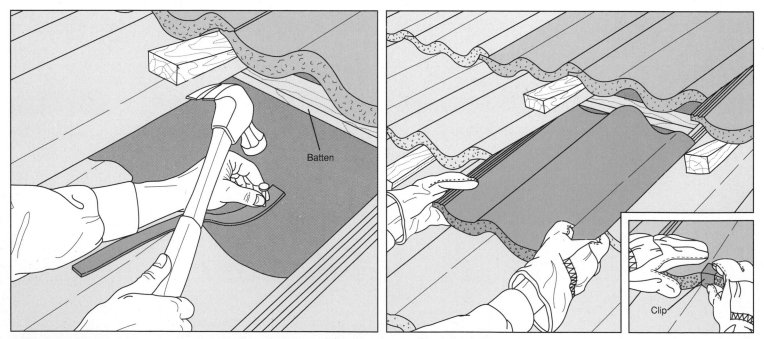

Batten

Clip

2 **Installing the replacement tile.** Buy a matching replacement tile at a building supply center. Wearing work gloves and safety goggles, cut a clip of 28-gauge galvanized sheet metal 1 inch wide and 12 inches long using tin snips. Nail one end of the clip at the center of the opening for the replacement tile *(above, left)* and apply a dab of plastic roofing cement to the nail head. Slide the replacement tile into position *(above, right)*, hooking it on any batten and aligning it with the tile on each side of it. Bend the protruding end of the clip up over the bottom edge of the replacement tile *(inset)*, then seat the tiles propped up; ensure that they lie flat and the interlocking channels fit properly.

REPLACING A SECTION OF INTERLOCKING TILES

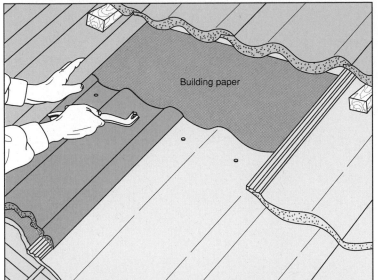

Removing and installing interlocking tiles. Work from the top to the bottom along each course of the damaged section to remove the tiles one at a time. Remove each tile of the first course *(page 36)*, then use a pry bar to take off each tile of the other courses. Using a wood block for leverage, work along the bottom of the tile to pry it up and raise its nail heads, then push it back down and pull out the nails *(above, left)*. Buy matching tiles for the replacement section at a build-

ing supply center and work from the bottom to the top along each course to install them. Slide each tile into position, overlapping one tile beside it and hooking it on any batten. To secure each tile of other than the last course, wear safety goggles to drive a roofing nail carefully through each opening in it *(above, right)* until the head just touches it. Then, install each tile of the last course *(page 36)*.

REPLACING AN S-SHAPED TILE

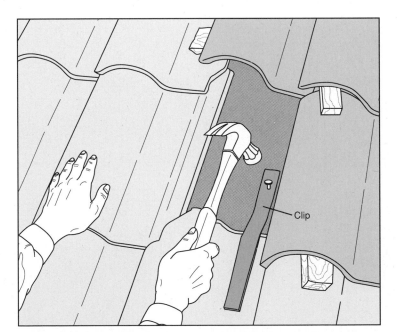

1 **Removing the damaged tile.** Work safely on a ladder *(page 127)* to prop up each tile overlapping the damaged tile: two tiles of the course above it; one tile beside it. Wearing work gloves, raise the tile enough to slip a wedge under it; consult a professional if the tiles are wired and cannot be raised. To remove the damaged tile, lift it slightly to raise its nail heads *(above)*, then push it back down and pull out the nails with a pry bar. If the nails are not accessible, prop up the damaged tile and wear safety goggles to break it into pieces using a ball-peen hammer, then pull out its nails.

2 **Installing the replacement tile.** Buy a matching replacement tile at a building supply center. Wearing work gloves and safety goggles, cut a clip of 28-gauge galvanized sheet metal 1 inch wide and 12 inches long using tin snips. Nail one end of the clip at the center of the opening for the replacement tile *(above)* and apply a dab of plastic roofing cement to the nail head. Slide the replacement tile into position and align it with the tile on each side of it, then bend the protruding end of the clip up over its bottom edge. Seat the tiles propped up, ensuring that they lie flat.

REPLACING A SECTION OF S-SHAPED TILES

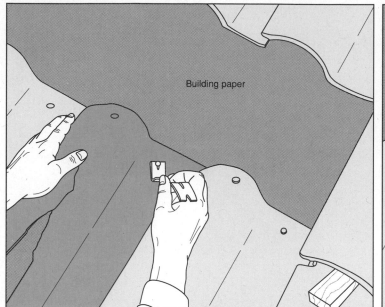

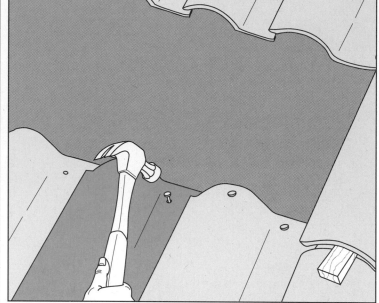

Removing and installing S-shaped tiles. Work from the top to the bottom along each course of the damaged section to remove the tiles one at a time. Remove each tile of the first course *(page 37)*, then use a pry bar to take off each tile of the other courses. Using a wood block for leverage, work along the bottom of the tile to pry it up and raise its nail heads, then push it back down and pull out the nails *(above, left)*.

Buy matching tiles for the replacement section at a building supply center and work from the bottom to the top along each course to install them. Slide each tile into position, overlapping one tile beside it. To secure each tile of other than the last course, wear safety goggles to drive a roofing nail carefully through each opening in it *(above, right)* until the head just touches it. Then, install each tile of the last course *(page 37)*.

REPLACING A CAP TILE AND A PAN TILE

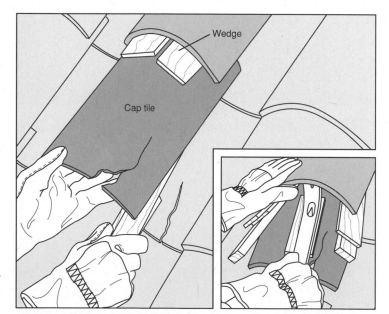

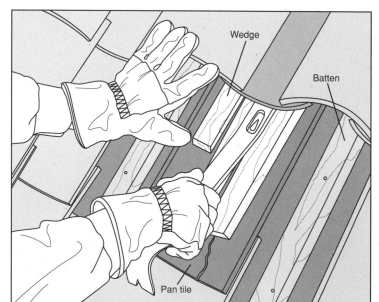

1 Removing the damaged cap tile. Work safely on a ladder *(page 127)* to prop up the cap tile overlapping the damaged cap tile one course above it. Wearing work gloves, raise the cap tile enough to slip wedges under it; consult a professional if it is wired and cannot be raised. To remove the damaged cap tile, raise its nail head by lifting it slightly with a wood block *(above)*, then push it back down and pull out the nail with a pry bar *(inset)*. If the nail is not accessible, prop up the damaged cap tile and wear safety goggles to break it into pieces using a ball-peen hammer, then pull out its nail.

2 Removing the damaged pan tile. If the pan tile is not damaged, install a replacement cap tile *(step 4)*. Otherwise, remove the other cap tile overlapping the damaged pan tile *(step 1)*, then prop up the pan tile overlapping it one course above it, raising it enough to slip wedges under it. To remove the damaged pan tile, raise its nail head by lifting it slightly, then push it back down and pull out the nail with a pry bar *(above)*. If the nail is not accessible, prop up the damaged pan tile and wear safety goggles to break it into pieces using a ball-peen hammer, then pull out its nail.

REPLACING A CAP TILE AND A PAN TILE (continued)

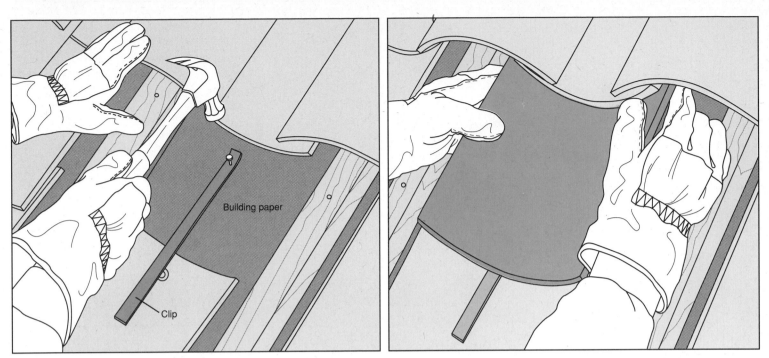

3 **Installing the replacement pan tile.** Buy a matching replacement pan tile at a building supply center. Wearing work gloves and safety goggles, cut a clip of 28-gauge galvanized sheet metal 1 inch wide and 12 inches long using tin snips. Nail one end of the clip at the center near the top of the opening in the roofing *(above, left)* and apply a dab of plastic roofing cement to the nail head. Slide the replacement pan tile into position *(above, right)* and align it with the pan tile on each side of it, then bend the protruding end of the clip up over its bottom edge. Seat the pan tile propped up, ensuring that it lies flat.

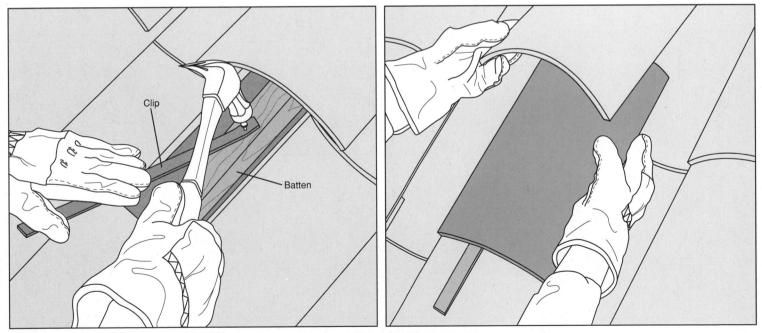

4 **Installing the replacement cap tile.** Buy a matching replacement cap tile at a building supply center. Wearing work gloves and safety goggles, cut a clip of 28-gauge galvanized sheet metal 1 inch wide and 12 inches long using tin snips. Nail one end of the clip to the batten near the top of the opening in the roofing *(above, left)* and apply a dab of plastic roofing cement to the nail head. Slide the replacement cap tile into position *(above, right)* and align it with the cap tile on each side of it, then bend the protruding end of the clip up over its bottom edge. If you replaced a pan tile, reinstall the other cap tile removed the same way. Seat each cap tile propped up, ensuring that it lies flat.

REPLACING A SECTION OF CAP AND PAN TILES

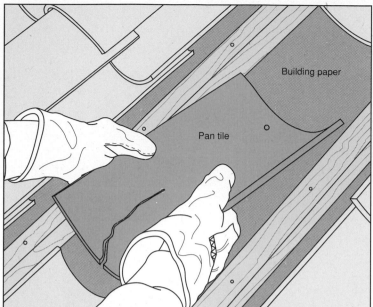

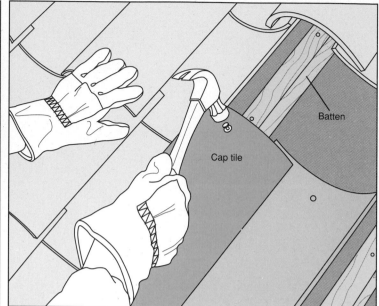

Removing and installing cap and pan tiles. Work from the top to the bottom along each course of the damaged section to remove the cap and pan tiles one at a time. Remove each cap tile of the first course *(page 38)*, then take off each cap tile of the other courses. Lift the cap tile slightly to raise its nail head, then push it back down and pull out the nail with a pry bar. Take off each pan tile the same way *(above, left)*. Buy matching cap and pan tiles for the replacement section at a building supply center and work from the bottom to the top along each course to install them. For each pan tile of other than the last course, slide it into position and wear safety goggles to drive a roofing nail carefully through the opening in it until the head just touches it. Then, install each pan tile of the last course *(page 39)*. Work the same way to nail each cap tile of other than the last course *(above, right)*, then install each cap tile of the last course *(page 39)*.

REPLACING A SHAKE

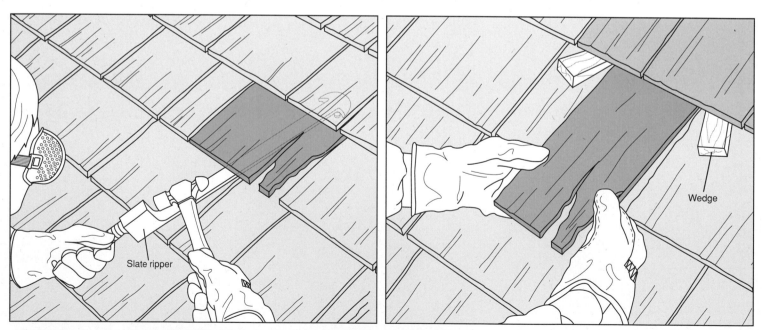

1 Removing the damaged shake. Work safely on a ladder *(page 127)* to remove the damaged shake using a slate ripper—available at a roofing supply center. Wearing work gloves and safety goggles, slide the tip of the slate ripper under the damaged shake and around a nail securing it—usually about 1 inch from each side of it a little above the bottom edge of the shakes above it. To cut the nail, strike the handle of the slate ripper sharply with a ball-peen hammer *(above, left)*. Cut off each nail of the damaged shake the same way, then pull it out; if necessary, prop up the bottom of each shake overlapping it with a wedge *(above, right)*.

REPLACING A SHAKE (continued)

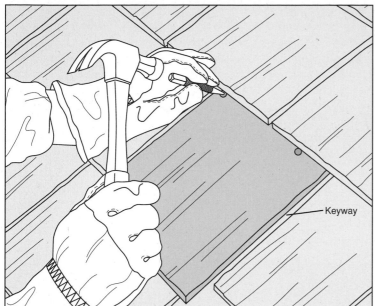

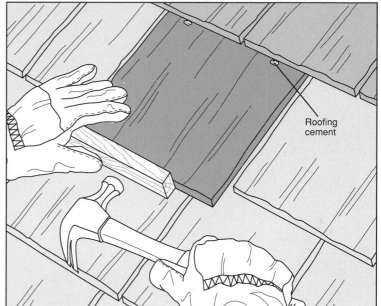

Roofing cement

Keyway

2 **Installing the replacement shake.** Buy a matching replacement shake at a building supply center and mark it to size: equal in length to the shake removed; 1 inch less in width than the opening in the roofing to allow for a keyway of 1/2 inch along each side of it. Cut the shake to size with a backsaw, trimming each end of it as necessary to match the thickness of its bottom edge with the other shakes. Apply a preservative or finish to the shake and let it dry. Slide the shake into position until its bottom edge is about 3/4 inch below the bottom edge of the shake on each side of it, then secure it with hot-dipped galvanized box nails 1 1/2 inches long. Using a nail set, drive a nail at a 45° angle through the shake about 1 inch from each side of it just below the bottom edge of the shakes above it *(above, left)*. Apply a dab of plastic roofing cement to the head of each nail, then tap the bottom edge of the shake into line with the shake on each side of it using a wood block and mallet *(above, right)*.

REPLACING A SECTION OF SHAKES

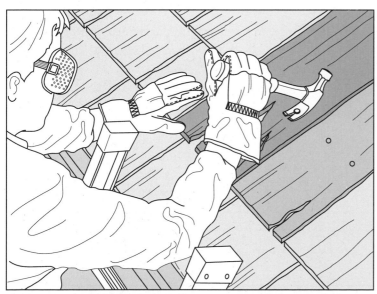

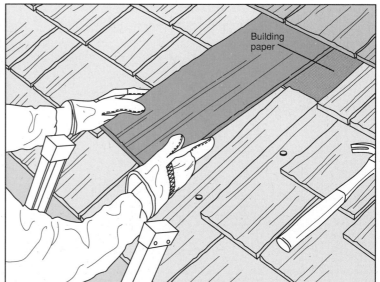

Building paper

Removing and installing shakes. Work from the top to the bottom along each course of the damaged section to remove the shakes one at a time. Remove each shake of the first course *(page 40)*, then use a hammer or pry bar to take off each shake of the other courses. Using a wood block for leverage, work along the bottom of the shake to pry it up and raise its nail heads, then push it back down and pull out the nails *(above, left)*. Buy matching shakes for the replacement section at a building supply center and apply a preservative or finish to them. Work from the bottom to the top along each course to install the shakes, offsetting the keyways of alternate courses by 1 1/2 inches. For each shake of other than the last course, slide it into position *(above, right)* and align it with the shake on each side of it, then secure it with hot-dipped galvanized box nails 1 1/2 inches long. Drive a nail through the shake about 1 inch from each side of it just above the bottom edge of the shakes of the course above it. Apply a dab of plastic roofing cement to the nail heads. Install each shake of the last course *(step 2, above)*.

DOORS

Doors are among the sturdiest components of an older home, rarely beset with major problems—but subject to a number of annoying minor problems with the passage of time. Refer to page 43 for illustrations of the typical hinged door and pocket doors that are common features of an older home. The most common problem with a hinged- or pocket-type of door is binding or rubbing as it is opened or closed. Failure to close properly is another frequent irritant: a hinged door that does not latch; pocket doors that do not meet squarely. For help in solving a particular problem with a door, use the Troubleshooting Guide below.

Most repairs to the doors of an older home are usually easily undertaken with only a few basic carpentry tools; refer to Tools & Techniques *(page 124)* for instructions on using tools properly. Keep in mind that the doors are often heavy and can be difficult to lift or awkward to maneuver. Work with a helper to remove a hinged door *(page 44)*, or a top-hung *(page 49)* or bottom-roller *(page 50)* pocket door; build a pair of door jacks and use them to support the door *(page 51)* while you work on it. Before starting any repair to a door, familiarize yourself with the information presented in the Emergency Guide *(page 8)*.

TROUBLESHOOTING GUIDE

SYMPTOM	POSSIBLE CAUSE	PROCEDURE
HINGED DOOR		
Door does not swing smoothly	Hinge pins lack lubricant	Lubricate hinge pins in turn with silicone-based lubricant
	Hinge screws loose	Tighten hinge screws
Door does not open or close freely	Hinge screws loose	Tighten hinge screws
	Finish buildup on edge or jamb	Remove excess finish from binding spots
	Top edge binds against head jamb	Shim top hinge *(p. 44)* □○ or trim binding spot *(p. 45)* ◧○
	Bottom edge binds against floor	Shim bottom hinge *(p. 44)* □○ or trim binding spot *(p. 45)* ◧○
	Top of latched edge binds against side jamb	Shim bottom hinge *(p. 44)* □○ or trim binding spot *(p. 45)* ◧○
	Bottom of latched edge binds against side jamb	Shim top hinge *(p. 44)* □○ or trim binding spot *(p. 45)* ◧○
	Center of latched edge binds against side jamb	Trim hinged edge *(p. 45)* ◧●
Door closes, but does not latch	Latch or strike plate screws loose	Tighten latch and strike plate screws
	Finish buildup on latch or strike plate	Remove excess finish from latch and strike plate
	Doorstop and door not aligned	Adjust doorstop *(p. 46)* □○
	Latch and strike plate not aligned	Adjust strike plate *(p. 46)* ◧○
	Gap between latch and strike plate	Shim strike plate *(p. 47)* □○ or shim each hinge *(p. 44)* □○ equally
TOP-HUNG POCKET DOORS		
Door does not slide smoothly	Roller assemblies lack lubricant	Lubricate roller assemblies *(p. 48)* □○
Door does not open or close freely	Pocket obstructed or dirty	Slide out door *(p. 48)* □○ and vacuum pocket
	Top or bottom edge binds	Adjust roller assemblies *(p. 48)* □○ or remove door *(p. 49)* ◧○ and trim binding edge *(p. 45)* ◧●
	Surface binds against stop molding	Adjust stop molding *(p. 49)* □○
	Roller assembly, track or studs of pocket damaged	Consult a professional
Doors close, but do not meet squarely	Doors not aligned	Adjust roller assemblies *(p. 48)* □○
BOTTOM-ROLLER POCKET DOORS		
Door does not slide smoothly	Roller assemblies lack lubricant	Service roller assemblies *(p. 51)* ◧○
Door does not open or close freely	Pocket obstructed or dirty	Remove center stop to slide out door and vacuum pocket
	Track sags	Level track *(p. 50)* □○
	Top or bottom edge binds	Remove door *(p. 50)* ◧○ and trim binding edge *(p. 45)* ◧●
	Surface binds against stop molding	Adjust stop molding *(p. 49)* □○
	Roller assembly damaged	Service roller assemblies *(p. 51)* ◧○
	Track or studs of pocket damaged	Consult a professional
Doors close, but do not meet squarely	Track sags	Level track *(p. 50)* □○

DEGREE OF DIFFICULTY: □ Easy ◧ Moderate ■ Complex
ESTIMATED TIME: ○ Less than 1 hour ◔ 1 to 3 hours ● Over 3 hours

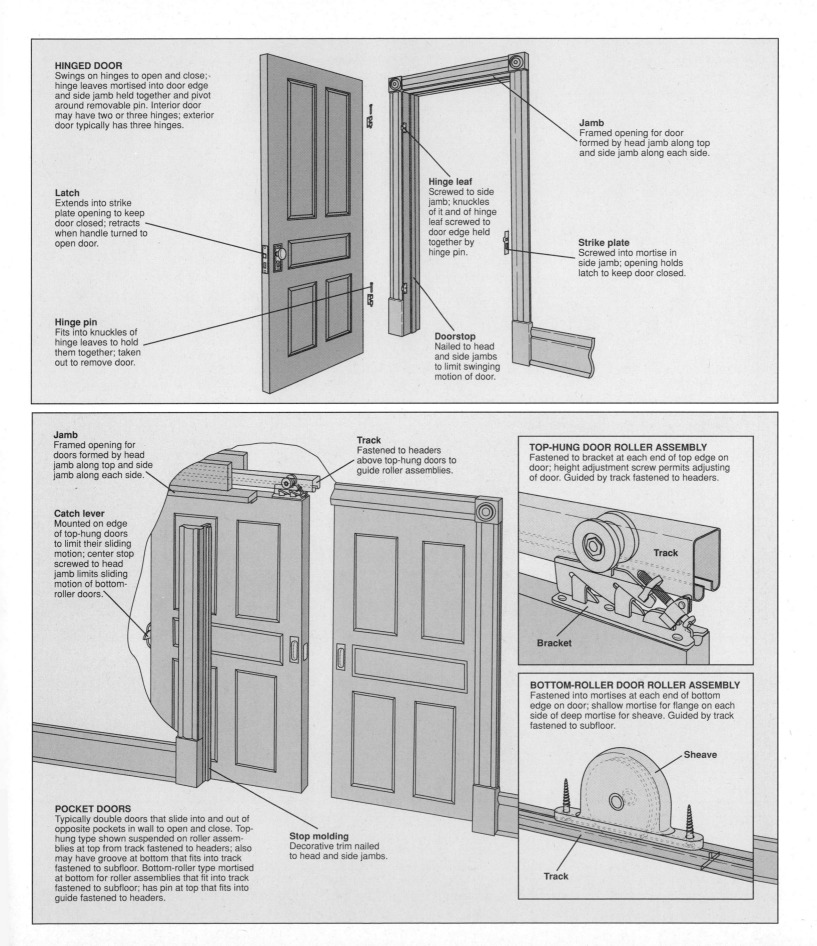

HINGED DOOR
Swings on hinges to open and close; hinge leaves mortised into door edge and side jamb held together and pivot around removable pin. Interior door may have two or three hinges; exterior door typically has three hinges.

Jamb
Framed opening for door formed by head jamb along top and side jamb along each side.

Latch
Extends into strike plate opening to keep door closed; retracts when handle turned to open door.

Hinge leaf
Screwed to side jamb; knuckles of it and of hinge leaf screwed to door edge held together by hinge pin.

Strike plate
Screwed into mortise in side jamb; opening holds latch to keep door closed.

Hinge pin
Fits into knuckles of hinge leaves to hold them together; taken out to remove door.

Doorstop
Nailed to head and side jambs to limit swinging motion of door.

Jamb
Framed opening for doors formed by head jamb along top and side jamb along each side.

Track
Fastened to headers above top-hung doors to guide roller assemblies.

TOP-HUNG DOOR ROLLER ASSEMBLY
Fastened to bracket at each end of top edge on door; height adjustment screw permits adjusting of door. Guided by track fastened to headers.

Track

Bracket

Catch lever
Mounted on edge of top-hung doors to limit their sliding motion; center stop screwed to head jamb limits sliding motion of bottom-roller doors.

BOTTOM-ROLLER DOOR ROLLER ASSEMBLY
Fastened into mortises at each end of bottom edge on door; shallow mortise for flange on each side of deep mortise for sheave. Guided by track fastened to subfloor.

Sheave

Stop molding
Decorative trim nailed to head and side jambs.

POCKET DOORS
Typically double doors that slide into and out of opposite pockets in wall to open and close. Top-hung type shown suspended on roller assemblies at top from track fastened to headers; also may have groove at bottom that fits into track fastened to subfloor. Bottom-roller type mortised at bottom for roller assemblies that fit into track fastened to subfloor; has pin at top that fits into guide fastened to headers.

Track

REMOVING AND REHANGING A HINGED DOOR

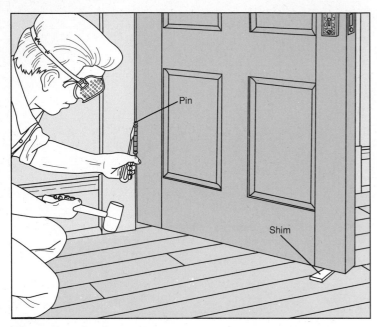

Removing the door. Wedge the door open with a wood shim or have a helper hold it open, then work up from the bottom to remove each hinge pin. If the pin is sealed at the bottom, place the tip of an old screwdriver under its head and tap it loose with a rubber mallet *(above)*. Otherwise, place the tip of a nail set on the bottom of the pin and use the mallet to tap it loose. Loosen the pin enough to pull out by hand. After removing each pin, lift the door off the hinges; if necessary, work with a helper.

Rehanging the door. Lubricate the hinge pins with light machine oil, then rest the door on a wood shim and maneuver it into position; if necessary, work with a helper. Working down from the top of the door, fit its hinge leaves with the hinge leaves on the jamb *(above)*; be careful not to pinch your fingers. Align the knuckles of each hinge in turn and slip its pin into it as far as possible by hand, then tap the pin down into place with a ball-peen hammer. After installing the pins in the hinges, remove the shim.

SHIMMING A HINGE

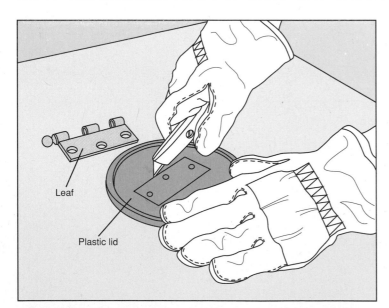

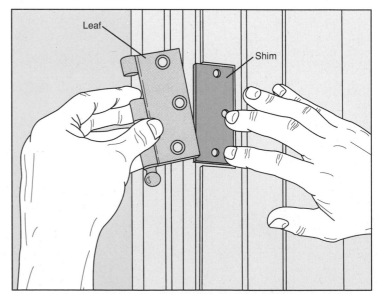

1 Making the shim. If the hinge leaves are not recessed below the door edge and the jamb, trim the binding spot *(page 45)*; otherwise, shim the leaf with the deepest mortise. To shim the leaf, remove the door; if it has more than two hinges, remove only the hinge pin *(step above, left)*. Unscrew the leaf, then use an old screwdriver to pry it out of its mortise. To make a shim, trace the leaf edges and screwholes onto a lid of thin plastic. Wearing work gloves, cut out the shim with a utility knife *(above)*, then punch the screwholes using an awl.

2 Installing the shim. Position the shim in the mortise and place the leaf on it *(above)*, then align the screwholes and drive in the screws. Rehang the door or reinstall the hinge pin *(step above, right)*, then close the door. If the door binds at the same location, make *(step 1)* and install as many shims as necessary for it to close and open freely. If the door still binds when the hinge leaves are flush with the door edge and the jamb, trim the binding spot *(page 45)*.

TRIMMING AN UNHINGED EDGE

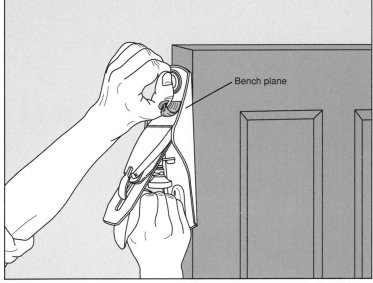

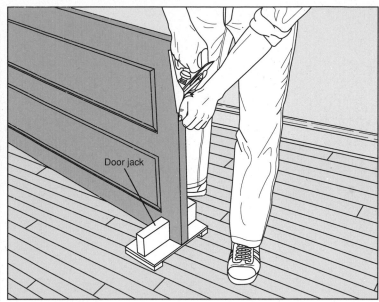

Bench plane

Door jack

Spot-planing an edge. Remove a hinged *(page 44)*, top-hung pocket *(page 49)* or bottom-roller pocket *(page 50)* door if its binding spot is not accessible. To trim a little off the binding spot, use sandpaper and a sanding block. Otherwise, trim the binding spot using a bench plane. For a binding spot along the latched edge of a hinged door, wedge the door open with a wood shim. Position the plane flat on the edge just to one side of the binding spot and apply moderate pressure to trim to the

other side of it *(above, left)*. For a binding spot along the bottom edge of a door, set the door lengthwise between door jacks *(page 51)* and trim the same way *(above, right)*. If the plane catches or gouges the wood, reverse its direction to smooth the cut. Continue trimming until the door can close and open freely, leaving enough clearance for any refinishing. Refinish the door, then rehang it if you removed it.

TRIMMING A HINGED EDGE

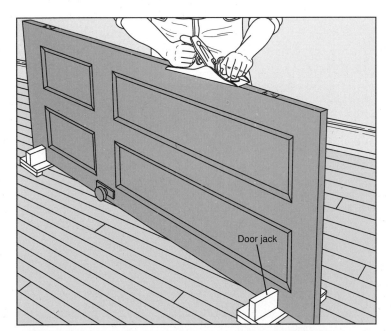

Door jack

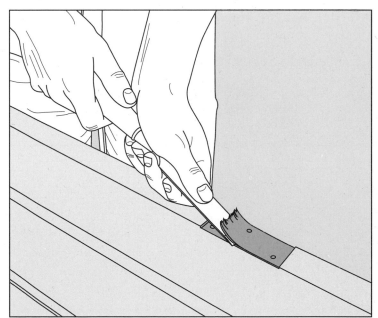

1 Planing the edge. Remove the door *(page 44)* and set it lengthwise on its latched edge between door jacks *(page 51)*. Unscrew each hinge leaf from the door edge and pry it out of its mortise, then trim the edge using a bench plane. Starting at one end of the edge, position the plane flat and apply moderate pressure to trim to the other end of it *(above)*. If the plane catches or gouges the wood, reverse its direction to smooth the cut. Continue trimming until the door can close and open freely, leaving enough clearance for any refinishing.

2 Deepening the mortises. Deepen each mortise until its hinge leaf can sit flush with the door edge. Score along the ends of the mortise using a wood chisel, tapping it with a wooden mallet. Then, work with the chisel bevel-side down to remove wood from the mortise, guiding it along the grain to pare off a thin shaving *(above)*. When the hinge leaf can sit flush with the door edge, screw it into place. Refinish the door, then rehang it *(page 44)*.

ADJUSTING A DOORSTOP

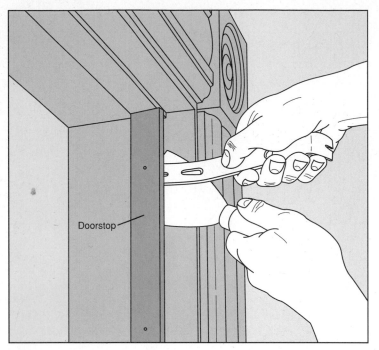

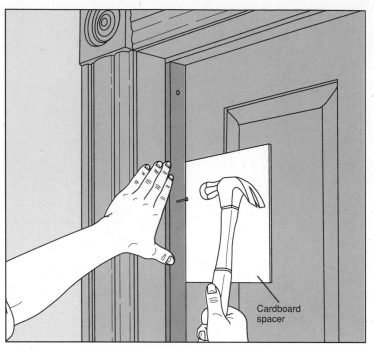

1 **Removing the stops.** To reposition each stop without removing it, use a utility knife to break any finish bond between it and the jamb, then hold a wood block against it and tap with a mallet. If the door still does not close freely, start along the latched edge to remove each stop. Fit the blade of a putty knife under one end of the stop to pull it from the jamb, then work carefully along it with a utility bar to pry it off *(above)*. Use a nail puller to pull out the nails.

2 **Reinstalling the stops.** Close the door and start along the hinged edge to reinstall each stop. Position the stop using a spacer of cardboard to maintain a narrow gap between it and the door. Then, drive a finishing nail through each hole in the stop into the jamb *(above)*. Set the nail heads using a nail set. Refinish the stops and the jambs, if necessary, or fill the nail heads.

ADJUSTING A STRIKE PLATE

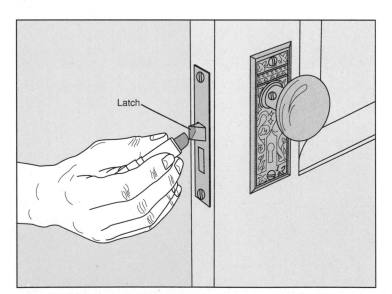

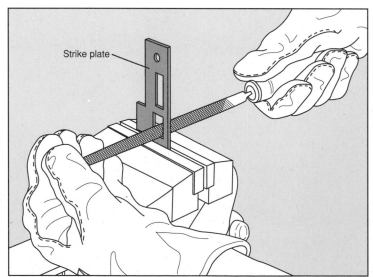

1 **Checking the strike plate.** Open the door and coat the tip of the latch with lipstick *(above)*, then retract it to close the door. Release the latch to mark the strike plate, then retract it to open the door. If the lipstick mark is to the side of the strike plate opening, adjust the doorstops *(steps above)*. Otherwise, measure the gap between the strike plate opening and the lipstick mark. If the gap is less than 1/8 inch, enlarge the strike plate opening *(step 2)*. If the gap is 1/8 inch or more, reposition the strike plate *(step 3)*.

2 **Enlarging the strike plate opening.** Unscrew the strike plate and take it off the jamb, using an old screwdriver to pry it out of its mortise. Secure the strike plate in a vise, aligning the lipstick mark on it slightly above the jaws; protect its face with masking tape, if necessary. Use a flat file to enlarge the strike plate opening *(above)*, removing material evenly from the edge until the lipstick mark disappears. Then, screw the strike plate back onto the jamb.

ADJUSTING A STRIKE PLATE (continued)

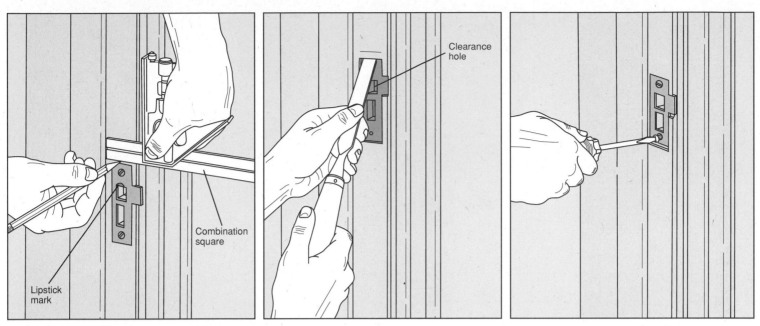

Clearance hole

Combination square

Lipstick mark

3 **Repositioning the strike plate.** Using a combination square, mark a horizontal line across the jamb the same distance above *(above, left)* or below the strike plate as the gap between the strike plate opening and the lipstick mark. Unscrew the strike plate and take it off the jamb, using an old screwdriver to pry it out of its mortise. Score the marked line across the jamb using a utility knife and a straightedge, then use a wood chisel to extend the mortise at the same depth to the scored line *(above, center)*. Extend each clearance hole in the jamb by an amount equal to the extension of the mortise using a wood chisel with a wooden mallet. Plug the screwholes in the jamb with glue-coated toothpicks and cut off the protruding ends. Position the strike plate in the mortise and mark new screwholes, then bore a pilot hole at each marked hole and screw the strike plate to the jamb *(above, right)*. Fill the excess mortise and refinish the jamb, if necessary.

SHIMMING A STRIKE PLATE

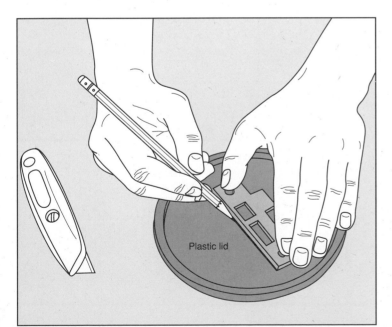

Plastic lid

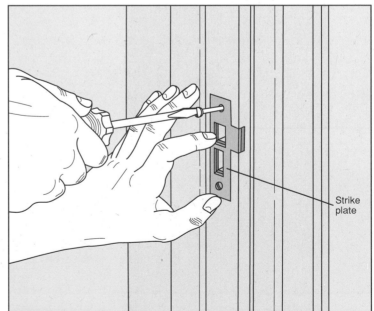

Strike plate

1 **Making the shim.** If the strike plate is not recessed below the jamb, shim each hinge of the door by an equal amount *(page 44)*; otherwise, shim the strike plate. Unscrew the strike plate and take it off the jamb, using an old screwdriver to pry it out of its mortise. To make a shim, trace the edges and screwholes of the strike plate onto a lid of thin plastic *(above)*. Wearing work gloves, cut out the shim with a utility knife, then punch the screwholes cosing an awl.

2 **Installing the shim.** Position the shim in the mortise and place the strike plate on it, then align the screwholes and drive in the screws *(above)*. If the door does not stay closed, repeat the procedure, making *(step 1)* and installing as many shims as necessary. If the door still does not stay closed when the strike plate is flush with the jamb, shim each hinge by an equal amount *(page 44)*.

LUBRICATING A TOP-HUNG POCKET DOOR ROLLER ASSEMBLY

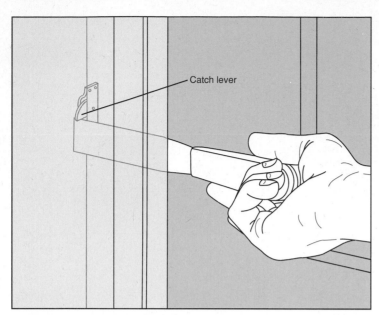

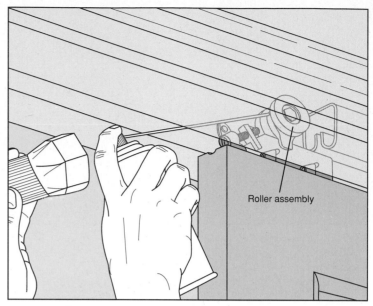

1 **Sliding the door out of the pocket.** Work with a helper to slide the door out of its pocket. If the stop moldings obstruct the door, remove them *(page 49)*. Holding the door by its exposed edge, rock and pull it out of the pocket a little at a time. As the opposite edge of the door reaches the wall opening, flip up its catch lever with a putty knife *(above)*, allowing it to clear the pocket. **Caution:** Support the door to keep it from toppling as it clears the pocket.

2 **Lubricating the roller assemblies.** With your helper supporting the door, use a stepladder and a flashlight to locate the roller assembly at each end of it. Lubricate each roller assembly with a silicone-based lubricant, using its extension tube to spray the axle, in particular *(above)*. Flipping up the catch lever to push the door into its pocket, slide it back and forth a few times, then lubricate each roller assembly again. Wipe up stray lubricant with a clean cloth.

ADJUSTING A TOP-HUNG POCKET DOOR ROLLER ASSEMBLY

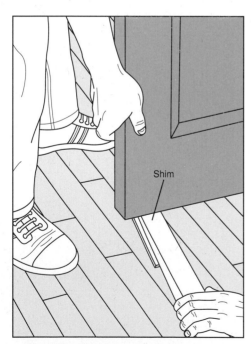

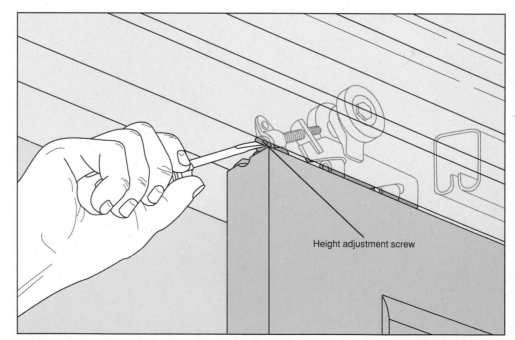

1 **Shimming the door.** Slide the door out of its pocket *(step 1, above)*; if it jams against the floor or the track before clearing its pocket, slide it back slightly. Prop the door on wood shims *(above)* to take the weight off the rollers, then adjust its height *(step 2)*.

2 **Adjusting the door height.** Use a stepladder and a flashlight to locate the height adjustment screw of each roller assembly. Use a screwdriver to turn the height adjustment screw: clockwise to raise the end of the door *(above)*; counterclockwise to lower it. Have a helper add wood shims under the door as it is raised or remove them as it is lowered. To keep the same alignment of the door, raise or lower each end of it equally. To adjust the alignment of the door, raise its low end and lower its high end. If the door binds when it is raised to its limit, remove it *(page 49)* and trim the binding spot or edge *(page 45)*.

REMOVING AND REHANGING A TOP-HUNG POCKET DOOR

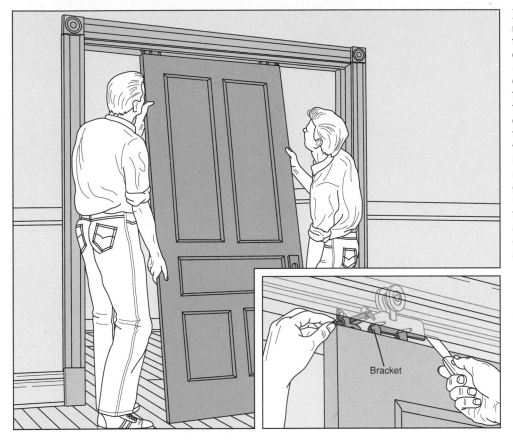

Removing and rehanging the door. To remove the door, take the stop molding off the top jamb *(step 1, below)*, then slide the door out of its pocket and lower each end of it *(page 48)* until the height adjustment screw comes out. Free each roller assembly from its bracket, then use a putty knife to slide it toward the center of the door. Work with a helper to swing the door out of the wall opening, pulling it at the bottom to clear the track *(left)*. To rehang the door, work with your helper to swing it into position under the track. Use a putty knife to fit each roller assembly into its bracket, engaging the fingers with the slots. Having your helper keep the roller assembly in position with a putty knife, fit the height adjustment screw into its hole *(inset)* and turn it clockwise a few turns to start it. Adjust each roller assembly *(page 48)* and reinstall the stop molding on the top jamb *(step 2, below)*.

Bracket

ADJUSTING A STOP MOLDING

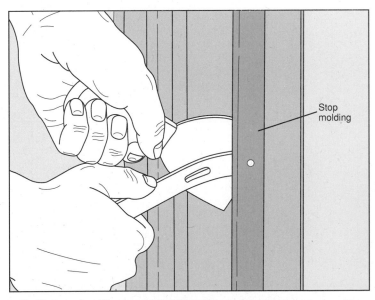

1 Removing the stop molding. To reposition each stop molding without removing it, use a utility knife to break any finish bond between it and the jamb, then hold a wood block against it and tap with a mallet. If the door still does not move freely, start along the pocket edge to remove each stop molding. Fit the blade of a putty knife under one end of the stop molding to pull it from the jamb, then work carefully along it with a utility bar to pry it off *(above)*. Use a nail puller to pull out the nails.

Stop molding

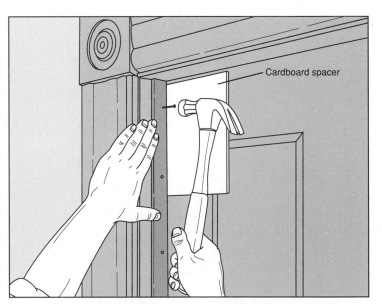

2 Reinstalling the stop molding. Close the door and start along the pocket edge to reinstall each stop molding. Position the stop molding using a spacer of cardboard to maintain a narrow gap between it and the door. Then, drive a finishing nail through each hole in the stop molding into the jamb *(above)*. Set the nail heads using a nail set. Refinish the stop molding and the jambs, if necessary, or fill the nail heads.

Cardboard spacer

LEVELING A BOTTOM-ROLLER POCKET DOOR TRACK

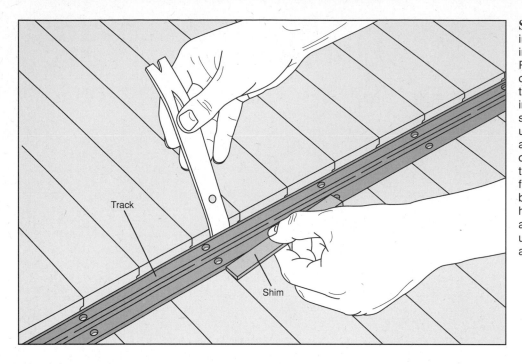

Track

Shim

Shimming the door track. Slide each door into its pocket and remove the screws securing the track to the subfloor in the wall opening. Run a string along the top of the track in the wall opening, fastening each end of it with a thumbtack pressed into the subfloor. To locate a sag in the track, check for a gap between it and the string. Gently lift the track at each sag with a utility bar and fit a wood shim under it *(left)*, adding as many as necessary to level it without causing the door to bind at the top. When the track is level, fill any gap between it and the subfloor with other shims. Use an electric drill to bore a pilot hole through each shim at a screwhole in the track, then put back the screws. Cut any protruding shim flush with the track using a utility knife, then caulk each edge of the track along the subfloor.

REMOVING AND REHANGING A BOTTOM-ROLLER POCKET DOOR

Center stop

Removing and rehanging the door. To remove the door, take the center stop off the top jamb *(inset)*, then work with a helper to slide the door out of its pocket. If the stop moldings obstruct the door, remove them *(page 49)*. Holding the door by its exposed edge, rock and pull it out of the pocket a little at a time. **Caution:** Support the door to keep it from toppling as it clears the pocket. When the door clears the pocket, swing it out of the wall opening, lifting it at the bottom to clear the track *(left)*. If the guide at the top of the wall opening obstructs the door, force it up slightly by wedging a 2-by-4 equal in length to the height of the door under it; use scrap wood to protect the floor. To rehang the door, work with your helper to swing it into position in the track, then slide it into its pocket. Screw the center stop back onto the top jamb and reinstall any stop molding removed.

SERVICING A BOTTOM-ROLLER POCKET DOOR ROLLER ASSEMBLY

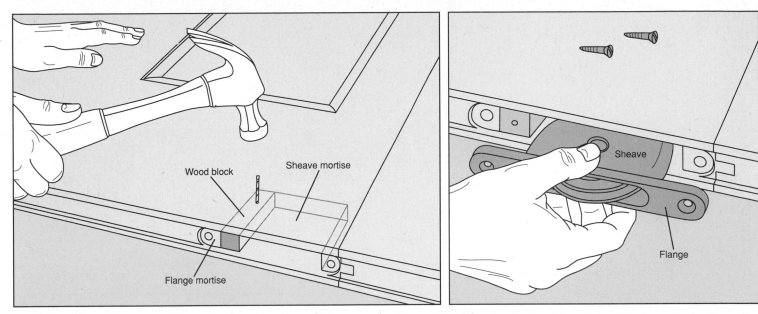

Replacing the roller assembly. Remove the door *(page 50)*, then take out the roller asssembly. To lubricate the roller assembly, use a silicone-based lubricant. If the roller assembly is damaged, buy a replacement or a large double-hung window sash cord pulley—usually available at an architectural or window salvage or hardware supply center, or through a specialty woodworking catalog. If the replacement sheave is smaller than the original, fill the gap along one side of the mortise with a wood block. Use a wood chisel to smooth the surfaces of the mortise, then glue the block into place. Drive a 1-inch finishing nail through the door into each end of the block *(above, left)* and set the nail heads with a nail set. To enlarge the mortise for the replacement sheave or deepen the mortise for a flange to sit flush, use a wood chisel. Fit the replacement sheave into its mortise to mark the screwholes of the flanges, then bore a pilot hole at each marked point. Reposition the replacement sheave *(above, right)* and drive in the screws, then rehang the door.

SUPPORTING A DOOR WITH DOOR JACKS

Propping up a door. Use door jacks to support a door securely while trimming it. To make a door jack, cut a piece of 1/4-inch plywood 18 inches long and 6 inches wide, two 2-by-4 pieces 8 inches long and two 1-by-3 pieces 6 inches long. Position the 2-by-4s end to end with a 2-inch space between them on their narrow edge under the center of the plywood, then bore pilot holes and fasten them with screws *(inset)*. Turn over the plywood, then position the 1-by-3s on their wide edge under the ends of it and fasten them with nails *(above, left)*. To support a door, position two jacks on the floor, then fit the top *(above, right)* and bottom of it into the space between their 2-by-4 pieces.

WINDOWS

There are few features of an older home that can match the artful technology and craftsmanship of the traditional double-hung and casement windows, leaded-glass panes, and skylights that usually grace it; refer to page 53 for illustrations showing the details of their typical construction. Yet, the windows are often an Achilles' heel, their functional elegance inevitably suffering from the cumulative wear of use as well as the natural cycles of temperature and humidity change. Thankfully, most problems with the windows are seldom difficult to correct—a blessing, since replacing one window poses the challenge of duplicating the others and replacing all the windows raises the unsettling question of cost. For assistance in undertaking a particular repair to a window, consult the Troubleshooting Guide below.

Most repairs to the windows of an older home are usually easily undertaken with only a few basic carpentry tools; refer to Tools & Techniques *(page 124)* for instructions on using tools properly, as well as for information on working safely from a ladder or on the roof. Keep in mind that some repairs to a window of leaded-glass panes may require specialized techniques. For example, replacing a leaded-glass pane is a job that is not complicated or time-consuming to conduct if the cames are flat or only gently rounded and flexible enough for their edges to be manipulated; if the cames are fully rounded or rigid, however, it is a delicate task that should be entrusted to a skilled professional. Before starting any repair to a window, familiarize yourself with the information presented in the Emergency Guide *(page 8)*.

TROUBLESHOOTING GUIDE

SYMPTOM	POSSIBLE CAUSE	PROCEDURE
DOUBLE-HUNG WINDOW		
Sash does not open	Sash nailed or screwed shut	Remove nails or screws holding sash shut
	Sash painted shut	Unjam double-hung sash *(p. 54)* □ ○
Sash does not slide open or closed smoothly	Channels lack lubricant	Lubricate sash channels with paraffin wax or silicone-based lubricant
	Finish buildup along channels	Remove excess finish from sash channels
	Surface binds against stop, stool or parting strip	Trim double-hung sash *(p. 56)* ◪ ◒
	Joint loose or cracked	Reinforce sash joint *(p. 56)* ◪ ◒
	Cord or chain broken	Replace sash cords or chains *(p. 57)* ◪ ◒
	Pulley lacks lubricant or damaged	Service sash pulley *(p. 58)* □ ○
Sash does not stay up	Cord or chain broken	Replace sash cords or chains *(p. 57)* ◪ ◒
CASEMENT WINDOW		
Sash does not open	Sash nailed or screwed shut	Remove nails or screws holding sash shut
	Sash painted shut	Unjam casement sash *(p. 59)* □ ○
Sash does not swing open or closed smoothly	Hinge screws loose	Tighten hinge screws
	Finish buildup on edge or jamb	Remove excess finish from binding spots
	Top edge binds against jamb	Shim top hinge *(p. 60)* □ ○ or trim binding spot *(p. 60)* ◪ ○
	Bottom edge binds against sill	Shim bottom hinge *(p. 60)* □ ○ or trim binding spot *(p. 60)* ◪ ○
	Top of latched edge binds against other sash	Shim bottom hinge *(p. 60)* □ ○ or trim binding spot *(p. 60)* ◪ ○
	Bottom of latched edge binds against other sash	Shim top hinge *(p. 60)* □ ○ or trim binding spot *(p. 60)* ◪ ○
	Center of latched edge binds against other sash	Trim hinged edge *(p. 61)* ◪ ◒
	Joint loose or cracked	Reinforce sash joint *(p. 56)* ◪ ◒
LEADED-GLASS WINDOW		
Pane loose; rattles	Glazing compound deteriorated	Replace leaded-glass glazing compound *(p. 61)* ◪ ○
Pane cracked or broken	Accidental blow or impact	Replace leaded-glass pane *(p. 62)* ■ ◒
Panes and cames bowed	Normal aging of cames	Reinforce leaded-glass sash *(p. 64)* ◪ ◒
SKYLIGHT		
Pane cracked or broken	Accidental blow or impact	Replace skylight pane *(p. 64)* ◪ ◒

DEGREE OF DIFFICULTY: □ Easy ◪ Moderate ■ Complex
ESTIMATED TIME: ○ Less than 1 hour ◒ 1 to 3 hours ● Over 3 hours

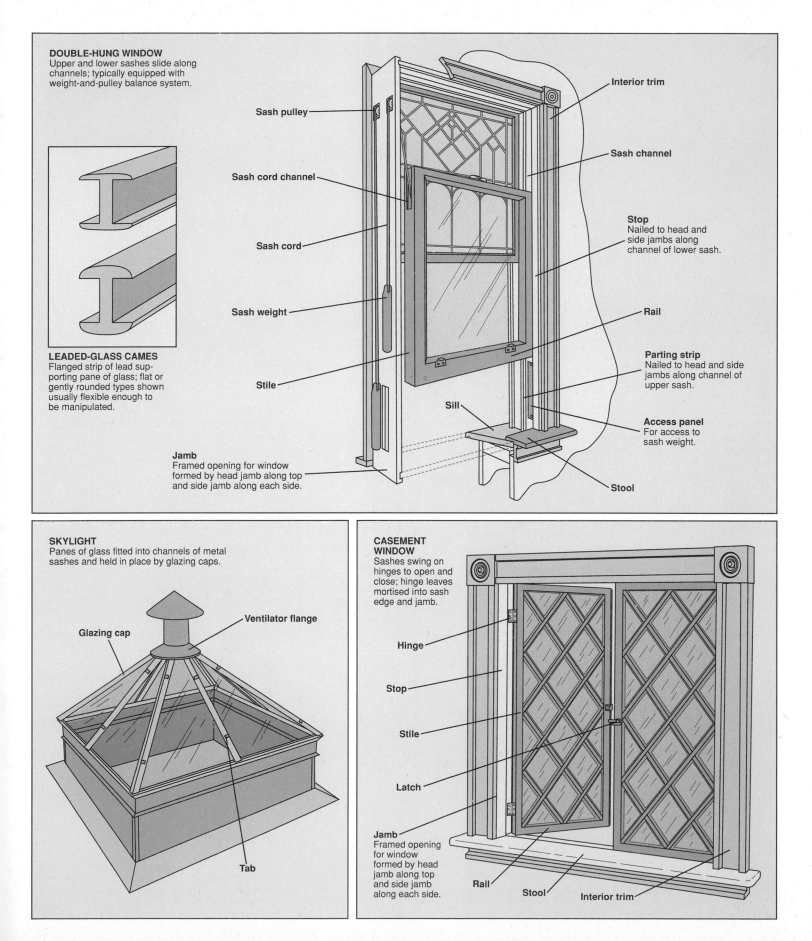

DOUBLE-HUNG WINDOW
Upper and lower sashes slide along channels; typically equipped with weight-and-pulley balance system.

LEADED-GLASS CAMES
Flanged strip of lead supporting pane of glass; flat or gently rounded types shown usually flexible enough to be manipulated.

Sash pulley

Sash cord channel

Sash cord

Sash weight

Stile

Jamb
Framed opening for window formed by head jamb along top and side jamb along each side.

Interior trim

Sash channel

Stop
Nailed to head and side jambs along channel of lower sash.

Rail

Parting strip
Nailed to head and side jambs along channel of upper sash.

Access panel
For access to sash weight.

Sill

Stool

SKYLIGHT
Panes of glass fitted into channels of metal sashes and held in place by glazing caps.

Glazing cap

Ventilator flange

Tab

CASEMENT WINDOW
Sashes swing on hinges to open and close; hinge leaves mortised into sash edge and jamb.

Hinge

Stop

Stile

Latch

Jamb
Framed opening for window formed by head jamb along top and side jamb along each side.

Rail

Stool

Interior trim

FREEING A DOUBLE-HUNG SASH

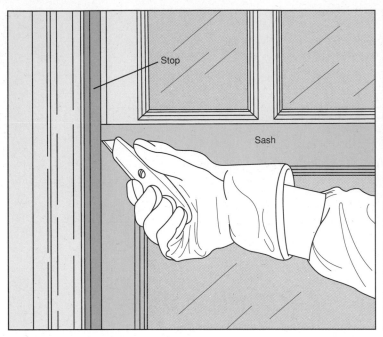

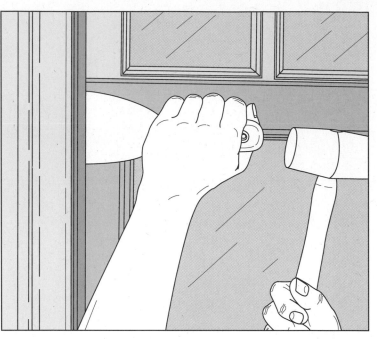

1 **Unjamming the sash.** Remove any nail or screw driven through the sash to lock it. Wearing work gloves, use a utility knife to break any finish bond along the joints at the perimeter of the sash; work carefully to avoid marring any surface. For the lower sash, run the utility knife between it and each stop *(above, left)*, the stool, and the bottom rail of the upper sash. To unjam the lower sash, work the blade of a wide putty knife as deep as possible along the joints, tapping gently

with a mallet along each stop until it bottoms out against the jamb *(above, right)*. For the upper sash, run the utility knife and work the blade of the putty knife in turn between it and each side parting strip, the top parting strip, and the top rail of the lower sash. If possible, work the same way on the exterior side of the sash; otherwise, pry the sash open indoors *(step 3)*.

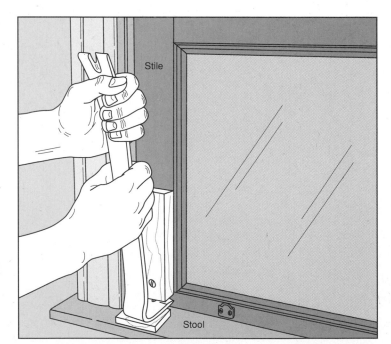

2 **Prying the sash open outdoors.** For the lower sash, work two wide putty knives into one end of the joint between it and the sill, then fit a pry bar between them and force the sash up about 1/4 inch *(above)*. Wedge a wood block under the corner of the sash and repeat the procedure at the other end of the joint between it and the sill. Continue the same way, using wood blocks and the pry bar to force up each corner of the sash a little at a time until it opens and closes. For the upper sash, screw a wood block to the top of each stile on its exterior side and pry it open as you would indoors *(step 3)*.

3 **Prying the sash open indoors.** For the lower sash, screw a wood block to the bottom of each stile about 3/4 inch from the stool. Protecting the stool with a wood block, fit a pry bar between the wood blocks at one corner of the sash and force it up about 1/4 inch *(above)*. Then, repeat the procedure at the other corner of the sash. Continue forcing up each corner of the sash a little at a time until it opens and closes. For the upper sash, screw a wood block to the top of each stile about 3/4 inch from the top parting strip and force down each corner of it the same way.

REMOVING AND REINSTALLING A DOUBLE-HUNG SASH

1 Removing a stop. Remove the stop along one side of the lower sash. To break any finish bond, run a utility knife along each joint between the stop and the jamb, opening the sashes as needed. Then, work the blade of a wide putty knife under one end of the stop and gently pull it away from the jamb. Protecting the jamb with the putty knife, fit a pry bar under the stop and work carefully along it to pry it off *(above)*. Use a nail puller to pull the nails out of the stop.

2 Removing the lower sash. Close the lower sash, then pull its sash cords or chains as far as possible out of the pockets and secure them in position with nails. Open the lower sash slightly and swing its side without a stop away from the jamb *(above)*, then hold it in position and have a helper remove the sash cord or chain from its side. Swing the other side of the lower sash away from the jamb and have the helper remove its sash cord or chain.

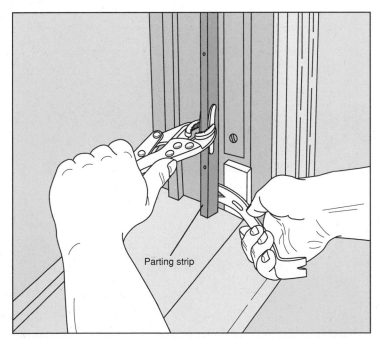

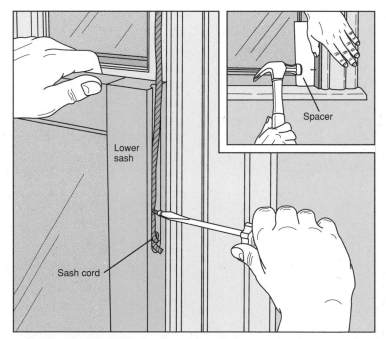

3 Removing the upper sash. Remove the parting strip along the side of the upper sash without a stop. To break any finish bond, run a utility knife along each joint between the parting strip and the jamb, opening the sash as needed. Using thin wood pads to protect the parting strip, grip one end of it with locking pliers and gently pull it away from the jamb. Fit a pry bar under the parting strip and work carefully along it to pry it off *(above)*, then pull out the nails. Take out the upper sash the same way as the lower sash *(step 2)*.

4 Reinstalling the sashes. To reinstall each sash, reverse the procedure used to remove it. For the upper sash, fasten its sash cords or chains to its sides and swing it back into place, then remove the nails used to secure the sash cords or chains. Position the parting strip using a spacer of cardboard to maintain a narrow gap between it and the upper sash, then drive finishing nails through its holes into the jamb and set the nail heads. For the upper sash, work the same way *(above)*, nailing the stop to the jamb *(inset)*. Refinish any damaged surface.

TRIMMING A DOUBLE-HUNG SASH

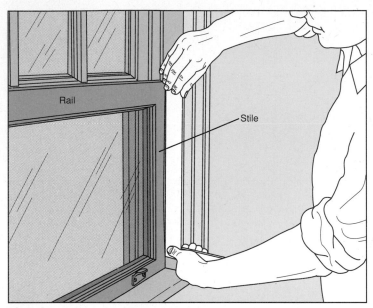

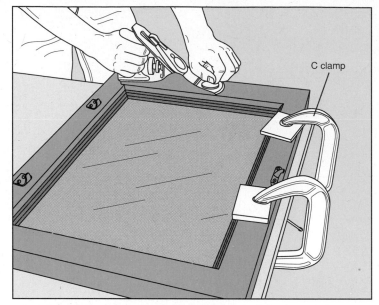

1 **Locating the binding surface.** To locate a binding spot on the sash, position a metal straightedge on its edge in turn along the surface of each stile *(above)* and rail. If the straightedge does not sit flat on the surface, check for the gaps. If there is a gap of more than 1/4 inch, consult a professional about replacing the sash. Otherwise, use the gaps to find the edges of each binding spot, then mark its outline on the surface with a pencil. Remove the sash *(page 55)* and clamp it to a work table, then spot-plane each binding surface *(step 2)*.

2 **Spot-planing the binding surface.** Take any hardware off the binding surface, then spot-plane it using a bench plane. Position the plane flat on the surface just to one side of the binding spot and apply moderate pressure to trim along the wood grain to the other side of it *(above)*. If the plane gouges or catches the wood, reverse its direction to smooth the cut. Continue until each binding spot is level, checking the surface with the straightedge *(step 1)*. Sand the surface and refinish it, then reinstall the sash *(page 55)*.

REINFORCING A SASH JOINT

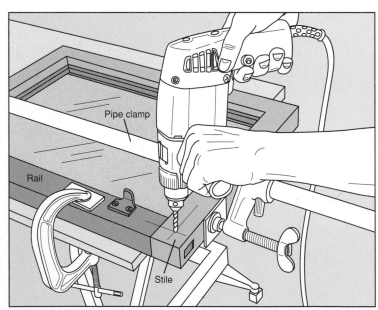

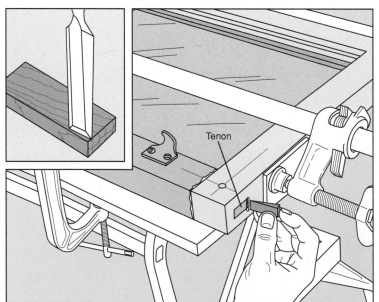

Tightening a mortise and tenon. Remove the double-hung *(page 55)* or casement *(page 59)* sash. Pull any loose wedge out of the mortise and use a putty knife to clean the joint between the rail and the stile. Clamp the sash to a work table and use a pipe clamp to close the joint between the rail and the stile. Mark a line along the center of the rail and the stile, then bore a hole through the sash at the intersection of the lines using an electric drill fitted with a 1/4-inch twist bit *(above, left)*. Cut a wedge for the mortise from a wood block

using a wood chisel *(inset)* and cut a 1/4-inch dowel for the hole in the sash. Remove the pipe clamp to coat the joint between the rail and the stile with wood glue, then reinstall it. Coat the wedge with wood glue and fit it into the mortise next to the tenon *(above, right)*, then coat the dowel with wood glue and fit it into the hole in the sash. Tap the wedge and the dowel into place with a mallet and wipe off extruded glue, then sand them flush with the surfaces of the sash. Refinish the sash and reinstall it.

REPLACING SASH CORDS OR CHAINS

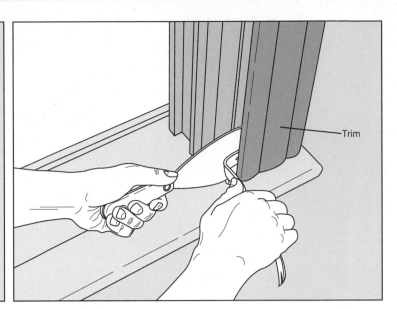

Access plate

Trim

1 **Gaining access to the sash weights.** Replace both sash cords or chains—even if only one is broken. Open the lower sash and unscrew the access plate for the weight attached to each sash cord or chain *(above, left)*. If there are no access plates, remove the trim covering the pocket of the weight attached to each sash cord or chain. To break any finish bond, run a utility knife along each joint between the trim and the jamb, the wall, and any corner block or other trim. Then, work the blade of a wide putty knife under one end of the trim and gently pull it away from the jamb. Protecting the jamb with the putty knife, fit a pry bar under the trim and work carefully along it to pry it off *(above, right)*. Use a nail puller to pull the nails out of the trim.

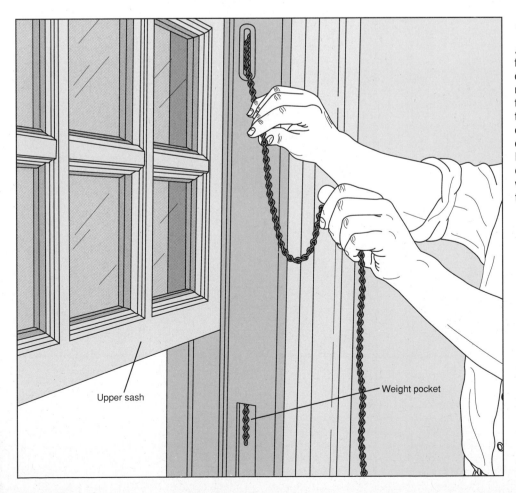

Upper sash

Weight pocket

2 **Positioning the replacement sash chains.** Remove the sash *(page 55)*, then unfasten its sash cords or chains from the weights. Buy replacement sash chains of the same length as the cords or chains removed at a building supply center; ensure that the sash chains are strong enough to support the sash and the weights. To position each sash chain, feed one end of it through the pulley and down to the bottom of the weight pocket *(left)*. Pull the end of the sash chain out of the bottom of the weight pocket far enough to fasten it to its weight, then fit a nail through its link at the pulley to secure it in place.

REPLACING SASH CORDS OR CHAINS (continued)

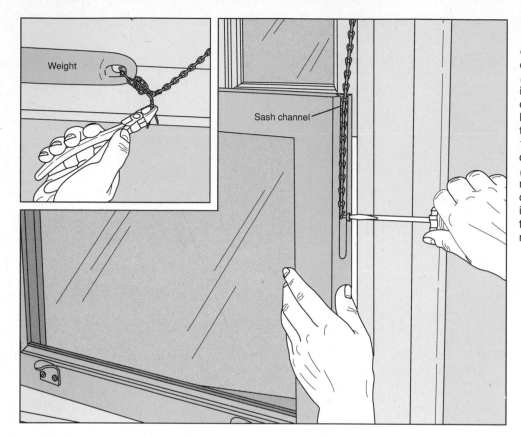

Weight

Sash channel

3 **Fastening the replacement sash chains.** Loop the end of each sash chain through the eye of its weight and use pliers to tie two of its links together with baling wire *(inset)*. Set each weight into its pocket and raise it to its maximum height by pulling the sash chain down from the pulley, then fit a nail through the link at the pulley to secure it in place. To fasten the end of each sash chain to the sash, use a 1-inch wood screw, fitting it with a washer and driving it through the end link into the channel *(left)*. Having a helper hold the sash in position, remove the nails securing the sash chains and open the sash fully. If the weights are less than 3 inches from the bottom of their pockets, shorten the sash chains. Screw in the access plates or nail on the trim, then reinstall the sash *(page 55)*.

SERVICING A SASH PULLEY

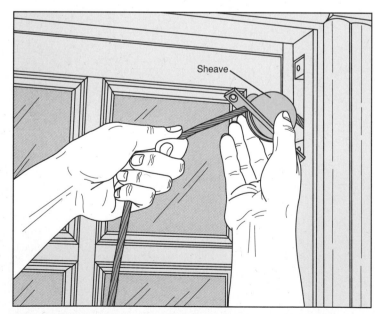

Sheave

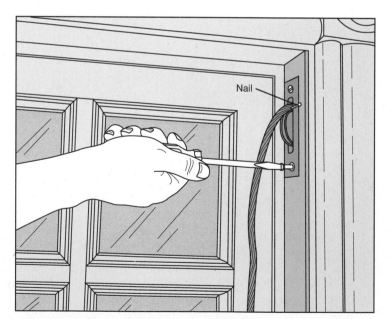

Nail

1 **Removing the pulley.** Remove the sash *(page 55)*, then unscrew the pulley sheave and take it off the jamb, using an old screwdriver to pry it out of its mortise. Hold the sash cord or chain and remove the nail used to secure it, then slide the pulley down off it *(above)* and resecure it with the nail. Clean the pulley and its sheave, then lubricate it with light machine oil. If the pulley is damaged, buy a replacement—usually available at an architectural or window salvage or hardware supply center, or through a specialty woodworking catalog.

2 **Reinstalling the pulley.** Feed the end of the sash cord or chain around the sheave and out through the pulley, then slide the pulley up it to the mortise in the jamb. Hold the sash cord or chain and remove the nail used to secure it, then fit the pulley sheave into the mortise in the jamb and resecure it with the nail. Tap the pulley sheave into place in the mortise with a mallet, if necessary, and screw it to the jamb *(above)*, then reinstall the sash *(page 55)*.

FREEING A CASEMENT SASH

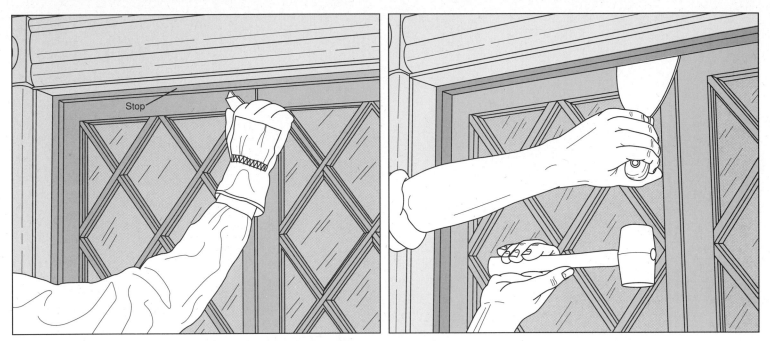

Unjamming the sash. Remove any nail or screw driven through the sash to lock it. Wearing work gloves, use a utility knife to break any finish bond along the joints at the perimeter of the sash *(above, left)*; work carefully to avoid marring any surface. To unjam the sash, work the blade of a wide putty knife as deep as possible along the joints, tapping gently with a mallet along each stop until it bottoms out against the jamb *(above, right)*. If possible, work the same way on the exterior side of the sash. If necessary, force the sash open by holding a wood block against the stile near the latch and tapping it with the mallet.

REMOVING AND REINSTALLING A CASEMENT SASH

Removing and reinstalling the sash. To remove the sash, open it fully and have a helper support it. Take out all but the top screw from each hinge leaf on the jamb *(left)*, then start at the top hinge leaf on the jamb to remove the top screws. Gently rock and pull the sash as necessary to free the hinge leaves from their mortises. To reinstall the sash, have a helper support it in position, then fit each hinge leaf into its mortise and start at the bottom hinge leaf to drive in the top screws. Then, drive the other screws through each hinge leaf into the jamb.

SHIMMING A SASH HINGE

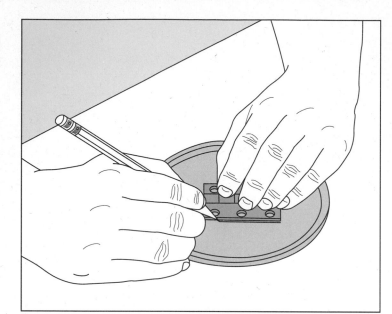

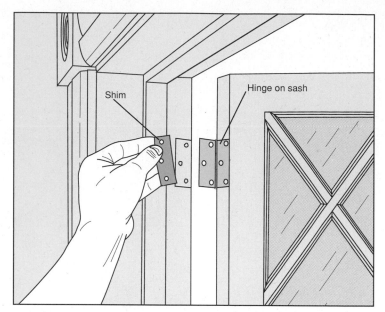

1 Making the shim. If the hinge leaves are not recessed below the sash edge and the jamb, trim the binding unhinged *(step below)* or hinged *(page 61)* edge of the sash; otherwise, shim the leaf with the deepest mortise. To shim the leaf, remove the sash *(page 59)* and unscrew the hinge, using an old screwdriver to pry it out of its mortise. To make a shim, trace the leaf edges and screwholes onto a lid of thin plastic *(above)*. Wearing work gloves, cut out the shim with a utility knife, then punch the screwholes using an awl.

2 Installing the shim. To shim the jamb leaf, screw the hinge to the sash, then fit the shim into the jamb mortise *(above)* to reinstall the sash *(page 59)*. To shim the sash leaf, fit the shim into the sash mortise and screw on the hinge, then reinstall the sash. If the sash binds at the same location, make *(step 1)* and install as many shims as necessary for it to open and close freely. If the sash still binds when the hinge leaves are flush with the sash edge and the jamb, trim its binding unhinged *(step below)* or hinged *(page 61)* edge.

TRIMMING AN UNHINGED SASH EDGE

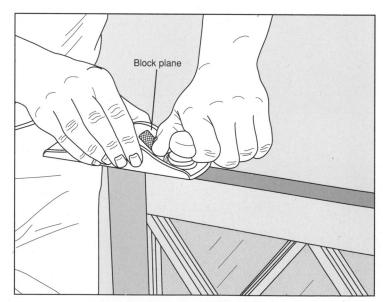

Spot-sanding an edge. Spot-plane a binding spot of more than 3 inches *(step right)*. Otherwise, remove any hardware from the edge and spot-sand it using coarse sandpaper on a sanding block. Wearing a dust mask, position the sanding block flat on the edge just to one side of the binding spot and apply moderate pressure to trim across it along the wood grain *(above)*; for the rabbeted edge shown, trim each surface of it in turn the same way. Continue until the sash can close and open freely, leaving enough clearance for refinishing. Put back any hardware removed.

Spot-planing the edge. Spot-sand a binding spot of up to 3 inches *(step left)*. Otherwise, remove the sash *(page 59)* and clamp it to a work table, then take any hardware off the edge and spot-plane. Apply moderate pressure to trim across the binding spot, using a block plane for end grain *(above)*; otherwise, using a bench plane along the wood grain. For a rabbeted edge, trim each surface. If the plane catches or gouges the wood, reverse its direction to smooth the cut. Continue until the sash can close and open freely, leaving enough clearance for refinishing. Put back any hardware removed and reinstall the sash.

TRIMMING A HINGED SASH EDGE

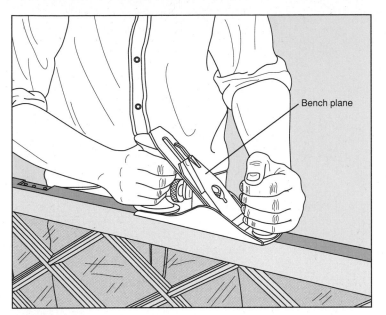

Bench plane

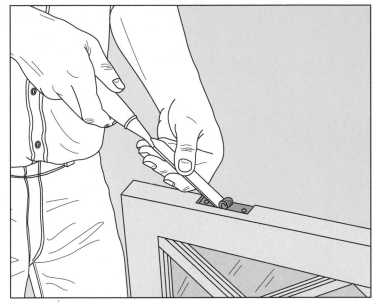

1 **Planing the edge.** Remove the sash *(page 59)* and clamp it on its latched edge to a work table. Unscrew each hinge leaf from the sash edge and pry it out of its mortise, then trim the edge using a bench plane. Starting at one end of the edge, position the plane flat and apply moderate pressure to trim to the other end of it *(above)*. If the plane catches or gouges the wood, reverse its direction to smooth the cut. Continue trimming until the sash can close and open freely, leaving enough clearance for refinishing.

2 **Deepening the mortises.** Deepen each mortise until its hinge leaf can sit flush with the sash edge. Score along the ends of the mortise using a wood chisel, tapping it with a wooden mallet. Then, work with the chisel bevel-side down to remove wood from the mortise, guiding it along the grain to pare off a thin shaving *(above)*. When the hinge leaf can sit flush with the sash edge, screw it into place. Refinish the sash, then reinstall it *(page 59)*.

REPLACING LEADED-GLASS GLAZING COMPOUND

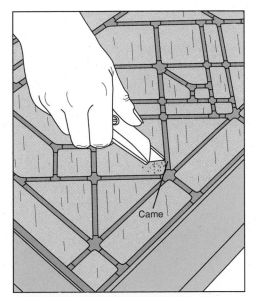

Came

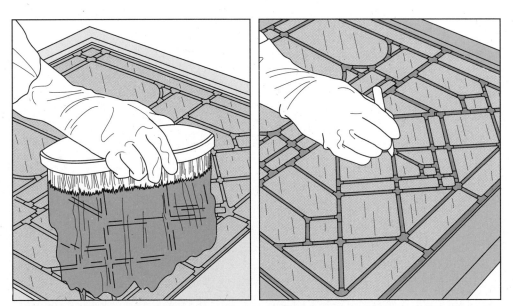

1 **Removing the old glazing compound.** Remove the double-hung *(page 55)* or casement *(page 59)* sash and set it on a work table. Clean dried or otherwise damaged glazing compound out of the cames of each pane with a utility knife *(above)*, then vacuum up particles and dust. Turn the sash over and repeat the procedure on the other side of it.

2 **Applying new glazing compound.** Work outdoors or in a well-ventilated area indoors. Wearing rubber gloves, safety goggles and a respirator, prepare 1 cup of metal-sash glazing compound at a time in a glass jar, adding 1 tablespoon of mineral spirits and mixing it with a stick into a thick, buttery consistency. Pour half the compound onto the panes and use a soft-bristled fiber brush to gently work it into the cames *(above, left)*. Wipe the panes dry with a soft cloth, then sprinkle sawdust on them and scrub gently with a clean brush to clean off oily residue. Scrape excess compound and sawdust out of the cames with a stick *(above, right)*. Clean the panes by scrubbing gently with whiting. Turn the sash over and repeat the procedure on the other side of it, then reinstall it.

REPLACING A LEADED-GLASS PANE

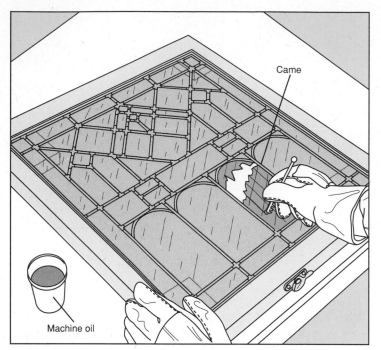

1 Removing the damaged pane. Remove the double-hung *(page 55)* or casement *(page 59)* sash and set it interior-side up on a work table, using wood blocks to support the pane at each corner of it and the damaged pane. Wearing work gloves and safety goggles, lubricate the cutting wheel of a glass cutter with light machine oil, then score across the damaged pane repeatedly with it *(above)*. Turn the sash over and use the ball end of the glass cutter to tap the damaged pane, breaking it into pieces, then turn the sash back over.

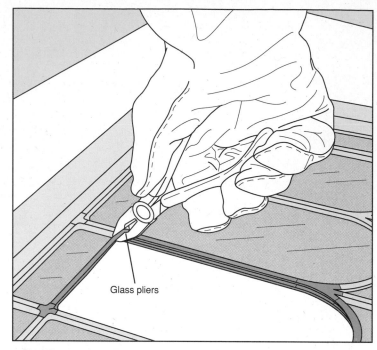

2 Preparing the cames. Wear work gloves to pull shards from the cames. Scrape glazing compound out of the cames and cut diagonally into each joint with a utility knife. Working carefully from one end to the other end along each came, bend its edge up vertical; if necessary, use glass pliers *(above)*. Buy glass for a replacement pane at an art glass dealer, taking a piece of the original pane to match it. Cut a template of cardboard 1/8 inch larger than the opening in the cames and use it to mark cutting lines for the replacement pane.

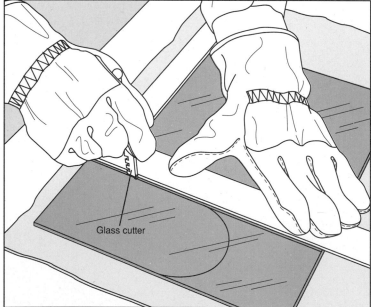

3 Cutting straight pane edges. If there is no straight edge to cut, cut each curved edge *(step 4)*. Otherwise, set the replacement pane smooth-side up onto a thick layer of papers on a work table, then wear work gloves and safety goggles to cut each straight edge. Position a straightedge along the cutting line just to the waste side, then lubricate the cutting wheel of a glass cutter with light machine oil and score once along it. Keeping the glass cutter vertical, apply firm pressure and draw it smoothly along the cutting line *(above, left)*, leav-

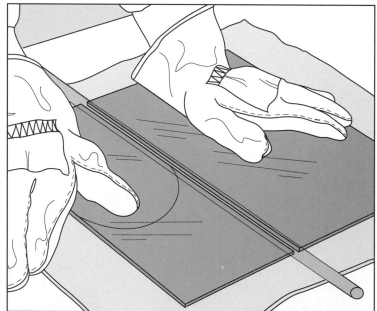

ing a visible scar. For a scored line of more than 3 inches, use a dowel longer than it to snap the pane. Set the dowel under the pane and aligned with the scored line, then apply uniform downward pressure on the pane with the heels of your hands to snap it cleanly *(above, right)*. For a scored line of up to 3 inches, snap the pane by hand. Grip the pane firmly along each side of the scored line and twist your wrists sharply away from you to snap it cleanly.

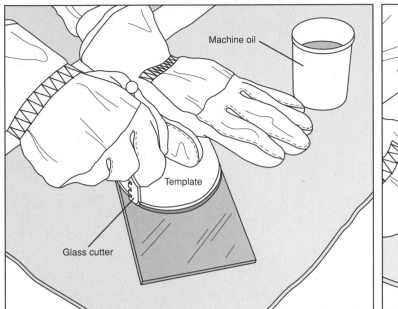

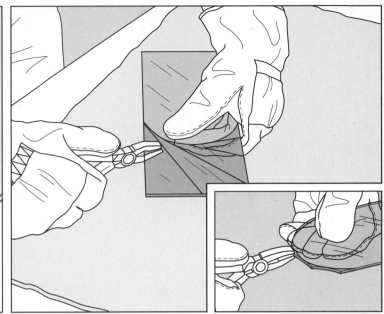

4 **Cutting curved pane edges.** If there is no curved edge to cut, install the replacement pane *(step 5)*. Otherwise, set the replacement pane smooth-side up onto a thick layer of papers on a work table, then wear work gloves and safety goggles to cut each curved edge. Position the template along the cutting line just to the waste side, then lubricate the cutting wheel of a glass cutter with light machine oil and score once along it. Keeping the glass cutter vertical, apply firm pressure and draw it smoothly along the cutting line *(above,* *left)*, leaving a visible scar. To help break the pane cleanly along the scored line, score a series of straight lines from it to the edge of the pane with the glass cutter, then snap off each segment. Grip the segment firmly with glass pliers *(above, right)* and twist your wrist sharply downward to snap it off cleanly. Nibble remaining bits off the curved edge of the pane by making bites of 1/16 inch with the glass pliers *(inset)*, then smooth it using fine sandpaper.

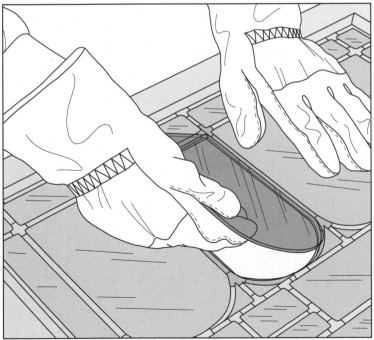

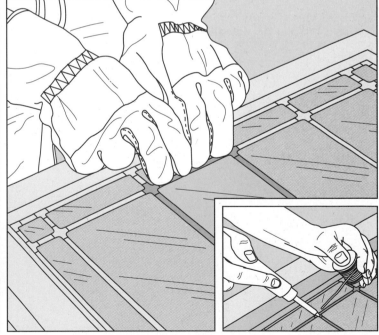

5 **Installing the replacement pane.** Wearing work gloves, seat one edge of the replacement pane into the came along one side of the opening *(above, left)*, then lower its other edges into place. Bend down the edge of each came flat onto the pane *(above,* *right)*; if necessary, use a wood block to apply even pressure. Clean the joints of the cames with medium steel wool, then work in a well-ventilated area to solder them. Buy solder and flux recommended for leaded glass at an art glass dealer. Wearing work gloves, safety goggles and a respirator, heat up a soldering iron following the manufacturer's instructions. To solder each joint, coat it with flux, then unroll a 6-inch length of solder. Without touching the soldering iron to the came or the solder, hold the tip near the joint for a few seconds to heat it, then quickly touch the solder to it *(inset)*. Apply just enough solder to coat the joint evenly, working carefully to avoid overheating and melting the came. Apply new glazing compound *(page 61)* and reinstall the sash.

REINFORCING A LEADED-GLASS SASH

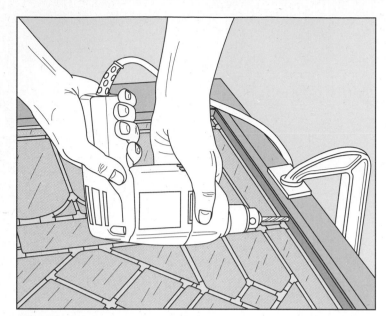

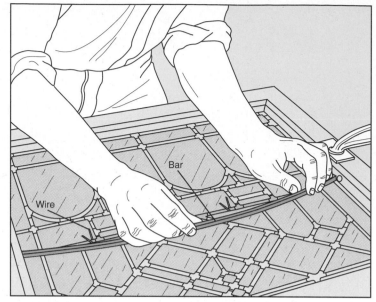

1 **Positioning the reinforcing bar.** Remove the double-hung *(page 55)* or casement *(page 59)* sash and set it bowed-side up in direct sunlight to flatten it; use a board across the panes as a weight. Secure the sash interior-side up to a work table and reinforce the panes with a 1/4-inch steel bar, aligning it with the cames to help disguise it. Cut the bar 1/2 inch longer than the distance across the panes with a hacksaw, then bore a hole 3/8 inch deep for each end of it into the edge of the sash using an electric drill fitted with a 1/4-inch twist bit *(above)*. Clean soldering points for wires on the cames every 8 inches across the panes with medium steel wool.

2 **Installing the reinforcing bar.** Work in a well-ventilated area to solder pairs of copper wires to the cames. Buy solder and flux recommended for leaded glass at an art glass dealer. Wearing work gloves, safety goggles and a respirator, heat up a soldering iron following the manufacturer's instructions and unroll a 6-inch length of solder. Without touching the soldering iron to the came or the solder, hold the tip to each wire to heat it, then quickly touch it to the solder and to the came. Fit the bar into the holes in the edge of the sash *(above)* and use pliers to twist each pair of wires together around it, then reinstall the sash.

REPLACING A SKYLIGHT PANE

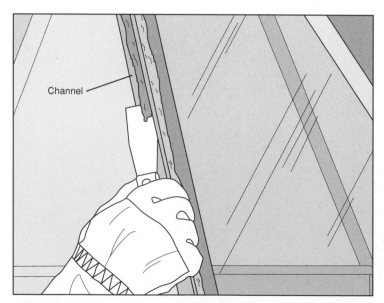

1 **Removing the glazing caps.** Block access to the area under the skylight, then work safely on the roof *(page 128)*. Wearing work gloves and safety goggles, remove each glazing cap from the edge of the damaged pane. Bend each tab securing the glazing cap up vertical *(above)*, then pull the bottom of the glazing cap off the skylight and slide the top of it out from under the ventilator flange.

2 **Removing the damaged pane.** Wearing work gloves and safety goggles, scrape glazing compound off the edges of the damaged pane using a putty knife. Work carefully to remove the damaged pane from the channels, then scrape glazing compound out of them with the putty knife *(above)*. Use a wire brush to clean particles and debris out of the channels, then apply a metal primer and paint.

REPLACING A SKYLIGHT PANE (continued)

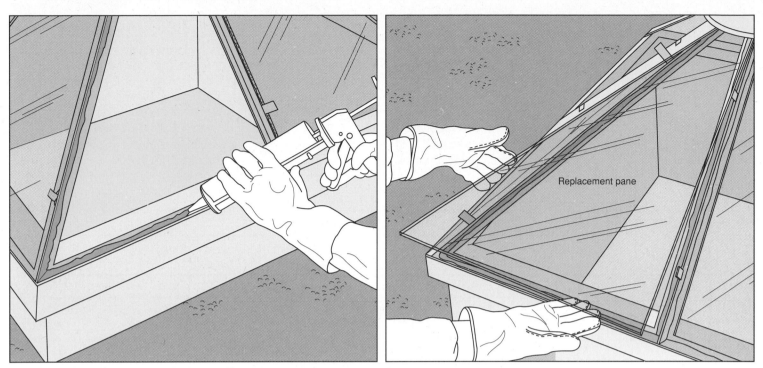

Replacement pane

3 **Installing the replacement pane.** Cut a template of cardboard 1/4 inch smaller than the opening in the skylight to use for a replacement pane. Check your local building code to find out if safety or wired glass is required for the skylight, then buy the pane and have it cut to size at a building supply center; also buy glazing compound recommended for metal sashes. Wearing work gloves, use a caulking gun to eject a continuous bead of glazing compound along each channel as a bed for the pane *(above, left)*. Set the pane into place along the channels *(above, right)* and check that it is centered, then press it into the glazing compound.

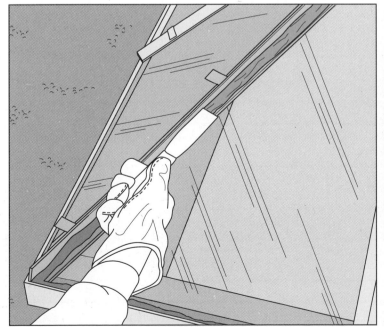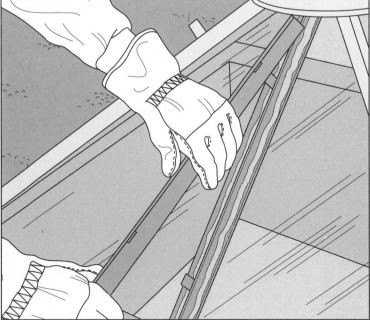

4 **Reinstalling the glazing caps.** Seal the replacement pane by ejecting a thick, continuous bead of glazing compound along each edge of it with the caulking gun. Smooth and shape the glazing compound by drawing a clean putty knife dipped in soapy water along it, beveling it at a 45° angle *(above, left)*. Wipe up stray glazing compound using a cloth dampened with mineral spirits. To reposition each glazing cap, slide the top of it under the ventilator flange and set it along the channel with its slots fitted on the tabs *(above, right)*. Press down on the glazing cap and bend each tab down flat against it to secure it.

INTERIOR WALLS AND TRIM

Interior walls and ceilings of plaster are classic features of an older home, gracefully accented by the usual complement of cornices, medallions, finely-appointed wood trim and other adornments; refer to the illustration on page 67 for details on their typical construction. Although ageless in charm, the interior walls and ceilings are nonetheless vulnerable to the passage of time, inevitably reflecting the normal settling of the foundation, the natural cycles of temperature and humidity change, as well as the cumulative wear of habitation. Fortunately, however, most problems with interior walls and ceilings are only cosmetic; for help in undertaking a particular repair, use the Troubleshooting Guide below.

Most repairs to the interior walls and ceilings of an older home are easily undertaken with only a few basic carpentry tools; the materials needed are usually readily available at a building supply center. Refer to Tools & Techniques *(page 124)* for instructions on using tools properly, as well as for information on working safely from a ladder, removing paint and replicating textured surfaces. Keep in mind that the particles and dust of plaster are hazardous; protect yourself by wearing safety goggles and a dust mask, and cover items near your work area with drop cloths. Before starting any repair to an interior wall or ceiling, familiarize yourself with the information presented in the Emergency Guide *(page 8)*.

TROUBLESHOOTING GUIDE

SYMPTOM	POSSIBLE CAUSE	PROCEDURE
PLASTER SURFACE		
Hairline crack: up to 1/4 inch wide	Normal house settlement; seasonal temperature and humidity changes; accidental blow or impact	Fill crack with joint or spackling compound using gloved fingertip
Crack: 1/4 to 1 inch wide; stable	Normal house settlement; seasonal temperature and humidity changes; accidental blow or impact	Repair crack *(p. 68)* □ ○
Crack: wider than 1 inch; expanding or contracting	Uneven house settlement	Consult a professional
Hole: less than 1 inch square	Hanger or other fastener removed	Fill hole with joint or spackling compound using putty knife
Hole: 1 inch to 8 inches square	Accidental blow or impact	Repair small hole *(p. 69)* □ ○ ; at inside corner *(p. 71)* ◨ ◔ or outside corner *(p. 72)* ◨ ◔
Hole: more than 8 inches square	Fixture or other item removed; accidental blow or impact	Repair large hole *(p. 69)* ◨ ◔ ; at inside corner *(p. 71)* ◨ ◔ or outside corner *(p. 72)* ◨ ◔
Inside corner damaged	Normal house settlement; seasonal temperature and humidity changes; accidental blow or impact	Repair inside corner *(p. 71)* ◨ ◔
Outside corner damaged	Normal house settlement; seasonal temperature and humidity changes; accidental blow or impact	Repair outside corner *(p. 72)* ◨ ◔
PLASTER CORNICE OR MEDALLION		
Hairline crack: up to 1/4 inch wide	Normal house settlement; seasonal temperature and humidity changes; accidental blow or impact	Fill crack with joint or spackling compound using gloved fingertip
Crack: 1/4 to 1 inch wide; stable	Normal house settlement; seasonal temperature and humidity changes; accidental blow or impact	Repair cornice *(p. 73)* ◨ ◔ ; cast plaster *(p. 74)* ◨ ◔
Crack: wider than 1 inch; expanding or contracting	Uneven house settlement	Consult a professional
Nick, dent or gouge	Accidental blow or impact	Repair cornice *(p. 73)* ◨ ◔ ; cast plaster *(p. 74)* ◨ ◔
Section damaged	Accidental blow or impact	Replace section of cast plaster *(p. 74)* ■ ●
WOOD TRIM		
Crack, nick, dent or gouge	Accidental blow or impact	Repair wood trim *(p. 76)* □ ○
Section damaged	Accidental blow or impact	Replace section of wood trim *(p. 76)* ◨ ◔

DEGREE OF DIFFICULTY: □ Easy ◨ Moderate ■ Complex
ESTIMATED TIME: ○ Less than 1 hour ◔ 1 to 3 hours ● Over 3 hours

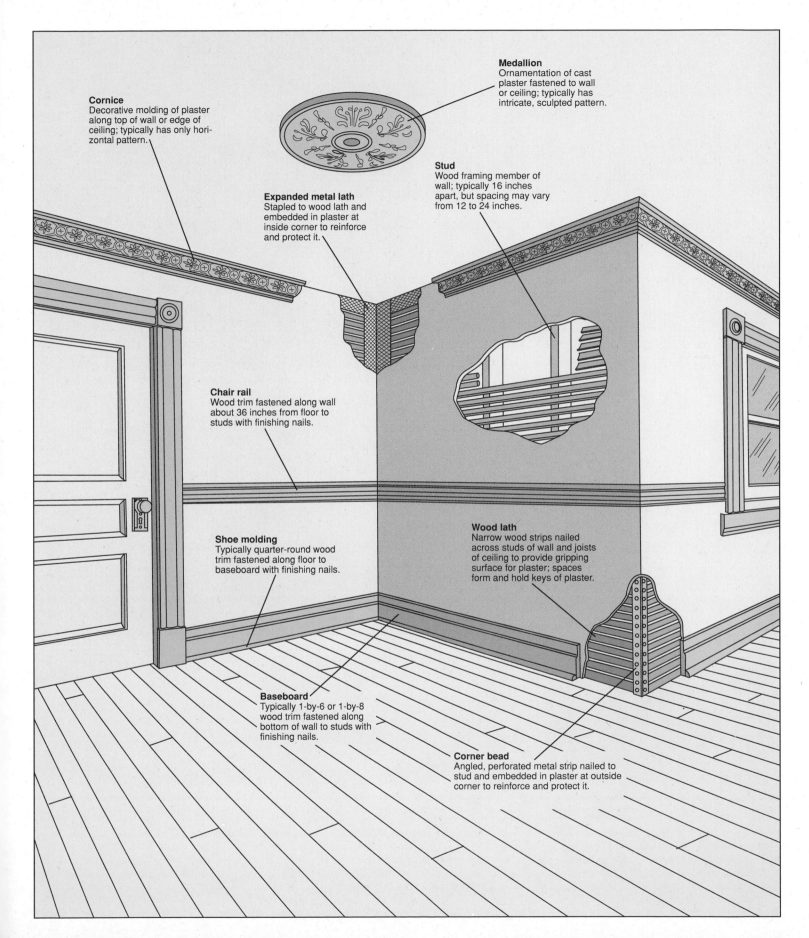

Medallion
Ornamentation of cast plaster fastened to wall or ceiling; typically has intricate, sculpted pattern.

Cornice
Decorative molding of plaster along top of wall or edge of ceiling; typically has only horizontal pattern.

Expanded metal lath
Stapled to wood lath and embedded in plaster at inside corner to reinforce and protect it.

Stud
Wood framing member of wall; typically 16 inches apart, but spacing may vary from 12 to 24 inches.

Chair rail
Wood trim fastened along wall about 36 inches from floor to studs with finishing nails.

Shoe molding
Typically quarter-round wood trim fastened along floor to baseboard with finishing nails.

Wood lath
Narrow wood strips nailed across studs of wall and joists of ceiling to provide gripping surface for plaster; spaces form and hold keys of plaster.

Baseboard
Typically 1-by-6 or 1-by-8 wood trim fastened along bottom of wall to studs with finishing nails.

Corner bead
Angled, perforated metal strip nailed to stud and embedded in plaster at outside corner to reinforce and protect it.

REPAIRING A PLASTER CRACK

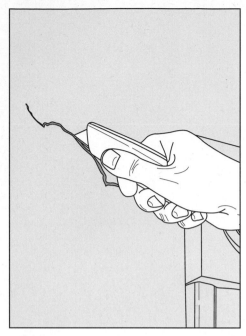

1 **Preparing the crack.** Use a utility knife to widen and deepen the crack to about 1/4 inch *(above)*, undercutting its edges to help patching compound lock into it. Brush loose particles and dust out of the crack with a scrub brush or an old paintbrush.

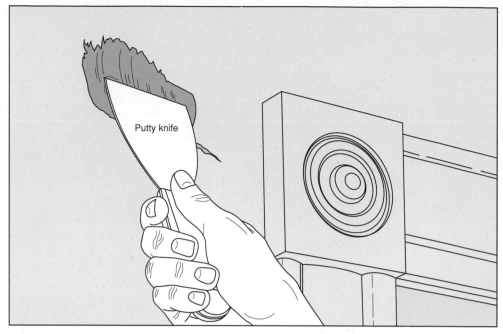

Putty knife

2 **Filling the crack.** Buy ready-mixed joint or spackling compound at a building supply center; if patching a flat surface, also self-adhesive fiber-mesh tape. To help the bonding of the compound, use a spray bottle or sponge to dampen the crack with water. Using a flexible putty knife, work compound into the crack and overfill it slightly, making short passes across it *(above)*. Draw the putty knife along the crack to scrape off excess compound. If patching a flat surface, let the compound dry, then tape the patch *(step 3)*; otherwise, texture the patch to match the surrounding surface.

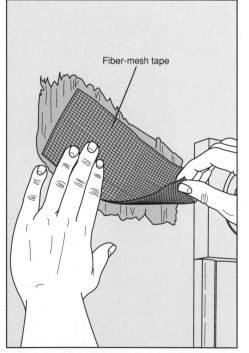

Fiber-mesh tape

3 **Taping the patch.** To help keep the crack from recurring, reinforce it with fiber-mesh tape. Cut a strip of tape and press it into place along the filled crack *(above)*. Apply as many strips of tape as necessary to cover the filled crack without overlapping them.

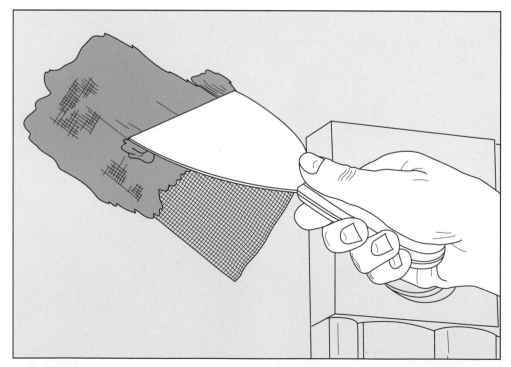

4 **Finishing the patch.** Cover the tape with a thin, even layer of compound, drawing it smoothly across the surface with a wide putty knife *(above)*. Make overlapping passes outward from the center of the patch to level it and feather its edges, disguising the repair. Let the compound dry, then sand the surface using medium sandpaper on a sanding block. Brush or wipe off particles and repeat the procedure, applying compound to fill depressions and feather the edges of the patch until it blends with the surrounding surface. Sand the surface and clean off particles, then apply a primer and paint.

REPAIRING A SMALL PLASTER HOLE

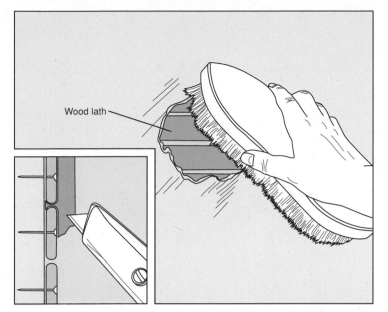

Wood lath

1 Preparing the hole. If hand pressure causes movement of the surface around the hole or any wood lath is damaged, prepare the hole as you would a large one *(step 1, below)*. Otherwise, use a utility knife to enlarge the hole slightly *(inset)*, clearing it of loose pieces and undercutting its edges to help patching compound lock into it. Brush loose particles and dust out of the hole with a scrub brush *(above)* or an old paintbrush.

2 Patching the hole. Buy ready-mixed joint or spackling compound at a building supply center. To help the bonding of the compound, use a spray bottle or sponge to dampen the hole with water. Using a flexible putty knife, work compound into the hole and overfill it slightly, making short passes across it *(above)*. Draw the putty knife along the surface to scrape off excess compound. If patching a flat surface, let the compound dry, then finish the patch as you would for a crack *(page 68)*; otherwise, texture the patch to match the surrounding surface.

REPAIRING A LARGE PLASTER HOLE

Wood lath

1 Preparing the hole. If hand pressure causes movement of the surface around the hole, the plaster keys or wood lath may be damaged. Wearing safety goggles and a dust mask, cut back the edges of the hole as far as necessary to reach a solid surface. Use a cold chisel and ball-peen hammer to chip out pieces of plaster, working carefully to avoid damaging the wood lath. If the wood lath is damaged, cut back to the center of the nearest stud to remove it. Mark a square-edged outline around the hole, then use an electric drill fitted with an abrasive wheel to cut along the marked outline *(above)*.

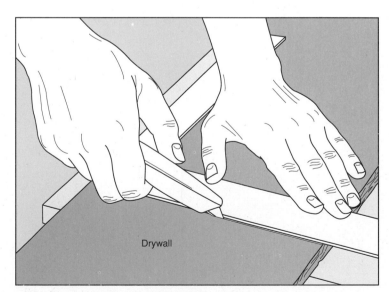

Drywall

2 Preparing the patch. To patch the hole, use a drywall sheet of a thickness less than the shallowest edge of the hole. Measure the dimensions of the hole and transfer them to the drywall sheet, using a pencil and a straightedge to mark the outline of the patch. Cut the patch out of the drywall sheet using a saber saw or score and snap its edges in turn. To score and snap the drywall sheet, cut it deeply using a utility knife and a straightedge *(above)*, then set it face down with the scored line along the edge of a work table and press down sharply on the back of it overhanging the work table.

REPAIRING A LARGE PLASTER HOLE (continued)

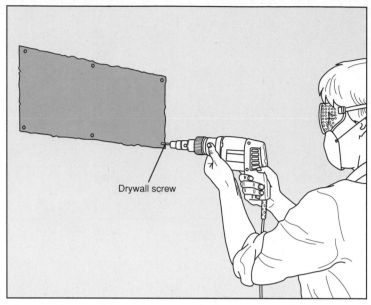

Drywall screw

3 **Fitting the patch.** Test-fit the patch in the hole and adjust it as necessary to sit securely, its edges flush with the surrounding surface. To trim the edges of the patch, use a utility knife and a straightedge. To support the edges of the patch uniformly, use wood shims. Calculate the thickness of the shims needed by measuring the thickness of each edge of the hole, then subtracting the thickness of the patch. Secure the shims in place to the back of the patch with masking tape *(above)*.

4 **Installing the patch.** Fasten the patch every 8 inches to a stud or wood lath with drywall screws about 1 inch longer than the deepest edge of the hole. Mark the location of studs or wood lath at the edges of the hole, if necessary, then position the patch. Keeping about 1 inch from any edge of the patch, drive in the screws using an electric drill fitted with a drywall-screw clutch driver *(above)*; or, using a screwdriver, setting them slightly below the surface to dimple it and disguise the repair.

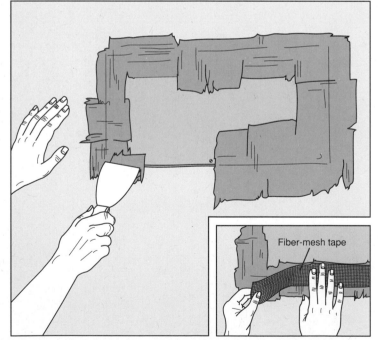

Fiber-mesh tape

5 **Taping the patch.** Buy ready-mixed joint or spackling compound at a building supply center; if patching a flat surface, also self-adhesive fiber-mesh tape. To help the bonding of the compound, use a spray bottle or sponge to dampen the edges of the patch with water. Using a flexible putty knife, work compound into the gap along each edge of the patch, overfilling it slightly *(above)* and scraping off excess. If patching a textured surface, texture the patch to match it; otherwise, let the compound dry, then apply strips of tape without overlapping them along the filled edges of the patch *(inset)*.

6 **Finishing the patch.** Cover the tape and screws with a thin, even layer of compound, drawing it smoothly across the surface with a wide putty knife *(above)*. Make overlapping passes outward from the center along each edge of the patch to level and feather it, disguising the repair. Let the compound dry, then sand the surface using medium sandpaper on a sanding block. Brush or wipe off particles and repeat the procedure, applying compound to fill depressions and feather the edges of the patch until it blends with the surrounding surface. Sand the surface and clean off particles, then apply a primer and paint.

REPAIRING AN INSIDE PLASTER CORNER

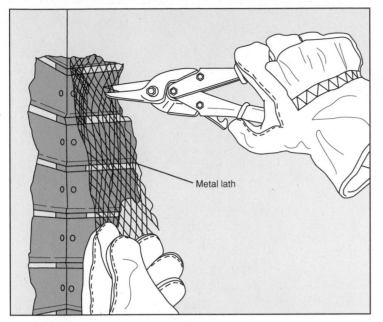

1 Preparing the corner. Repair a crack as you would any other crack *(page 68)*. Otherwise, wear work gloves, safety goggles and a dust mask to cut back the edges of the damaged section as far as necessary to reach a solid surface. Use a cold chisel and ball-peen hammer to chip out pieces of plaster, working carefully to avoid damaging the metal or wood lath. Cut out damaged metal lath with tin snips *(above)*. Using a utility knife, clean and undercut each edge of the damaged section to help patching compound lock into it. Brush away loose particles and dust with a scrub brush or an old paintbrush.

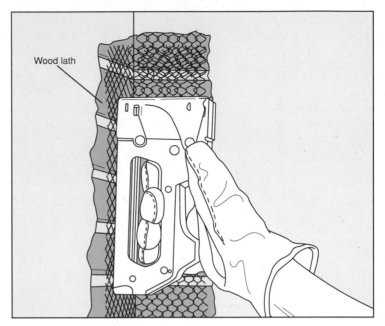

2 Installing metal lath. If the damaged section is not missing metal lath, patch it *(step 3)*. Otherwise, buy expanded metal lath for the damaged section at a building supply center. Wearing work gloves and safety goggles, use tin snips to cut a piece of lath to the size needed for the damaged section; cut it long enough to overlap the ends of any lath still in place. Shape the lath to fit the damaged section by folding it at a 90° angle along the edge of a work table. Position the lath in the damaged section, then use a staple gun to staple it every 1 to 2 inches to the wood lath *(above)*.

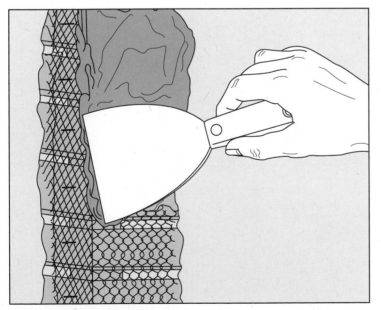

3 Patching the corner. Buy ready-mixed joint or spackling compound at a building supply center. To help the bonding of the compound, use a spray bottle or sponge to dampen the edges of the damaged section with water. Using a flexible putty knife, work compound into the damaged section along each edge of it, overfilling it slightly *(above)*. Draw the putty knife along the surface on each side of the corner to scrape off excess compound. If patching a corner of flat surfaces, let the compound dry, then finish the patch *(step 4)*; otherwise, texture the patch to match the surrounding surfaces.

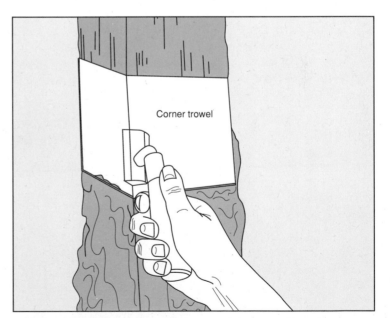

4 Finishing the patch. Apply a thin, even layer of compound on the patch with a wide putty knife, overlapping passes outward from the corner to level each surface and feather the edges, disguising the repair. Shape the corner of the patch by drawing a corner trowel along it, keeping the blades flat against the surfaces *(above)*. Let the compound dry, then sand the surfaces with medium sandpaper on a sanding block. Brush or wipe off particles and repeat the procedure, applying compound to fill depressions and feather the edges of the patch until it blends with the surrounding surfaces. Sand the surfaces and clean off particles, then apply a primer and paint.

REPAIRING AN OUTSIDE PLASTER CORNER

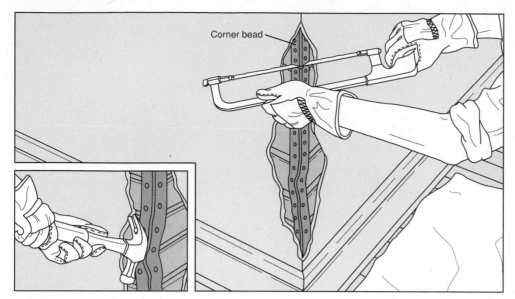

Corner bead

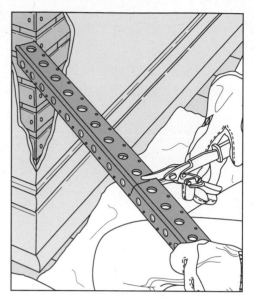

1 Preparing the corner. Repair a crack as you would any other crack *(page 68)*. Otherwise, wear work gloves, safety goggles and a dust mask to cut back the edges of the damaged section as far as necessary to reach a solid surface. Use a cold chisel and ball-peen hammer to chip out pieces of plaster, working carefully to avoid damaging the corner bead or wood lath. To remove damaged corner bead, use a hacksaw to cut as far as possible across its flanges *(above)* without damaging any wood lath or stud, then pull out its nails *(inset)* and finish cutting the flanges with tin snips. Using a utility knife, clean and undercut each edge of the damaged section to help patching compound lock into it. Brush away loose particles and dust with a scrub brush or an old paintbrush.

2 Preparing replacement corner bead. If the damaged section is not missing corner bead, patch it *(step 3)*; otherwise, cut a piece 1/4 inch shorter than the damaged section missing it. Wearing work gloves and safety goggles, set the corner bead along the edge of a work table and use a hacksaw to cut as far as possible without damaging the table, then finish the cuts with tin snips *(above)*.

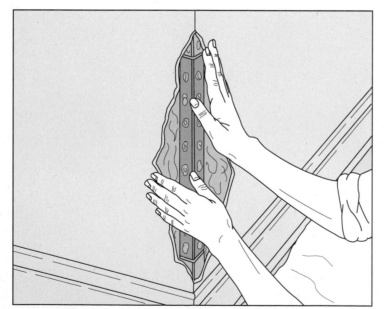

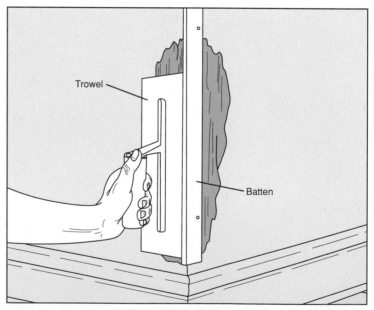

Trowel

Batten

3 Patching the corner. Buy ready-mixed joint or spackling compound at a building supply center. To help the bonding of the compound, use a spray bottle or sponge to dampen the edges of the damaged section with water. Using a flexible putty knife, work compound into the damaged section, then press any replacement corner bead into place *(above)* and drive in a 1 1/2-inch drywall nail every 6 inches along each flange. Continue applying compound to the damaged section, overfilling it slightly, then scrape off excess. If patching a corner of flat surfaces, let the compound dry, then finish the patch *(step 4)*; otherwise, texture the patch to match the surrounding surfaces.

4 Finishing the patch. Apply a thin, even layer of compound on the patch with a wide putty knife, overlapping passes outward from the corner to level each surface and feather the edges, disguising the repair. Shape the corner of the patch by drawing a trowel along each surface, extending it beyond the surface to use the corner bead as a guide; or nail a 1-by-4 batten extending beyond the opposite surface to use as a guide *(above)*. Let the compound dry, then sand the surfaces with medium sandpaper on a sanding block. Brush or wipe off particles and repeat the procedure, filling depressions and feathering the edges until the patch blends with the surrounding surfaces. Sand the surfaces and clean off particles, then apply a primer and paint.

REPAIRING A PLASTER CORNICE

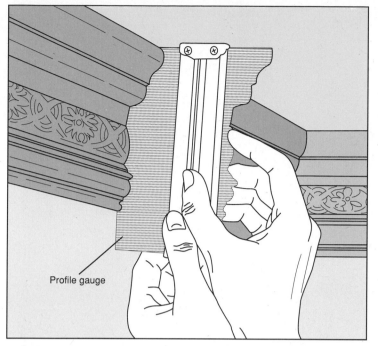

1 **Taking the molding profile.** To repair the damaged section, use the profile of an undamaged section with the same pattern. Take the profile of the undamaged section using a profile gauge—available at a building supply center. Following the manufacturer's instructions, hold the profile gauge vertically by its handle and press its needles against the undamaged section *(above)*, then lock the needles in position, if necessary.

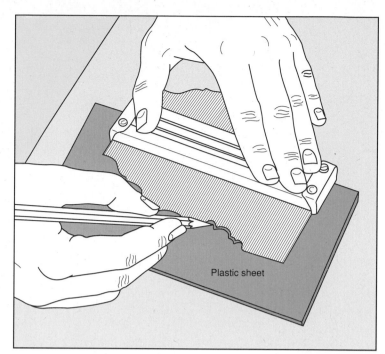

2 **Making the molding jig.** To make a jig for the damaged section, set a thin sheet of plastic or metal on a work table and position the profile gauge on it. Holding the profile gauge in place, carefully trace the edges of its needles onto the sheet with a pencil *(above)*, then cut the jig out of the sheet using tin snips. Test-fit the jig against the undamaged section and use a file to adjust it as necessary, smoothing any rough edge.

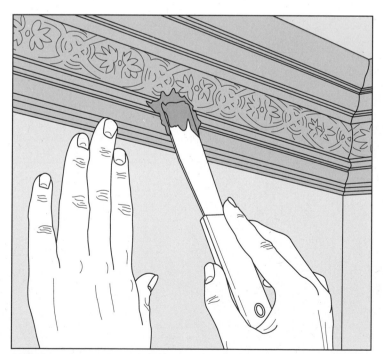

3 **Patching the surface.** Remove the paint from the damaged section, then patch it with plaster of paris. Buy plaster of paris at a building supply center and follow the manufacturer's instructions to prepare it. Score the surface of the damaged section lightly using the tip of a nail, then use a spray bottle or sponge to dampen it with water. Using a stiff putty knife, work plaster of paris into the damaged section, overfilling it slightly *(above)*.

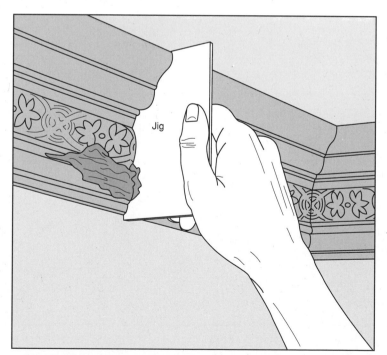

4 **Finishing the patch.** Draw the jig slowly and smoothly across the patch *(above)*, shaping it and scraping off excess plaster of paris. If necessary, apply more plaster of paris and repeat the procedure, continuing until the patch blends with the surrounding surfaces. Let the plaster of paris dry, then sand with medium sandpaper; wrap it around a dowel or other tool for contours and indentations. Brush or wipe off particles, then apply a primer and paint.

REPAIRING CAST PLASTER

Patching the surface. If the damaged section is large, replace it *(steps below)*; otherwise, remove the paint from it, then patch it with plaster of paris. Buy plaster of paris at a building supply center and follow the manufacturer's instructions to prepare it. Score the surface of the damaged section lightly using the tip of a nail, then use a spray bottle or sponge to dampen it with water. Work plaster of paris into the damaged section with a stick *(left)* or stiff putty knife, then shape the patch to match the surrounding surface using toothpicks, sharp knives or other tools. Let the plaster of paris dry, then sand with medium sandpaper; wrap it around a dowel or other tool for contours and indentations. Brush or wipe off particles, then apply a primer and paint.

REPLACING A SECTION OF CAST PLASTER

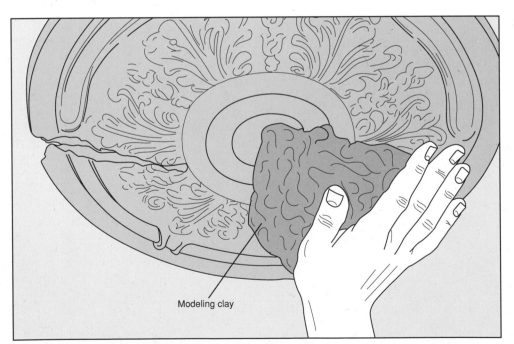

Modeling clay

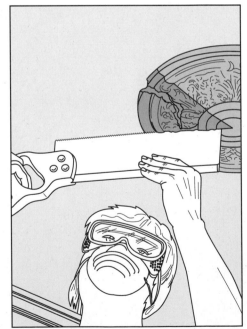

1 Making the mold. If the damaged section is small, repair it *(step above)*; otherwise, replace it using a mold of an undamaged section with the same pattern. To make the mold, buy air-hardening modeling clay at a hobby store. Using a paintbrush, coat the undamaged section and a little beyond its edges evenly with a thin film of petroleum jelly. Prepare the modeling clay following the manufacturer's instructions, then press a layer of it 1/2 inch thick firmly into place against the undamaged section coated with petroleum jelly *(above)*. Let the modeling clay harden, then carefully pry off the mold.

2 Removing the damaged section. Wearing safety goggles and a dust mask, use a backsaw to cut through each edge of the damaged section *(above)*; work carefully to avoid marring undamaged surfaces. Free the damaged section by hand, prying it gently with a putty knife or cold chisel only if necessary.

REPLACING A SECTION OF CAST PLASTER (continued)

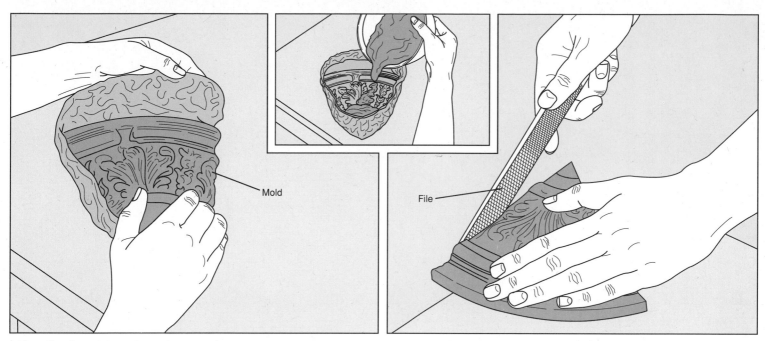

Mold

File

3 **Casting the replacement section.** Set the mold on a work table and build up its edges with modeling clay *(above, left)* to a height equal to the thickness of the damaged section. Let the modeling clay harden, then use a paintbrush to coat the interior of the mold evenly with a thin film of petroleum jelly. Buy plaster of paris at a building supply center and follow the manufacturer's instructions to pre-

pare it. Pour plaster of paris slowly into the mold *(inset)*; to eliminate air pockets, fill the mold about half full and gently agitate it, then finish filling it. Let the plaster of paris dry. Carefully break the edges of the mold to take out the cast section, then let it set for 24 hours. Test-fit the cast section in position and mark it to size, then trim it as necessary using a back-saw or file *(above, right)*.

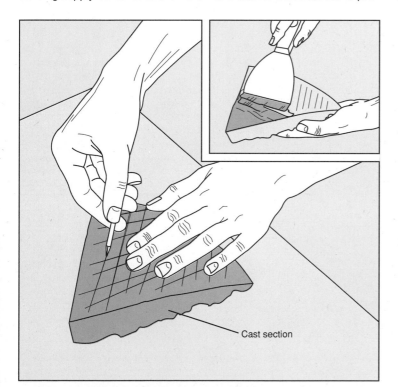

Cast section

4 **Installing the replacement section.** Score the bottom of the cast section lightly with the tip of a nail, working at opposite angles across it to form a diamond-shaped pattern *(above)*. Prepare more plaster of paris and use a putty knife to coat the bottom of the cast section evenly with it *(inset)*. Fit the cast section into position and hold it in place until the plaster of paris sets; if necessary, gently wedge it in place using 1-by-2s cut to fit between it and the floor.

5 **Finishing the patch.** Prepare more plaster of paris and use a stiff putty knife to work it into the gap along each edge of the cast section *(above)*, scraping off excess. Shape the plaster of paris to match the surrounding surfaces using toothpicks, sharp knives or other tools. Let the plaster of paris dry, then sand with medium sandpaper; wrap it around a dowel or other tool for contours and indentations. Brush or wipe off particles, then apply a primer and paint.

REPAIRING WOOD TRIM

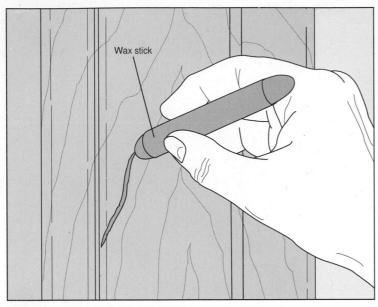

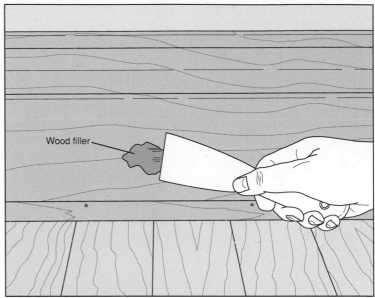

Patching the surface. If the damaged section is large, replace it *(steps below)*; otherwise, repair the surface with a wax stick or wood filler of a color that matches the wood, if possible. Cut damaged wood fibers off the surface with a utility knife, then wipe it using a soft cloth dampened with mineral spirits and blot it dry. To patch a small crack, nick or hole in trim along a door, for example, rub the tip of a wax stick back and forth across it *(above, left)*, filling it level with the surrounding surface. To patch a deep gouge or dent in a baseboard, for example, use a flexible putty knife to work wood filler into it, overfilling it slightly *(above, right)*, then scrape off excess to level it with the surrounding surface. If necessary, sand the patch using fine sandpaper and wipe or brush off particles, then finish it to match the surrounding surface.

REPLACING A SECTION OF WOOD TRIM

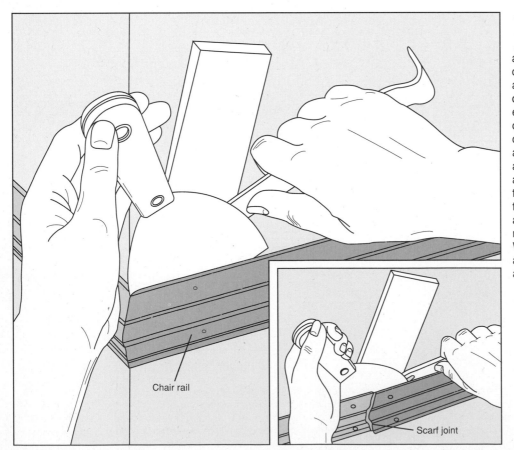

1 Removing the damaged section.
If the damaged surface is small, repair it *(step above)*; otherwise, replace the damaged section. To remove a damaged section of chair rail, for example, work along its edges with a utility knife to break any finish bond. Pry off the damaged section, starting at its most accessible end—such as at an outside corner *(left)* or the overlap at a scarf joint *(inset)*. Work the blade of a wide putty knife far enough under the damaged section to fit a pry bar behind it. Wedging a wood block behind the pry bar to protect the adjacent surface, work along the damaged section to gently pull it out a little at each nail. Return to the starting end of the damaged section and continue the same way, pulling it out at the nails a little farther each time until it comes off. Work carefully at an overlapped end of the damaged section—such as at an inside corner or at a scarf joint.

REPLACING A SECTION OF WOOD TRIM (continued)

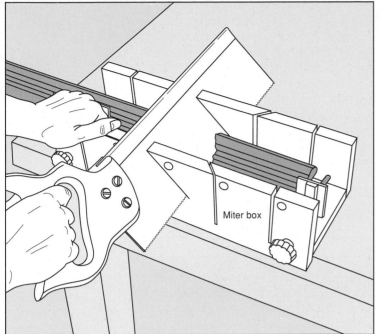

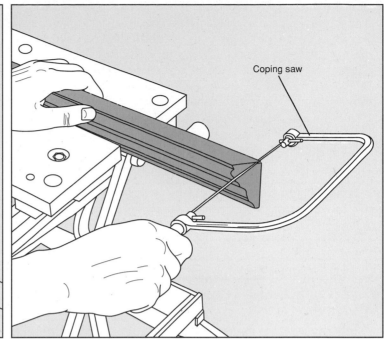

Coping saw

2 **Preparing the replacement section.** Buy a replacement section at a building supply center or take it from an inconspicuous spot in the house; if necessary, have it custom-made. Cut the replacement section to the length needed, using the ends of the damaged section as templates for marking and cutting any special angles. To cut an end of the replacement section for a butt joint, use a backsaw in the 90° slot of a miter box. To cut an end of the replacement section for a scarf joint, use the backsaw in the 45° face-cut slot of the miter box: placing the replacement section face up for an overlapped end; face down for an overlapping end. To cut a coped end, first make the 45° face cut needed for an overlapped end *(above, left)*, then cut along the contours of the face with a coping saw *(above, right)*.

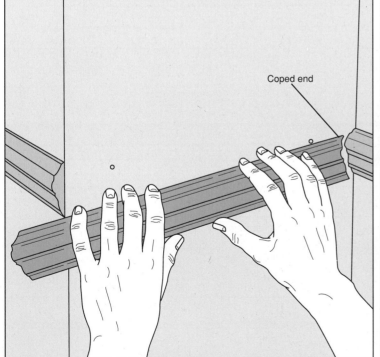

Coped end

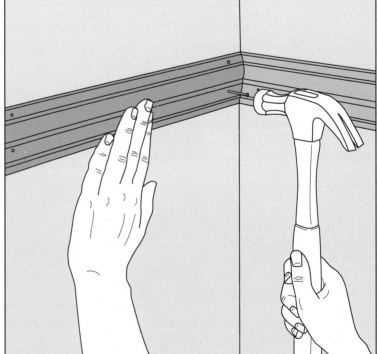

3 **Installing the replacement section.** Test-fit the replacement section, first positioning any end that is coped *(above, left)* or cut to be overlapped. Trim the ends of the replacement section as necessary to fit using a rasp or medium sandpaper; wrap sandpaper around a dowel or other tool for contours and indentations. To install the replacement section, mark the location for nails at studs; find them using the old nail holes as a guide or with an electronic density sensor, available at a building supply center. Position the replacement section and use an electric drill to bore pilot holes for 1 1/2-inch finishing nails, then drive in the nails *(above, right)* and set the heads with a nail set. Sand the replacement section using fine sandpaper and wipe or brush off particles, then finish it to match the original section.

FLOORS AND STAIRS

Flooring of hardwood and of ceramic tiles and the staircase are usually highly-prized features of an older home, evoking the fine craftsmanship of an earlier era; refer to the illustration on page 79 for details on their typical construction. Although durable, the flooring and staircase can often betray their age, reflecting the normal wear and tear of years of daily living as well as the effects of wood shrinkage and the shifting of wood joints. Fortunately, however, the flooring and staircase usually can be restored to a like-new appearance; for help in undertaking a particular repair, use the Troubleshooting Guide below.

Most repairs to the floors and stairs of an older home are easily undertaken with only a few basic carpentry tools; the materials needed are usually readily available at a building supply center. Refer to Tools & Techniques *(page 124)* for instructions on using tools properly, as well as for information on applying finishes. To refinish wood flooring, a few special tools are required: a drum sander, a floor edger and a commercial floor polisher—all available at a tool rental center. Before starting any repair to the flooring or staircase, familiarize yourself with the information presented in the Emergency Guide *(page 8)*.

TROUBLESHOOTING GUIDE

SYMPTOM	POSSIBLE CAUSE	PROCEDURE
WOOD FLOORING		
Surface stained or discolored	Finish damaged; wear or accidental spill	Spot-refinish *(p. 80)* □ ◐ or refinish *(p. 80)* ◼ ● ▲ wood flooring
Surface splinter	Accidental blow or impact	Repair board or slat *(p. 82)* □ ◐
Board squeaky or springy	Normal wood shrinkage or shifting of joints with age; board loose	Secure board *(p. 83)* □ ○
Board split, cracked, dented or gouged	Normal wood shrinkage or shifting of joints with age; accidental blow or impact	Replace board *(p. 84)* ◼ ◐ or section of boards *(p. 85)* ◼ ●
Boards cupped (curling edges) or crowned (bulging center)	Chronic high humidity; water damage	Replace section of boards *(p. 85)* ◼ ●
Slat split, cracked, dented or gouged	Normal wood shrinkage or shifting of joints with age; accidental blow or impact	Replace slat or section of slats *(p. 86)* ◼ ◐
Slats cupped (curling edges) or crowned (bulging center)	Chronic high humidity; water damage	Replace section of slats *(p. 86)* ◼ ◐
Flooring sagging or humped	Understructure damaged	Consult a professional
CERAMIC-TILE FLOORING		
Grout stained or discolored	Grout damaged; wear or accidental spill	Regrout tiles *(p. 90)* ◼ ○
Grout cracked or crumbling	Normal shifting of joints with age	Regrout tiles *(p. 90)* ◼ ○
Tile stained or discolored	Tile damaged; wear or accidental spill	Replace tile or section of tiles *(p. 91)* ◼ ◐
Tile loose	Normal shifting of joints with age	Regrout tiles *(p. 90)* ◼ ○
Tile chipped or broken	Accidental blow or impact	Replace tile or section of tiles *(p. 91)* ◼ ◐
Tiles sunken or heaved	Understructure damaged	Consult a professional
STAIRCASE		
Baluster loose or crooked	Normal settlement; wood shrinkage or shifting of joints with age	Tighten baluster *(p. 87)* □ ○
Newel post loose or crooked	Normal settlement; wood shrinkage or shifting of joints with age	Secure newel post *(p. 88)* □ ○
Handrail loose or sagging	Normal wear; wood shrinkage or shifting of joints with age	Secure handrail *(p. 88)* □ ○
	Newel post loose or crooked	Secure newel post *(p. 88)* □ ○
Tread squeaky	Wood shrinkage or shifting of joints with age; tread loose or springy	Work talcum powder into joints of tread; secure tread *(p. 89)* □ ○
Tread loose or springy	Normal wear; wood shrinkage or shifting of joints with age	Secure tread *(p. 89)* □ ○
	Stringer damaged	Consult a professional
Staircase sagging or crooked	Stringer damaged	Consult a professional

DEGREE OF DIFFICULTY: □ Easy ◼ Moderate ◼ Complex
ESTIMATED TIME: ○ Less than 1 hour ◐ 1 to 3 hours ● Over 3 hours   ▲ Special tool required

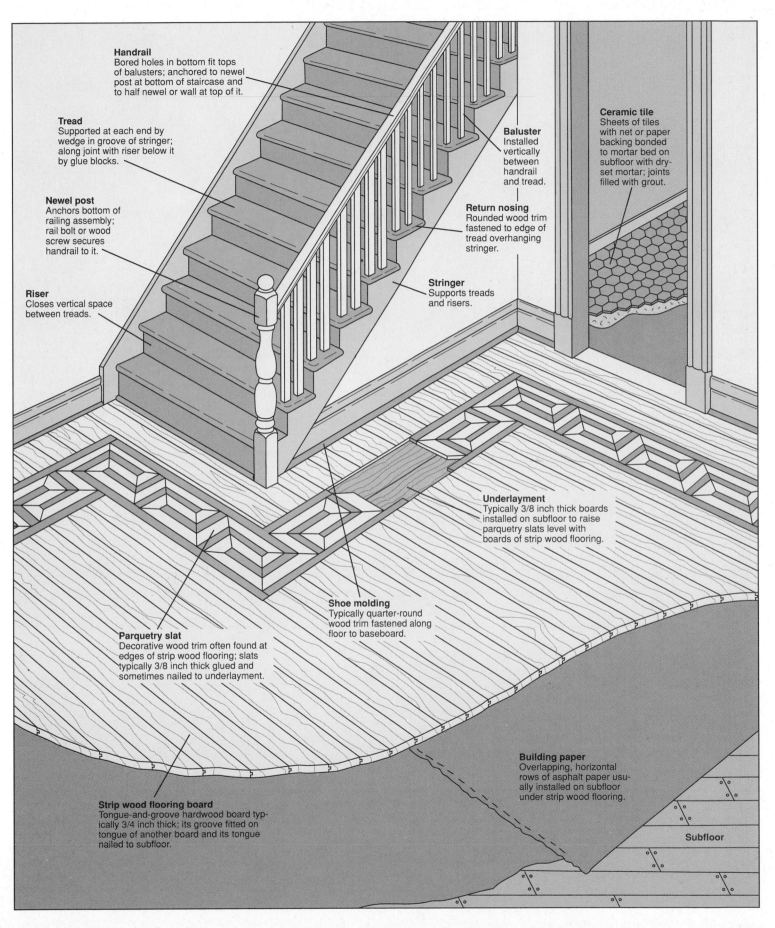

Handrail
Bored holes in bottom fit tops of balusters; anchored to newel post at bottom of staircase and to half newel or wall at top of it.

Tread
Supported at each end by wedge in groove of stringer; along joint with riser below it by glue blocks.

Newel post
Anchors bottom of railing assembly; rail bolt or wood screw secures handrail to it.

Riser
Closes vertical space between treads.

Baluster
Installed vertically between handrail and tread.

Return nosing
Rounded wood trim fastened to edge of tread overhanging stringer.

Stringer
Supports treads and risers.

Ceramic tile
Sheets of tiles with net or paper backing bonded to mortar bed on subfloor with dry-set mortar; joints filled with grout.

Underlayment
Typically 3/8 inch thick boards installed on subfloor to raise parquetry slats level with boards of strip wood flooring.

Shoe molding
Typically quarter-round wood trim fastened along floor to baseboard.

Parquetry slat
Decorative wood trim often found at edges of strip wood flooring; slats typically 3/8 inch thick glued and sometimes nailed to underlayment.

Strip wood flooring board
Tongue-and-groove hardwood board typically 3/4 inch thick; its groove fitted on tongue of another board and its tongue nailed to subfloor.

Building paper
Overlapping, horizontal rows of asphalt paper usually installed on subfloor under strip wood flooring.

Subfloor

SPOT-REFINISHING WOOD FLOORING

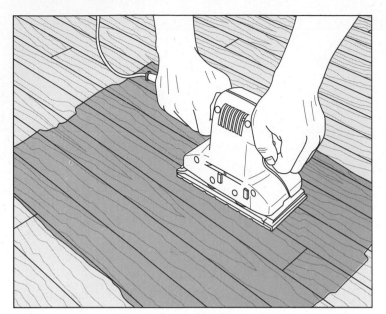

1 Preparing the surface. For superficial damage, wear rubber gloves and scrub the surface gently along the wood grain using fine steel wool moistened with mineral spirits. Otherwise, wear a dust mask and use an orbital sander fitted with fine sandpaper, sanding back and forth along the surface in smooth overlapping passes *(above)*. Work carefully to remove only the damaged finish, feathering the edges of the surface slightly to help disguise the repair. Vacuum particles off the surface and wipe it with a tack cloth.

2 Refinishing the surface. Buy a finish that matches the original at a building supply center. Wearing rubber gloves, use a paintbrush to apply a thin, even coat of finish on the surface, working along the wood grain in smooth overlapping passes *(above)*. Continue until the surface is uniformly coated, feathering the edges slightly and smoothing any unevenness immediately. Let the finish dry, then sand it *(step 1)* and apply another coat of finish. Repeat the procedure as necessary to disguise the repair.

REFINISHING WOOD FLOORING

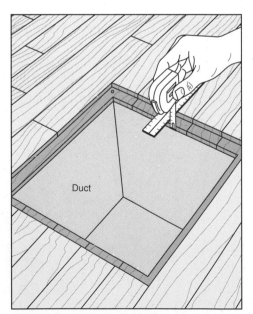

Duct

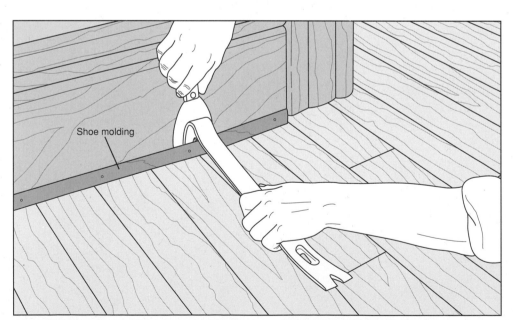

Shoe molding

1 Assessing the flooring. Remove the vent of a heating duct, the collar of a radiator pipe or the threshold of a door, then measure the thickness of the flooring using a tape measure and straightedge *(above)*. If the flooring is less than 11/16 inch thick, prepare it using an orbital sander *(step 1, above)*, then apply a finish *(step 5)*.

2 Preparing the flooring. To prepare the flooring, set the heads of protruding nails with a nail set and remove the shoe moldings. To remove each shoe molding, run a utility knife along its edges to break any finish bond, then work the blade of a wide putty knife far enough behind one end of it to fit in a pry bar *(above)*. Protecting the baseboard with the putty knife, work along the shoe molding with the pry bar to gently pull it out a little at each nail. Return to the end of the shoe molding to continue, pulling it out a little farther each time until it comes off. Ventilate the work area and seal it off from the rest of the interior with plastic sheeting.

REFINISHING WOOD FLOORING (continued)

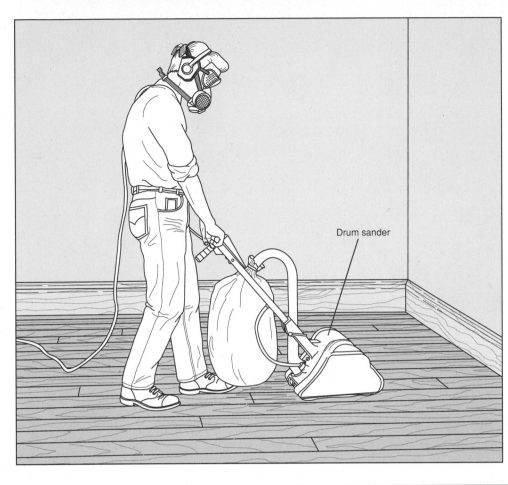

Drum sander

3 **Sanding the flooring.** Rent a drum sander at a tool rental center. For more than superficial damage, sand first diagonally across the wood grain using very coarse sandpaper; otherwise, sand only along the wood grain using coarse sandpaper. Wearing safety goggles, a respirator, hearing protection and work boots, position the drum sander: face-on at an angle to a corner to work diagonally across the wood grain; face-on to a wall at a corner to work along the wood grain. **Note:** Do not use the drum sander on a border of parquetry slats. Tilt the drum sander back to turn it on, then slowly lower it to the flooring—immediately moving it steadily backward to sand one strip. At the center of the flooring, tilt the drum sander back to change direction. Slowly lower the drum sander to the flooring and immediately move it steadily forward back over the same strip. Working back and forth the same way, sand parallel and overlapping strips diagonally across or along *(left)* the wood grain until half of the flooring is sanded. Sand the other half of the flooring using the same procedure. Sand the flooring edges and corners *(step 4)* between sandings diagonally across and along the wood grain.

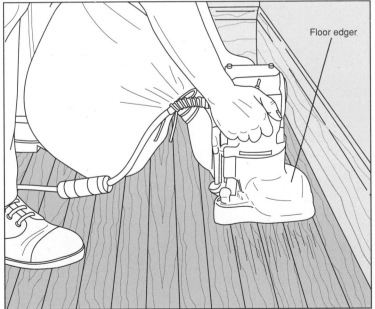

Floor edger

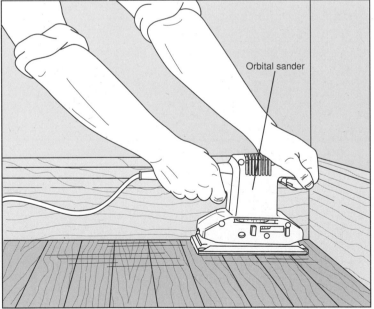

Orbital sander

4 **Sanding the flooring edges and corners.** Sand the flooring edges with a floor edger, available at a tool rental center; use sandpaper of the coarseness used with the drum sander *(step 3)*. Wearing safety goggles, a respirator, hearing protection and work boots, position the floor edger face-on to a wall at a corner. Tilt the floor edger back to turn it on, then slowly lower it to the flooring—immediately moving it steadily to sand one strip: back and forth sideways if the edge runs along the wood grain *(above, left)*; back and forth in a slight arcing motion if the edge runs across the wood grain. Working back and forth the same way, sand parallel and overlapping strips out to the drum-sanded flooring. For corners of the flooring that cannot be reached with the floor edger, sand parallel and overlapping strips using an orbital sander *(above, right)*. For surfaces of the flooring that cannot be reached with the orbital sander, work along the wood grain using a paint scraper; round its corners slightly with a file to avoid gouging. Vacuum particles off the flooring and wipe it with a tack cloth.

REFINISHING WOOD FLOORING (continued)

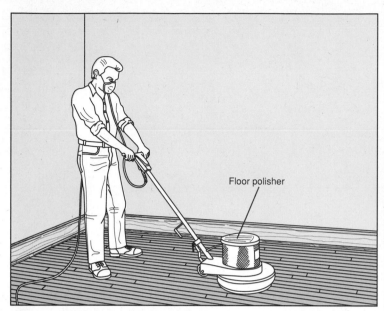

Floor polisher

5 **Applying a finish to the flooring.** Rent a commercial floor polisher with a medium sanding screen and a scrubbing pad at a tool rental center. Wearing a dust mask, work in sections across the flooring using the floor polisher fitted with the sanding screen, moving it steadily along the wood grain *(above, left)* to avoid gouging. Vacuum particles off the flooring and wipe it with a tack cloth. Buy a finish at a building supply center and apply it using a paint pad. Wearing a respirator and working in stockinged feet, start at a corner of the flooring and draw the paint pad lightly in one direction along the wood grain. Continue in sections across the flooring *(above, right)*, overlapping passes slightly and smoothing any unevenness immediately. Let the finish dry, then smooth the flooring using the floor polisher fitted with the scrubbing pad. Vacuum the flooring and wipe it with a tack cloth, then apply another coat of finish. Repeat the procedure as necessary, smoothing with the scrubbing pad, vacuuming and wiping before each coat of finish. When the last coat of finish is dry, reinstall the shoe moldings.

REPAIRING A BOARD OR SLAT

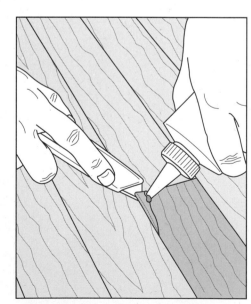

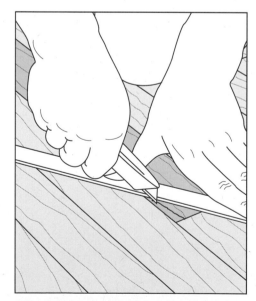

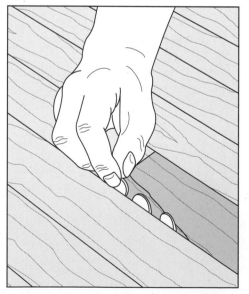

1 **Lifting and gluing the splinter.** Gently lift the splinter using a utility knife. If the splinter begins to widen or break or it is dirty, remove it *(step 2)*; otherwise, squeeze wood glue into the gap under it *(above)*. Gently lower and lift the splinter to work in the glue, then press it into place. Wipe up extruded glue using a damp cloth and secure the splinter *(step 3)*.

2 **Cutting and gluing the splinter.** Use a utility knife and a straightedge to cut off the splinter, scoring repeatedly across it *(above)*. Clean the splinter and the opening using a toothbrush dampened with mineral spirits. Apply wood glue to the splinter and the opening, then press the splinter into place. Wipe up extruded glue with a damp cloth.

3 **Securing the splinter.** To hold the splinter against an edge, wedge metal washers or coins between it and the board *(above)* or slat next to it. To hold down the splinter, cover it with a piece of waxed paper, then position a stick on the waxed paper in line with it and place a heavy weight on the stick. Allow the glue to cure, then spot-refinish the flooring *(page 80)*.

SECURING BOARDS

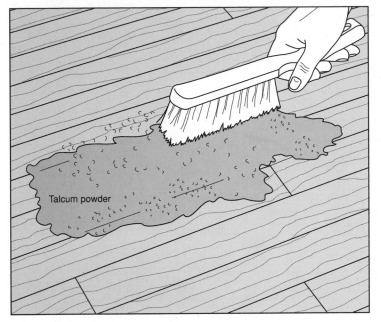

Lubricating boards. If the boards are springy, secure them from below *(step below)* or above *(step right)*. If the boards only squeak, brush talcum powder into their joints using a whisk broom *(above)* or pour liquid buffing wax into them. Lay a dropcloth on the boards, then walk back and forth along them a few times to work in the talcum powder or buffing wax. Remove the dropcloth and wipe off excess talcum powder or buffing wax using a damp cloth. If the boards still squeak, secure them from below or above.

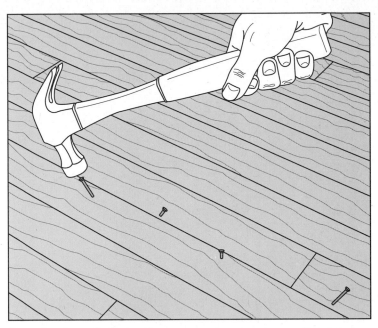

Securing boards from above. If the boards only squeak, lubricate them *(step, left)*. If the boards are springy and there is access from below, secure them *(step below)*; otherwise, secure them from above with 2 1/2-inch finishing nails. Wearing safety goggles, bore pilot holes for the nails at alternating 45° angles every 4 to 6 inches along the boards 1/2 inch from their joints, then drive in the nails *(above)* and use a nail set to set their heads. Cover the nail heads with a wax stick of a color that matches the boards.

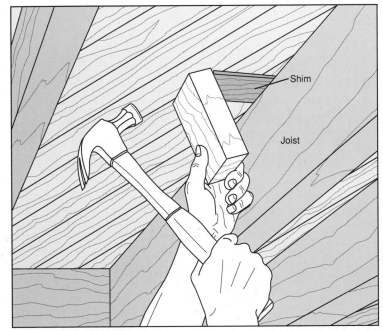

Securing boards from below. If the boards only squeak, lubricate them *(step above, left)*. If the boards are springy, work from below to locate their joint along a joist or between joists under the subfloor; if there is no access from below, secure them from above *(step above, right)*. To secure boards along a joist, wedge a shim into each gap between the joist and the subfloor. Coat the top and bottom of the shim with wood glue, then drive it into the gap using a wood block and a hammer *(above, left)* until it fits snugly. To secure boards between joists, work from above to bore a pilot hole for a 2 1/2-inch

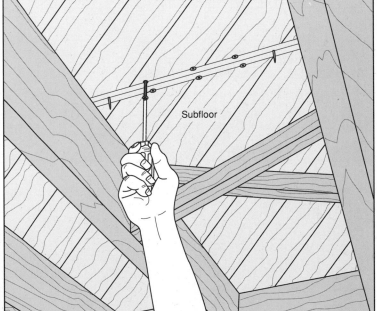

finishing nail into each end of their joint, then drive a nail into each hole until it is flush with the boards. Working from below, mark a centerline between the nails and a parallel line 1/2 inch from it on each side of it. To calculate the thickness of the flooring, subtract the length of the protruding tip of a nail from the length of the nail. Bore holes for countersinking wood screws 1/2 inch shorter than the thickness of the flooring every 4 to 6 inches along the line on each side of the centerline, then drive in the screws *(above, right)* and remove the nails.

REPLACING A BOARD

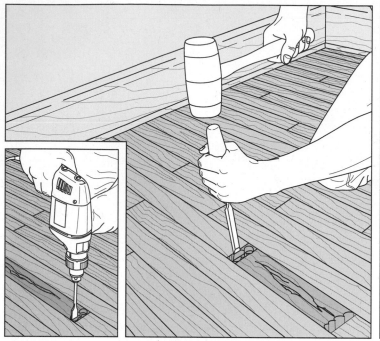

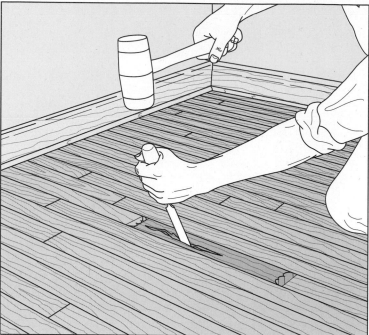

1 **Removing the damaged board.** Use a utility knife and a straightedge to score a cutting line across each end of the board or a section of it at least 12 inches long and 16 inches from an end of it. Wearing safety goggles, use an electric drill fitted with a 1/2-inch spade bit to bore holes for a cutout through the board to the subfloor at each cutting line *(inset)*. Complete the cutouts in the board with a wood chisel and a mallet *(above, left)*, clearing the tongue from the groove of the adjacent board. Cut a strip about 1 inch wide out of the center of the board between the cutouts using the chisel and mallet *(above, right)*, then use a pry bar to pull out the remaining strips: the nailed tongue of one strip from the groove of one adjacent board; the groove of the other strip off the nailed tongue of the other adjacent board. Vacuum debris and dust out of the opening in the flooring.

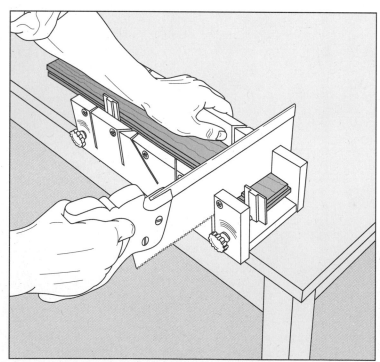

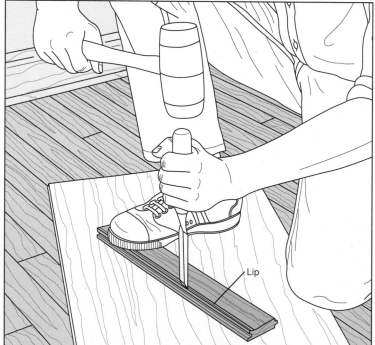

Lip

2 **Cutting and trimming the replacement board.** Buy a replacement board at a building supply center and cut it to size using a backsaw and a miter box *(above, left)*, trimming any tongue off each end of it to square it. To fit the replacement board into the opening in the flooring, trim the bottom lip off its groove. Lay the replacement board face-down on scrap plywood and score its bottom lip along the inside edge of the groove using a utility knife and a straightedge. Wear safety goggles to trim the bottom lip off the replacement board with a wood chisel and a mallet, making shallow cuts along the scored line *(above, right)*, then gradually deepening the cuts. Pare splinters off the chiseled edge of the replacement board using the utility knife.

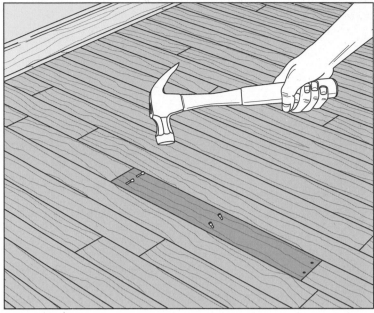

3 **Installing the replacement board.** Fit the replacement board into the opening in the flooring, pushing its tongue into the groove of the adjacent board and tapping it into place on the subfloor with a wood block and a mallet *(above, left)*. To fasten the replacement board, nail it to the subfloor with 2 1/2-inch finishing nails. Wearing safety goggles, bore pilot holes for the nails at alter-

nating 45° angles every 6 to 8 inches along the replacement board about 1/2 inch from each edge of it. Drive the nails through the replacement board into the subfloor *(above, right)* and use a nail set to set their heads. Cover the nail heads with a wax stick of a color that matches the replacement board and spot-refinish the flooring *(page 80)*.

REPLACING A SECTION OF BOARDS

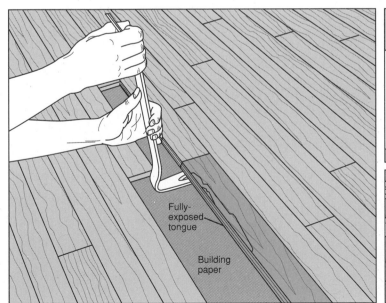

Fully-exposed tongue

Building paper

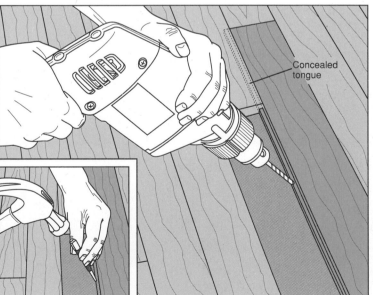

Concealed tongue

Removing and installing boards. Work one row at a time to remove each board or section of a board, offsetting the ends of alternate rows by at least 6 inches. For a board or section of a board without its tongue or groove fully exposed, cut a strip out of the center between cutouts and pry out the remaining strips to remove it *(page 84)*. For a board or section of a board with its tongue or groove fully exposed, use a pry bar to remove it *(above, left)*. Buy boards for the replacement section at a building supply center and work one row at a time to install each board, cutting and trimming it as needed *(page 84)*, then nailing

every 8 inches along it. For a board that can be positioned with its tongue fully exposed, bore pilot holes at a 45° angle along its tongue for 2 1/4-inch finishing nails. For a board that can be positioned only with its tongue partially or fully concealed, trim the bottom lip off its groove and fit it into place, then bore pilot holes: at a 45° angle along its exposed tongue for 2 1/4-inch finish nails *(above, right)*; at alternating 45° angles 1/2 inch from its edge along its concealed tongue and groove for 2 1/2-inch finishing nails. Drive in the nails and use a nail set to set their heads *(inset)*. Spot-refinish or refinish the flooring *(page 80)*.

REPLACING A SLAT OR SECTION OF SLATS

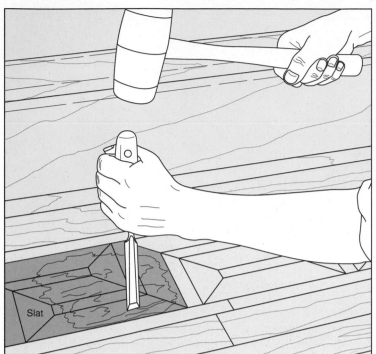

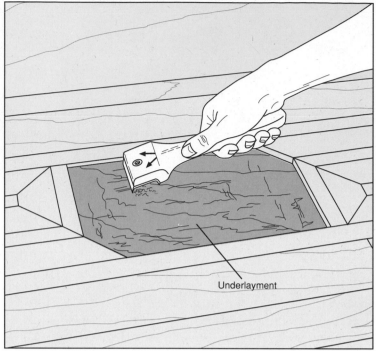

Underlayment

1 **Removing the damaged slats.** Wearing safety goggles, remove each slat with a wood chisel and a mallet. For one slat or the first slat of a section, drive the chisel into the center of it along the wood grain *(above, left)*, splitting it into pieces and prying them off the underlayment. For each other slat of a section, drive the chisel bevel-side down under its exposed edge to pry it off the underlayment.

Clean old adhesive and backing material out of the opening in the flooring with a paint scraper, applying firm pressure along the wood grain *(above, right)*; for the edges or a small opening in the flooring, use an old wood chisel or a utility knife. Secure loose underlayment to the subfloor with 1 1/2-inch spiral finishing nails. Vacuum particles and dust out of the opening in the flooring.

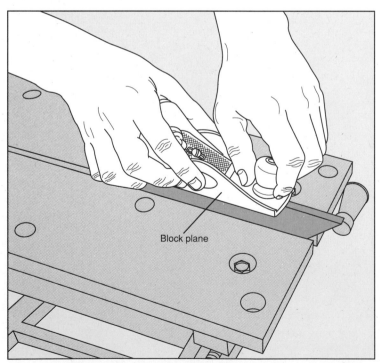

Block plane

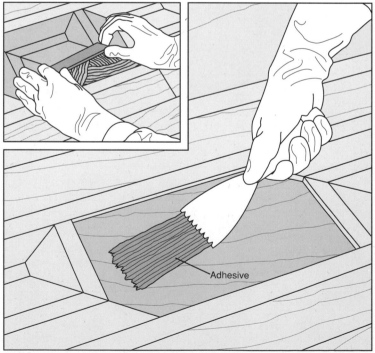

Adhesive

2 **Installing the replacement slats.** Buy a replacement slat or slats for the replacement section and adhesive at a building supply center; or, buy matching wood of the same thickness as the flooring and cut each slat to size. Test-fit each slat and trim its edges as needed using a block plane *(above, left)*, a rasp or medium sandpaper on a sanding block. Wear rubber gloves to apply the adhesive following

the manufacturer's instructions, using a notched knife to coat the opening in the flooring evenly with it *(above, right)*; for a small opening in the flooring, use a putty knife to coat the back of each slat evenly with it. Let the adhesive set, then fit each slat into the opening in the flooring *(inset)* and press it into place. Allow the adhesive to cure, then spot-refinish or refinish the flooring *(page 80)*.

TIGHTENING A BALUSTER

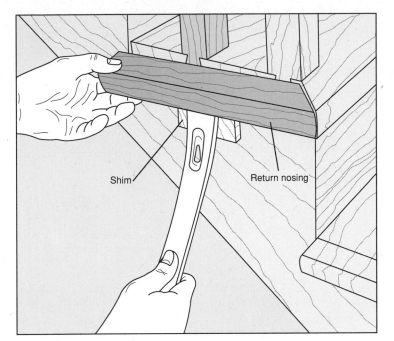

Shim

Return nosing

1 **Removing the return nosing.** If the bottom of the baluster is not loose at the tread, secure the top of it at the handrail *(step 4).* To secure the bottom of the baluster at the tread, remove the return nosing from the edge of the tread. Work the blade of a putty knife far enough into the joint along the bottom of the return nosing to fit in a wood shim. Using the wood shim as leverage, work along the return nosing with a pry bar to gently pry it off *(above).* Pull the nails out of the return nosing using a nail puller.

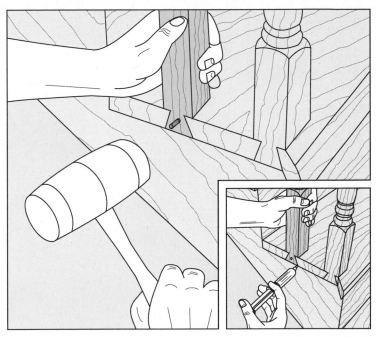

2 **Securing the baluster at the tread.** Clean the joint of the baluster with an old knife. Using an electric drill fitted with a 3/8-inch spade bit, bore a hole 2 1/8 inches deep through the tenon of the baluster into the tread. Coat a 3/8-inch serrated dowel 2 inches long with wood glue and drive it into the hole *(above).* Force glue into the joint of the baluster using a syringe *(inset)* and fill any gap with toothpicks, cutting off the ends with a wood chisel. Wipe off extruded glue using a cloth dampened with water.

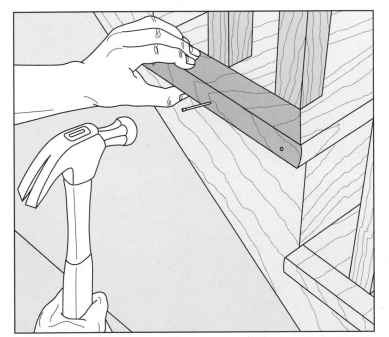

3 **Reinstalling the return nosing.** Lightly sand the back of the return nosing and the edge of the tread using medium sandpaper on a sanding block, then coat them evenly with wood glue. Position the return nosing on the edge of the tread and drive finishing nails 1 inch longer than the ones removed into the holes *(above),* using a nail set to set their heads. Wipe off extruded glue using a cloth dampened with water and cover the nail heads with a wax stick of a color that matches the wood.

4 **Securing the baluster at the handrail.** Clean the joint of the baluster with an old knife. Using an electric drill fitted with a twist bit, bore a pilot hole for a 2-inch finishing nail at a 45° angle through the top of the baluster into the handrail. Force wood glue into the joint of the baluster using a syringe and fill any gap with toothpicks, cutting off the ends with a wood chisel. Drive the nail into the hole and use a nail set to set its head *(above).* Wipe off extruded glue using a cloth dampened with water.

SECURING A NEWEL POST

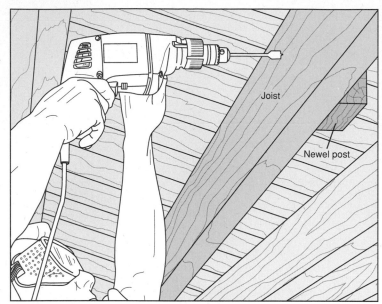

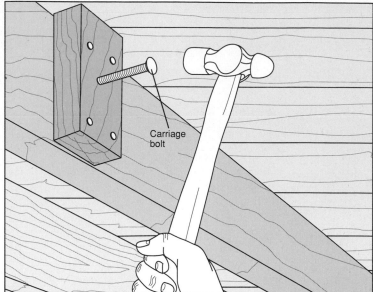

Bolting a newel post to a joist. If the base of the newel post cannot be bolted to a joist it butts against under the flooring, consult a professional about bolting it to the stringer. Otherwise, have the newel post plumbed from above by a helper using a carpenter's level and work from below to nail the base of it to the joist with common nails. Then, secure the base of the newel post to the joist with a carriage bolt. Wear-

ing safety goggles, use an electric drill fitted with a spade bit of the same diameter as the carriage bolt to bore a hole through the joist and the newel post; work from the side of the joist for greatest maneuvering room *(above, left)*. Slide the carriage bolt into the hole and tap it into place with a ball-peen hammer *(above, right)*, then fit it with a washer and thread a nut onto it; tighten the nut using a wrench.

SECURING A HANDRAIL

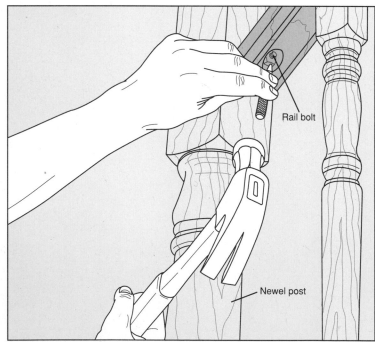

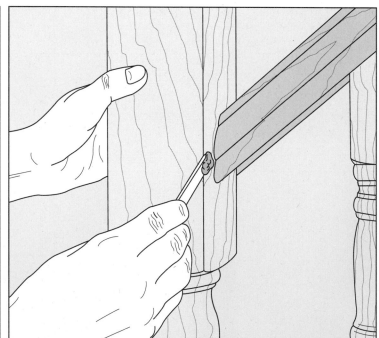

Tightening a handrail to a newel post. Wearing safety goggles, use a wood chisel and a mallet to remove the wood plug covering the rail bolt or wood screw in the bottom of the handrail near the newel post. If the handrail is fastened to the newel post with a rail bolt, loosen the nut using a wrench; if it is not a standard hex or square type, use a nail set and a hammer *(above, left)*. If the handrail is fastened to the newel post with a wood screw, remove it. Loosen the handrail enough

to clean the joint using a putty knife and apply wood glue, working it in with a wood stick *(above, right)* or forcing it in using a syringe. To close the joint between the handrail and the newel post, tighten the nut of the rail bolt or drive in a wood screw slightly longer than the one removed. Cover the rail bolt or wood screw with a wood plug, coating it with wood glue and seating it firmly. Wipe off extruded glue using a cloth dampened with water.

SECURING A TREAD

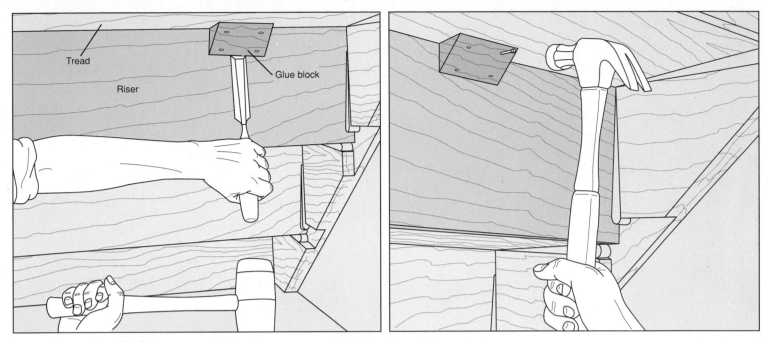

Replacing a glue block. Wearing safety goggles, use a wood chisel and a mallet to remove the glue block *(above, left)*; if it is not damaged, try to pry it off intact. For a replacement glue block, use a piece of very dry 2-by-2 softwood about 4 inches long. Having a helper stand on the tread, position the glue block and bore a pilot hole for a 2-inch finishing nail or No. 8 wood screw through each end of it into the tread and into the riser; offset the holes slightly. Lightly sand the contacting surfaces of the glue block, tread and riser using medium sandpaper, then coat them evenly with wood glue. Reposition the glue block and drive in the nails *(above, right)* or screws. Wipe off extruded glue using a cloth dampened with water.

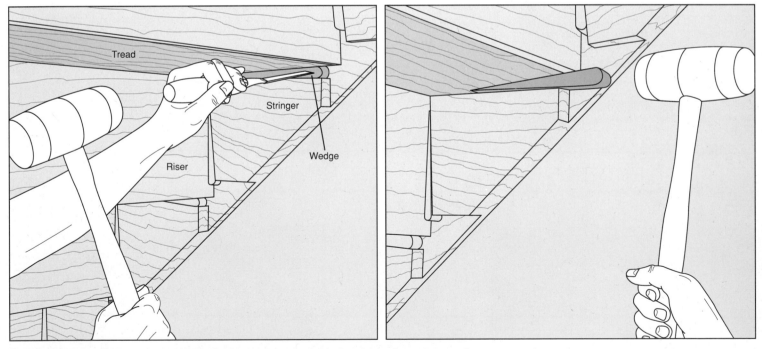

Replacing a wedge. Wearing safety goggles, use a wood chisel and a mallet to remove the wedge *(above, left)*; if it is not damaged, try to pry it out intact. For a replacement wedge, use a piece of very dry 1-by-2 hardwood 8 to 10 inches long tapered to a maximum thickness of 3/4 inch. Lightly sand the contacting surfaces of the wedge, stringer and tread using medium sandpaper, then coat them evenly with wood glue. Position the wedge in the groove of the stringer under the tread and drive it with a mallet *(above, right)* until it fits snugly; avoid driving it in too far and splitting the stringer. Wipe off extruded glue using a cloth dampened with water.

REGROUTING CERAMIC TILES

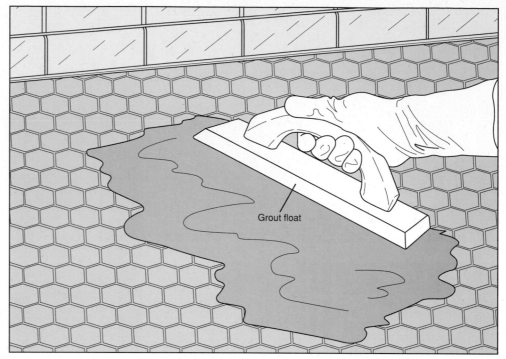

1 Removing the old grout. Wearing safety goggles and a dust mask, scrape damaged grout out of the joints using a carbide-tipped scriber *(above)* or grout saw, raking them to a uniform depth. Vacuum particles and dust from the flooring, then wipe the joints using a cloth dampened with water.

2 Applying the new grout. Buy latex-based grout at a building supply center and wear rubber gloves to prepare it following the manufacturer's instructions, mixing the dry ingredients and adding the latex slowly for grout that is spreadable but not runny. To fill one joint at a time, press the grout into it with a finger. Otherwise, apply the grout using a grout float, sweeping at an angle diagonally across the tiles to force it into the joints *(above)*. Keep the grout float flat against the tiles and sweep diagonally across them to scrape off excess grout without digging into a joint.

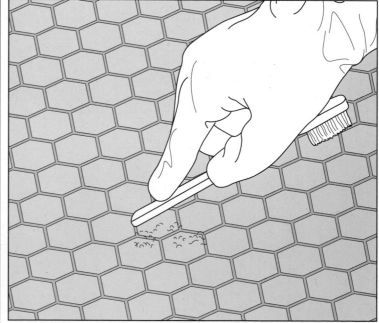

3 Cleaning the tiles and striking the joints. Wait 2 to 3 minutes for the joints to harden slightly, then wipe grout off the tiles. Wearing rubber gloves, soak an old towel with water and wring it out, then drag it unfolded across the tiles *(above, left)*. Continue until the tiles are free of grout, rinsing the towel periodically. If the edges of the tiles are beveled, smooth and shape each joint with the end of an old toothbrush, pressing ceramic grout into it in a slightly concave shape

(above, right). Wait about 15 minutes, then wipe the tiles clean using a cloth soaked in water and wrung almost dry; work carefully to avoid rubbing grout out of a joint. Continue until the tiles are clean, rinsing the cloth periodically. Let the tiles dry and wipe them clean again. Allow the grout to harden overnight, then rub particles off the tiles using a non-metallic kitchen scouring pad.

REPLACING A CERAMIC TILE OR SECTION OF CERAMIC TILES

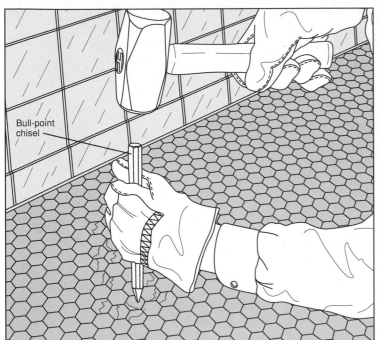

Bull-point chisel

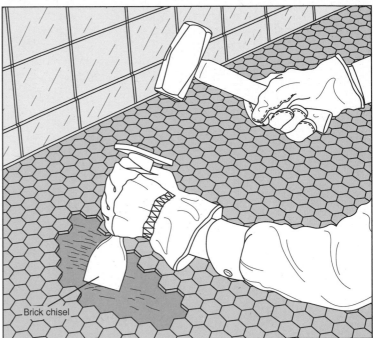

Brick chisel

1 Removing the damaged tiles. Remove the grout from the joints along the edges of each tile *(page 90)*, then wear safety goggles to break it into pieces using a bull-point chisel and a small sledgehammer *(above, left)*; work carefully to avoid marring undamaged tiles. Clean pieces of tile and particles out of the opening in the flooring with a whisk broom and a dustpan. Using a brick chisel with the small sledgehammer, chip a thin layer of the mortar bed out of the opening in the flooring *(above, right)*, digging at least 1/8 inch deeper than needed for each replacement tile to sit level with the other tiles. Sweep particles of mortar and dust out of the opening in the flooring, then vacuum it thoroughly.

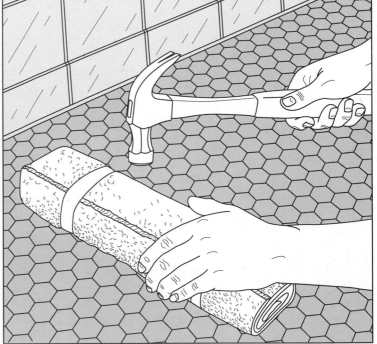

2 Installing the replacement tiles. Buy replacement tiles and dry-set latex mortar at a tile dealer. Position the tiles in the opening in the flooring, using a utility knife to cut the backing of sheets as needed to fit them. Set a straightedge across the tiles and measure the gap under it; if the gap is less than 1/8 inch, chip out more of the mortar bed *(step 1)*. Otherwise, wear rubber gloves to prepare the mortar following the manufacturer's instructions. Dampen the opening in the flooring with water, then use a putty knife to coat it with enough mortar for the tiles to sit level *(above, left)*. Press the tiles into the mortar and align them, then seat them level by setting a straight board wrapped in thick carpet across them and tapping it with a hammer *(above, right)*. Scrape off extruded mortar using a stick. Let the mortar cure, then grout the tiles *(page 90)*.

FAUCETS AND PIPES

Double-handle, compression faucets, supply pipes of galvanized steel or copper and drainpipes of cast iron are characteristic elements of the original plumbing system that in most instances distinguishes an older home—sometimes as the bane; refer to page 93 for illustrations on their usual construction and information on their identifiable traits. Although these elements of the plumbing system are seldom beset with major problems, their steadfast performance for decades is often of little redemption at the time of the troubling leak that inevitably occurs.

Faucets and supply pipes are vulnerable to leaking with the high pressure of the potable water they hold; drainpipes depending on gravity to carry waste water are prone to leaking with their natural shifting and settling. Fortunately, a small, isolated leak need not provoke undue worry about pending major problems with the plumbing system; many additional years of reliable functioning usually can be gained by a simple repair conducted without delay. For help in repairing a leaky faucet, supply pipe or drainpipe, use the Troubleshooting Guide below.

However, even a small, isolated leak should prompt an overall assessment of the plumbing system; if it is due to extensive corrosion or at an inaccessible spot behind a wall or under a floor, professional help may be needed. Consult a professional for any question about poor water quality, inadequate water pressure, recurring drainpipe blockages or slow-draining fixtures; also if the odor of sewer gas is ever detected. Check your local building code to replace supply pipes of lead—dull gray in color and easily scratched; they can contaminate the water.

Most repairs to a leaky faucet, supply pipe or drainpipe of an older home are easily undertaken with only a few basic plumbing tools; the materials needed are usually readily available at a plumbing supply center. Refer to Tools & Techniques (*page 124*) for instructions on using tools properly; a ratchet pipe cutter for replacing a damaged section of drainpipe can be obtained at a tool rental center. Before starting any repair to a leaky faucet, supply pipe or drainpipe, familiarize yourself with the information presented in the Emergency Guide (*page 8*).

TROUBLESHOOTING GUIDE

SYMPTOM	POSSIBLE CAUSE	PROCEDURE
FAUCET (COMPRESSION TYPE)		
Spout drips; leaks	Seat washer worn or split	Replace seat washer *(p. 94)* □ ○
	Seat pitted or corroded	Dress seat *(p. 95)* □ ○ ▲
	Faucet damaged	Replace faucet
Stem leaks	Packing nut loose	Tighten packing nut with adjustable wrench
	Stem packing worn	Replace stem packing *(p. 96)* □ ○
	Faucet damaged	Replace faucet
Handle leaks	Stem packing worn	Replace stem packing *(p. 96)* □ ○
	Faucet damaged	Replace faucet
DRAINPIPE (CAST IRON)		
Pipe drips; leaks	Pipe corroded; pinhole	Repair drainpipe pinhole *(p. 97)* □ ○
	Hub-and-spigot joint leaks	Repair drainpipe joint *(p. 97)* ◨ ○
	Pipe cracked or extensively corroded	Replace section of drainpipe *(p. 98)* ◨ ◕ ▲
SUPPLY PIPE (GALVANIZED STEEL)		
Pipe drips; leaks	Condensation (cold-water supply pipe)	Fit cold-water supply pipes with insulation sleeves or tape
	Pipe corroded; pinhole	Repair supply pipe pinhole *(p. 97)* □ ○
	Joint leaks; threaded union loose	Tighten threaded union; replace section of supply pipe *(p. 99)* ◨ ◕
	Pipe cracked or extensively corroded	Replace section of supply pipe *(p. 99)* ◨ ◕
SUPPLY PIPE (COPPER)		
Pipe drips; leaks	Condensation (cold-water supply pipe)	Fit cold-water supply pipes with insulation sleeves or tape
	Pipe corroded; pinhole	Repair supply pipe pinhole *(p. 97)* □ ○
	Joint leaks	Repair supply pipe joint *(p. 100)* ◨ ○
	Pipe cracked or extensively corroded	Replace section of supply pipe *(p. 100)* ◨ ◕

DEGREE OF DIFFICULTY: □ **Easy** ◨ **Moderate** ■ **Complex**
ESTIMATED TIME: ○ **Less than 1 hour** ◕ **1 to 3 hours** ● **Over 3 hours**
▲ **Special tool required**

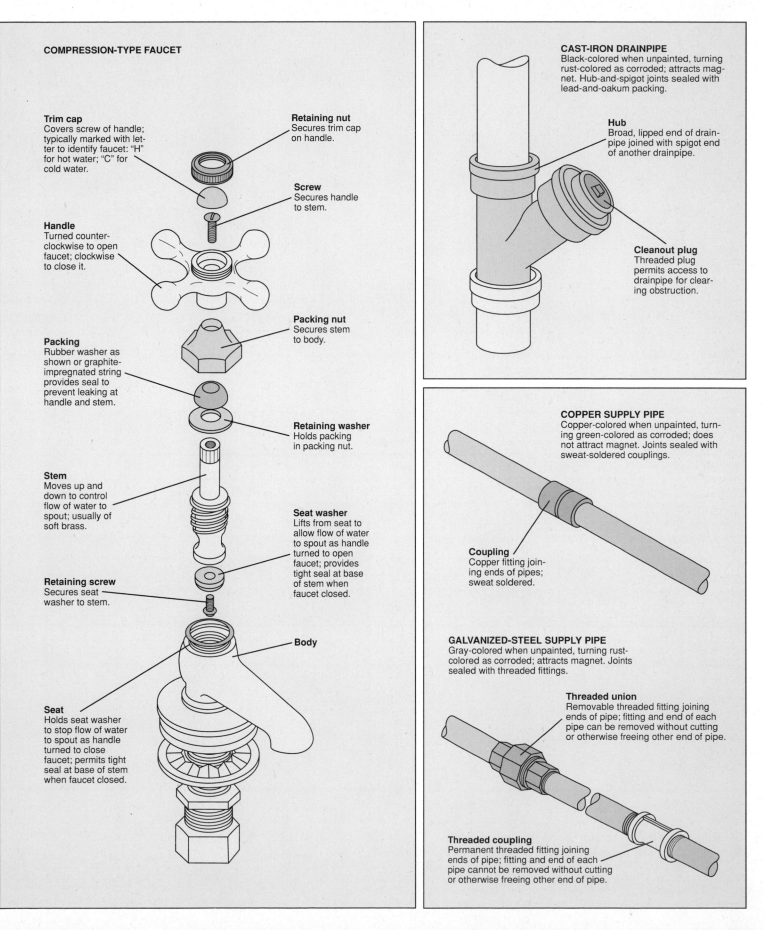

COMPRESSION-TYPE FAUCET

Trim cap
Covers screw of handle; typically marked with letter to identify faucet: "H" for hot water; "C" for cold water.

Retaining nut
Secures trim cap on handle.

Screw
Secures handle to stem.

Handle
Turned counterclockwise to open faucet; clockwise to close it.

Packing nut
Secures stem to body.

Packing
Rubber washer as shown or graphite-impregnated string provides seal to prevent leaking at handle and stem.

Retaining washer
Holds packing in packing nut.

Stem
Moves up and down to control flow of water to spout; usually of soft brass.

Seat washer
Lifts from seat to allow flow of water to spout as handle turned to open faucet; provides tight seal at base of stem when faucet closed.

Retaining screw
Secures seat washer to stem.

Body

Seat
Holds seat washer to stop flow of water to spout as handle turned to close faucet; permits tight seal at base of stem when faucet closed.

CAST-IRON DRAINPIPE
Black-colored when unpainted, turning rust-colored as corroded; attracts magnet. Hub-and-spigot joints sealed with lead-and-oakum packing.

Hub
Broad, lipped end of drainpipe joined with spigot end of another drainpipe.

Cleanout plug
Threaded plug permits access to drainpipe for clearing obstruction.

COPPER SUPPLY PIPE
Copper-colored when unpainted, turning green-colored as corroded; does not attract magnet. Joints sealed with sweat-soldered couplings.

Coupling
Copper fitting joining ends of pipes; sweat soldered.

GALVANIZED-STEEL SUPPLY PIPE
Gray-colored when unpainted, turning rust-colored as corroded; attracts magnet. Joints sealed with threaded fittings.

Threaded union
Removable threaded fitting joining ends of pipe; fitting and end of each pipe can be removed without cutting or otherwise freeing other end of pipe.

Threaded coupling
Permanent threaded fitting joining ends of pipe; fitting and end of each pipe cannot be removed without cutting or otherwise freeing other end of pipe.

93

SHUTTING OFF THE WATER SUPPLY

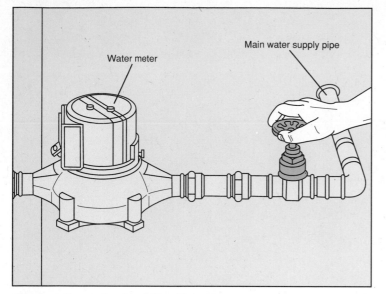

Closing the main shutoff valve. Locate the main shutoff valve on the main water supply pipe for the house—usually indoors at the entry point of the main water supply pipe. Turn the handle fully clockwise to close the valve *(above)*, shutting off the water supply to the house. Open a faucet on each story of the house to drain the supply pipes. To restore the water supply, close the faucets and open the main shutoff valve, slowly turning the handle fully counterclockwise. Wait a few minutes to let water enter the supply pipes, then open each faucet slowly to release trapped air.

Closing a faucet shutoff valve. Locate the shutoff valve for the faucet on its water supply pipe under the sink. Turn the handle fully clockwise to close the valve *(above)*, shutting off the water supply to the faucet. If there is no shutoff valve or it leaks, close the main shutoff valve *(step left)*; if it is stuck, apply penetrating oil and wait 24 hours. Open the faucet to drain its supply pipe. To restore the water supply to the faucet, close it and open its shutoff valve, turning the handle fully counterclockwise. Let water enter the supply pipe, then open the faucet to release trapped air.

REPLACING A FAUCET SEAT WASHER

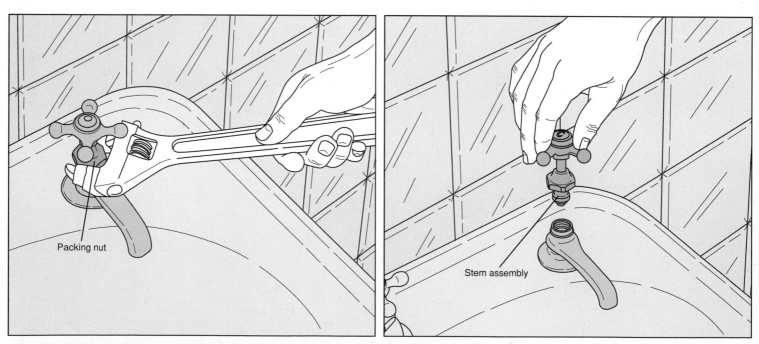

1 Removing the stem assembly. Shut off the water supply to the faucet and drain its supply pipe *(step above, right)*. Cover the drain of the sink to avoid losing parts. Loosen the packing nut of the stem assembly with an adjustable wrench, protecting the finish by wrapping masking tape around the jaws *(above, left)*. Avoid exerting extreme force; if the packing nut is stuck, apply penetrating oil and wait 1 hour to loosen it. When the packing nut is loosened, turn the handle clockwise to take it, the stem and the packing nut off the body *(above, right)*.

REPLACING A FAUCET SEAT WASHER (continued)

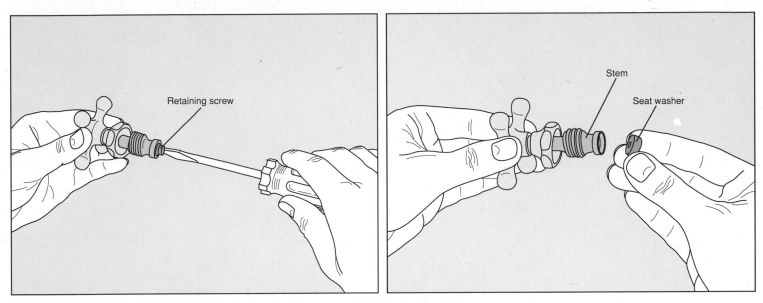

2 **Replacing the seat washer.** Remove the retaining screw of the seat washer *(above, left)*; if it is stuck, apply penetrating oil and wait 1 hour. If the retaining screw breaks, remove it with pliers. Pry the seat washer off the stem with an old screwdriver. Scrub deposits off the stem using fine steel wool. Buy a replacement seat washer and retaining screw at a plumbing supply center. Install the seat washer *(above, right)* with its marked side against the stem. Tighten the retaining screw until it holds the seat washer in place. Coat the stem with plumber's grease and reinstall the stem assembly, then restore the water supply. If the problem persists, dress the faucet seat *(step below)*.

DRESSING A FAUCET SEAT

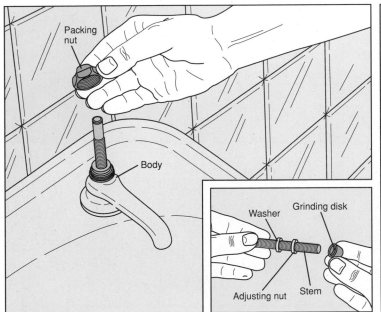

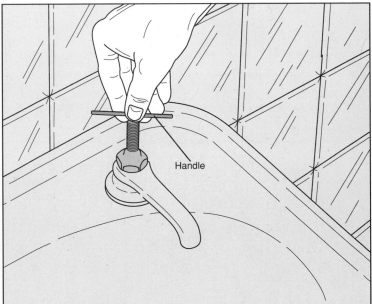

Grinding a faucet seat. Remove the stem assembly *(page 94)* and pull off the packing nut. Buy a faucet seat dresser with a grinding disk slightly larger than the seat washer at a plumbing supply center and use it following the manufacturer's instructions. For the model of dresser shown, screw the grinding disk onto the stem *(inset)* and insert it into the body. Turn the adjusting nut until it sits slightly above the body and slide the washer down to it, then screw the packing nut onto the stem *(above, left)* to hold the grinding disk flat against the seat. To grind the seat, fit the handle into the stem and turn it clockwise *(above, right)* three revolutions, tightening the packing nut each revolution. Loosen the packing nut and pull out the dresser to inspect the seat; use a flashlight, if necessary. If the seat is pitted or scored, grind it again. When the seat is smooth and polished, uncover the drain and pour water into the body to flush out grindings. Fit the packing nut back onto the stem assembly, coat the stem with plumber's grease and reinstall the stem assembly, then restore the water supply. If the problem persists, replace the faucet.

REPLACING A FAUCET STEM PACKING

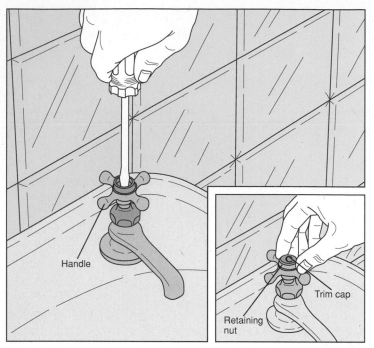

Handle

Trim cap

Retaining
nut

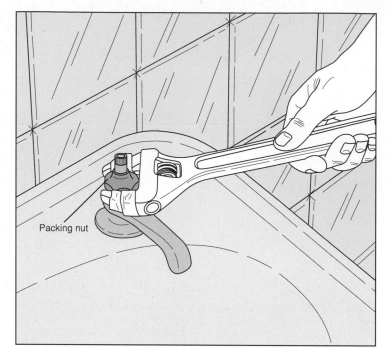

Packing nut

1 Taking off the handle. Shut off the water supply to the faucet and drain its supply pipe *(page 94)*. Cover the drain of the sink to avoid losing parts. Unscrew the retaining nut of the trim cap *(inset)* and take the trim cap off the handle; pry it off with an old screwdriver, if necessary. Remove the screw from the handle *(above)* and pull the handle off the stem; if the screw is stuck, apply penetrating oil and wait 1 hour to remove it.

2 Removing the old stem packing. Remove the packing nut from the stem using an adjustable wrench, protecting the finish by wrapping masking tape around the jaws *(above)*. Avoid exerting extreme force; if the packing nut is stuck, apply penetrating oil and wait 1 hour to remove it. Take the retaining washer out of the packing nut and pry out the packing washer or the packing string with an old screwdriver. Scrub deposits off the stem using fine steel wool.

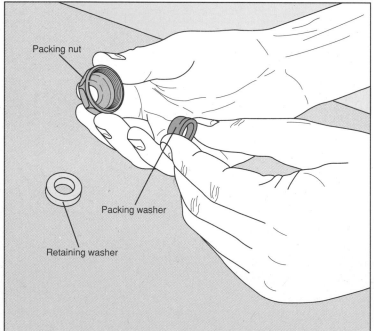

Packing nut

Packing washer

Retaining washer

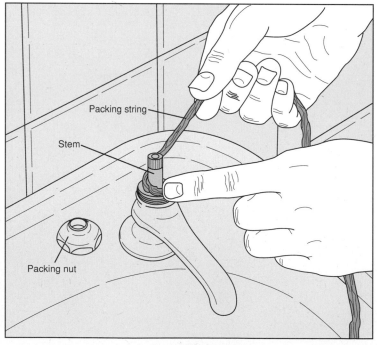

Packing string

Stem

Packing nut

3 Installing a replacement packing washer or string. Buy replacement packing at a plumbing supply center: a replacement packing washer that fits the packing nut; or, replacement graphite-impregnated packing string. To install a packing washer, position its beveled side into the packing nut *(above, left)* and insert the retaining washer, then reinstall the packing nut. To install packing string, insert the retaining washer into the packing nut and wrap two or three turns of packing string snugly around the base of the stem *(above, right)*, then reinstall the packing nut. Tighten the packing nut using an adjustable wrench, protecting the finish by wrapping masking tape around the jaws. Screw the handle back onto the stem, put back the trim cap and screw its retaining nut back onto it, then restore the water supply. If the problem persists, replace the faucet.

REPAIRING A PIPE PINHOLE

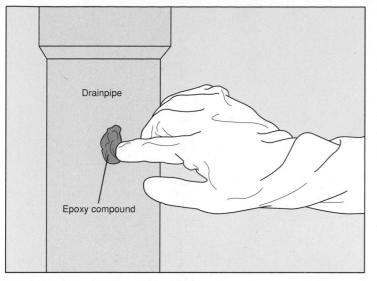

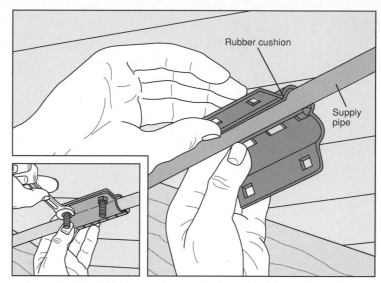

Plugging a drainpipe pinhole. Turn off the main water supply *(page 94)* and leave a note at each drain warning others not to use it. Buy epoxy compound at a plumbing supply center and follow the manufacturer's instructions to use it. Dry the drainpipe at the pinhole using a cloth and clean it with a wire brush; remove rust with coarse steel wool. Wearing rubber gloves, work compound into the pinhole and apply a thin layer to the drainpipe within 2 inches of it *(above)*. Allow the compound to cure, then restore the water supply. If the problem persists, replace the section of drainpipe *(page 98)*.

Clamping a supply pipe pinhole. Turn off the main water supply *(page 94)* and open the faucet nearest to the pinhole to drain the supply pipe. Buy a pipe-leak clamp of the same diameter as the supply pipe at a plumbing supply center. Dry the supply pipe at the pinhole using a cloth and fit the clamp around it, the rubber cushion centered on and completely covering the pinhole *(above)*. Insert the bolts into the clamp and tighten each nut in turn with a wrench *(inset)*, then restore the water supply. If the problem persists, replace the section of steel *(page 99)* or copper *(page 100)* supply pipe.

REPAIRING A DRAINPIPE JOINT

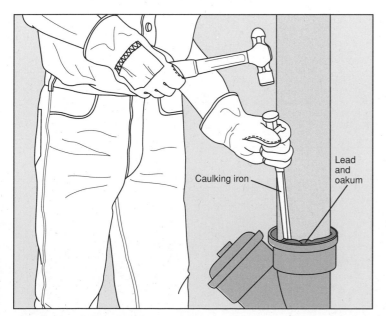

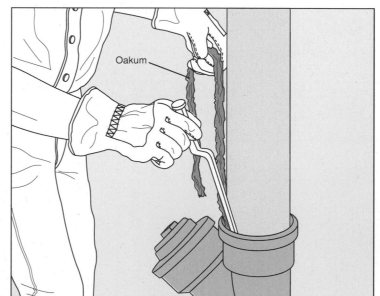

1 Tamping the joint. Turn off the main water supply *(page 94)* and leave a note at each drain warning others not to use it. Wearing work gloves and safety goggles, work along the joint with a caulking iron or cold chisel and a ball-peen hammer, tamping the lead and oakum into the hub *(above)*; work carefully to avoid damaging the drainpipe. Restore the water supply to check the joint. If the problem persists, turn off the main water supply and leave a note at each drain warning others not to use it, then repack the joint *(step 2)*.

2 Repacking the joint. Wearing work gloves, safety goggles and a dust mask, pry the lead and oakum out of the joint with an old screwdriver. To repack the joint, buy oakum and cold caulking compound at a plumbing supply center. Wrap oakum along the joint and tamp it using a caulking iron *(above)*, packing it to within 1 inch of the top of the hub; tamp the last layer with the caulking iron and a ball-peen hammer. Dampen a length of caulking compound twice the circumference of the joint and pack it the same way. Let the caulking compound cure, then restore the water supply.

REPLACING A SECTION OF DRAINPIPE

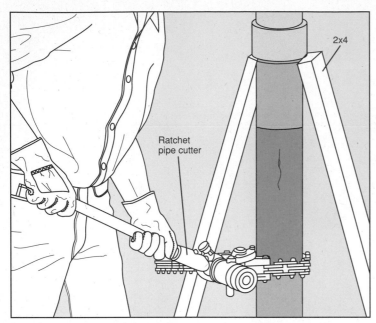

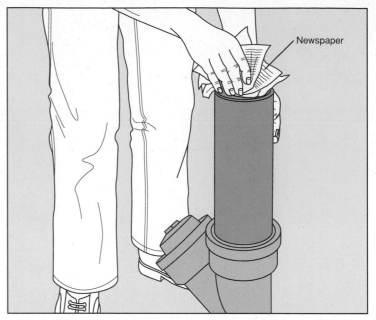

1 **Removing the damaged section.** Turn off the main water supply *(page 94)* and leave a note at each drain warning others not to use it. Rent a ratchet pipe cutter at a tool rental center and have its use demonstrated. Brace the drainpipe with 2-by-4s, wedging them between the hub of a joint above the damaged section and the floor. Mark a cutting line on the drainpipe at each end of the damaged section, then wear work gloves and safety goggles to cut along each marked line with the pipe cutter *(above)*. If the drainpipe crumbles, cut farther beyond the end of the damaged section.

2 **Preparing the replacement section.** Immediately stuff newspapers into each end of the open drainpipe to block sewer gas *(above)*. For the replacement section, use pipe of the same inside and outside diameter as the drainpipe and 1/4 inch shorter than the opening in it. Choose pipe of Schedule 40 PVC or ABS if permitted by your local plumbing code; of cast iron otherwise. Buy the pipe and two hubless fittings at a plumbing supply center. To cut PVC or ABS pipe, use a hacksaw and a miter box, then deburr the edges with a utility knife. To cut cast-iron pipe, use a ratchet pipe cutter.

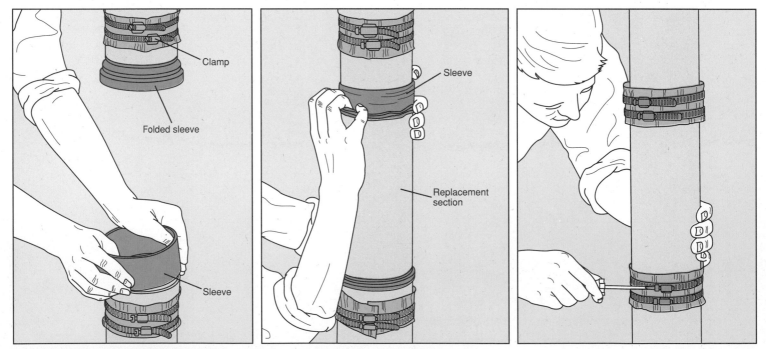

3 **Installing the replacement section.** Install a hubless fitting at each end of the open drainpipe. Position each clamp about 6 inches from the end of the drainpipe and temporarily tighten it. Slide each sleeve onto the drainpipe *(above, left)* until the interior separator ring bottoms out against the end of it, then fold the lip back onto it. Remove the newspapers and work the replacement section into position, then unfold the lip of each sleeve onto it *(above, center)*. Loosen each clamp and slide it onto the sleeve at the center of the joint between the replacement section and the drainpipe, then tighten it *(above, right)*. Restore the water supply.

REPLACING A SECTION OF STEEL SUPPLY PIPE

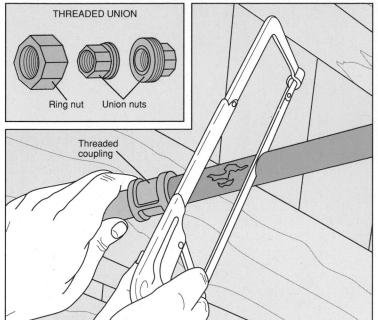

THREADED UNION

Ring nut   Union nuts

Threaded coupling

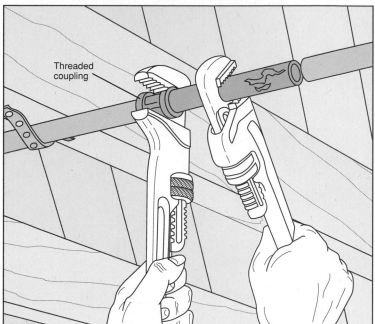

Threaded coupling

1 **Removing the damaged section.** Turn off the main water supply and drain the supply pipes *(page 94)*. If the damaged section is near a threaded union *(inset)*, unscrew the ring nut to free one end of it, then unscrew the other end of it from the nearest threaded coupling. Otherwise, wear safety goggles to cut through the damaged section using a hacksaw *(above, left)*, then unscrew each end of it from the nearest threaded coupling. To unscrew the ring nut of a

threaded union, use a double-wrench technique and orient the jaws in the direction of the force being applied. Steady the exposed union nut with one pipe wrench and turn the ring nut counterclockwise with another pipe wrench. Unscrew the end of a damaged section from a threaded coupling the same way, steadying the threaded coupling and turning the damaged section *(above, right)*.

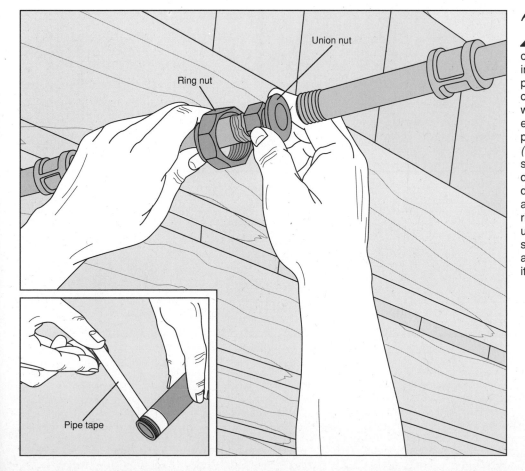

Union nut

Ring nut

Pipe tape

2 **Installing the replacement section.** For the replacement section, buy galvanized steel pipe of the same inside and outside diameter as the supply pipe at a plumbing supply center. If an end of the open supply pipe has a threaded union, have a single pipe cut to length; otherwise, have two pipes fitted with a threaded union cut to length. To install each end of the replacement section, wrap pipe tape snugly around its threads 1 1/2 turns *(inset)*. To screw an end of the replacement section onto a threaded coupling, apply the double-wrench technique used to unscrew the damaged section. To install a threaded union at a joint of the replacement section, slide the ring nut onto the end of one pipe and screw a union nut onto the end of each pipe *(left)*, then screw the ring nut onto the union nuts and apply the double-wrench technique to tighten it. Restore the water supply.

REPAIRING A COPPER SUPPLY PIPE JOINT

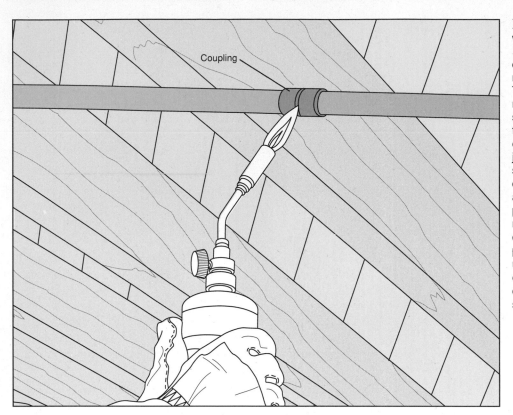

Coupling

Replacing a coupling. Turn off the main water supply and drain the supply pipes *(page 94)*, then use a propane torch to remove the coupling from the joint. **Caution:** Shield flammable surfaces nearby with tin or sheet metal. To avoid heating other couplings, wrap damp rags around them. Wearing work gloves and safety goggles, light the torch and play the flame steadily along the coupling to heat it evenly and melt the solder *(left)*, then bend the joint slightly to pull it off. Buy a replacement sweat-solder coupling at a plumbing supply center. Burnish the inside ends of the coupling and outside end of each pipe using fine emery paper, then wipe them with a clean cloth. Apply non-corrosive soldering flux to the inside end of the coupling and each pipe using a small paintbrush. Slide the coupling onto one pipe until the interior bottoms out, then slide the other pipe into the coupling until the end bottoms out. Twist the coupling 1/4 turn to distribute the soldering flux, then solder it *(page 101)*.

REPLACING A SECTION OF COPPER SUPPLY PIPE

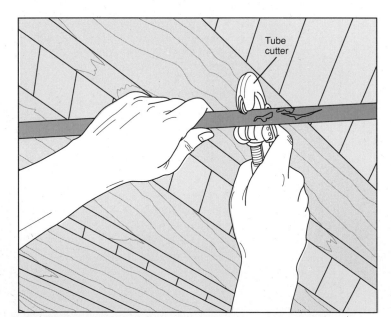

Tube cutter

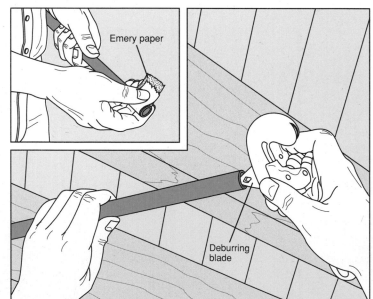

Emery paper

Deburring blade

1 **Removing the damaged section.** Turn off the main water supply and drain the supply pipes *(page 94)*. Mark a cutting line on the supply pipe at each end of the damaged section, then wear safety goggles to cut along each marked line with a tube cutter. Position the tube cutter on the supply pipe and align its cutting disk with the marked line. Tighten the knob until the rollers grip firmly and the cutting disk bites into the supply pipe, then rotate the tube cutter once around the supply pipe *(above)*. Continue tightening the knob and rotating the tube cutter until the supply pipe is severed.

2 **Preparing the replacement section.** For the replacement section, buy rigid copper tubing of the same inside and outside diameter as the supply pipe and two standard sweat-solder couplings at a plumbing supply center. Slide a coupling onto each end of the open supply pipe and cut the tubing to fit between the center ridges using a tube cutter; use its deburring blade to deburr each end of the open supply pipe *(above)* and replacement section. Using fine emery paper, burnish the inside ends of each coupling and outside ends of the replacement section *(inset)* and open supply pipe.

REPLACING A SECTION OF COPPER SUPPLY PIPE (continued)

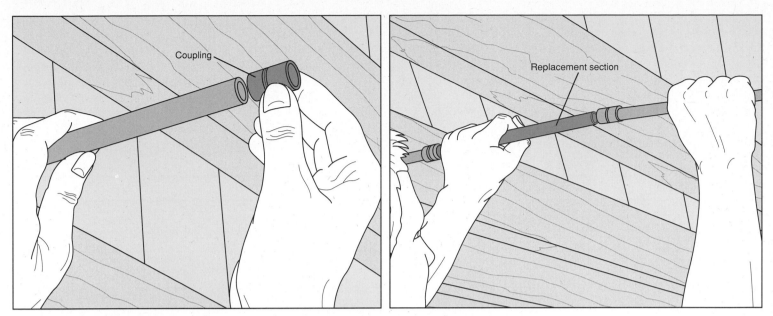

Coupling

Replacement section

3 **Installing the replacement section.** Wipe the inside ends of each coupling and outside ends of the replacement section and open supply pipe using a clean cloth, then apply non-corrosive soldering flux to them using a small paintbrush. Slide a coupling onto each end of the open supply pipe *(above, left)* until the interior bottoms out, then slide each end of the replacement section in turn into a coupling *(above, right)* until it bottoms out. Twist the couplings 1/4 turn to distribute the soldering flux, then solder them *(step below)*.

SOLDERING A COPPER SUPPLY PIPE JOINT

Coupling

Solder

Soldering a coupling. Buy lead-free solder at a plumbing supply center and apply it to each joint of the coupling using a propane torch. **Caution:** Shield flammable surfaces nearby with tin or sheet metal. To avoid heating other couplings, wrap damp rags around them. Wearing work gloves and safety goggles, light the torch and play the flame steadily along the coupling to heat it evenly. Unroll a 6-inch length of solder and touch the tip of it to the joint of the coupling—not to the flame. Continue heating the coupling *(left)* until the solder is drawn into the joint, forming a bead completely around it. Wipe off excess solder with a clean cloth, then restore the water supply.

ELECTRICAL FIXTURES

Few problems with a feature of an older home are as intimidating as with the electrical system: an unreliable switch, a flickering light fixture, an outlet that does not work or a doorbell that fails to sound. However, a repair to an element of the electrical system need not be daunting—if it is performed methodically, following all safety precautions. Refer to page 103 for illustrations of a typical single-pole wall switch, wall-mounted light fixture, duplex outlet and doorbell characteristic of an original electrical system; for help in undertaking a repair, use the Troubleshooting Guide below.

Most repairs to elements of the electrical system of an older home are easily undertaken with only a few basic electrical tools; the materials needed are usually readily available at an electrical supply center. Refer to Tools & Techniques (page 124) for instructions on using tools properly and working safely with electricity. Before starting any repair to the electrical system, conduct a careful assessment of it (page 104); it may need to be inspected or upgraded by an electrician. Also, familiarize yourself with the information presented in the Emergency Guide (page 8).

TROUBLESHOOTING GUIDE

SYMPTOM	POSSIBLE CAUSE	PROCEDURE
WALL SWITCH (SINGLE POLE)		
Light fixture does not light or lights intermittently	Bulb faulty; fuse blown or breaker tripped	Replace bulb; replace fuse (p. 104) □○ or reset breaker
	Switch faulty	Service switch (p. 106) □○
	Light fixture faulty	Service wall-mounted (p. 107) ◨◕ or ceiling-mounted light fixture
	Electrical box faulty	Consult an electrician
Switch sparks; shocks	Switch faulty	Shut off electricity (p. 10) and service switch (p. 106) □○
	Light fixture faulty	Shut off electricity (p. 10) and service wall-mounted (p. 107) ◨◕ or ceiling-mounted light fixture
	Electrical box faulty	Shut off electricity (p. 10) and consult an electrician
Fuse blows or breaker trips repeatedly	Circuit overloaded or shorted; electrical system capacity inadequate	Consult an electrician
LIGHT FIXTURE (WALL MOUNTED)		
Light fixture does not light or lights intermittently	Bulb faulty; fuse blown or breaker tripped	Replace bulb; replace fuse (p. 104) □○ or reset breaker
	Switch faulty	Service switch (p. 106) □○
	Light fixture faulty	Service light fixture (p. 107) ◨◕
	Electrical box faulty	Consult an electrician
Light fixture sparks; shocks	Switch faulty	Shut off electricity (p. 10) and service switch (p. 106) □○
	Light fixture faulty	Shut off electricity (p. 10) and service light fixture (p. 107) ◨◕
	Electrical box faulty	Shut off electricity (p. 10) and consult an electrician
Fuse blows or breaker trips repeatedly	Circuit overloaded or shorted; electrical system capacity inadequate	Consult an electrician
WALL OUTLET (DUPLEX)		
Lamp or other electrical unit does not work or works intermittently	Lamp or other electrical unit faulty	Test by plugging working lamp into outlet
	Fuse blown or breaker tripped	Replace fuse (p. 104) □○ or reset breaker
	Outlet faulty	Service outlet (p. 110) ◨○
	Electrical box faulty	Consult an electrician
Outlet sparks; shocks	Outlet faulty	Shut off electricity (p. 10) and service outlet (p. 110) ◨○
	Electrical box faulty	Shut off electricity (p. 10) and consult an electrician
Fuse blows or breaker trips repeatedly	Circuit overloaded or shorted; electrical system capacity inadequate	Consult an electrician
DOORBELL		
Doorbell does not sound	Fuse blown or breaker tripped	Replace fuse (p. 104) □○ or reset breaker
	Push button, transformer or bell unit faulty	Service doorbell (p. 112) ◨◕
	Junction box faulty	Consult an electrician

DEGREE OF DIFFICULTY: □ Easy ◨ Moderate ■ Complex
ESTIMATED TIME: ○ Less than 1 hour ◕ 1 to 3 hours ● Over 3 hours

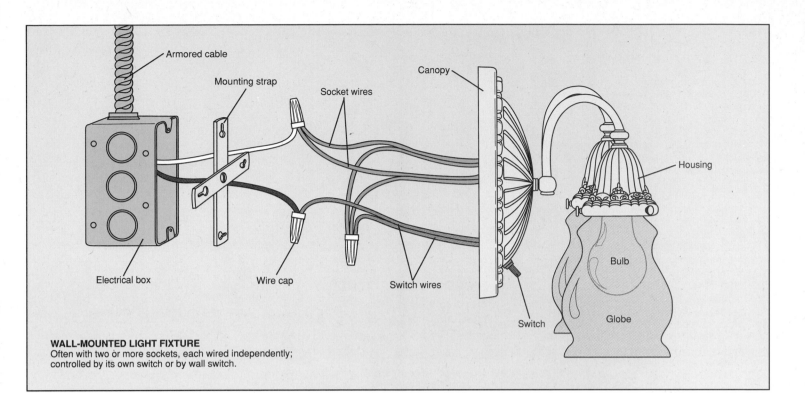

WALL-MOUNTED LIGHT FIXTURE
Often with two or more sockets, each wired independently; controlled by its own switch or by wall switch.

CAUTION:
The electrical system of an older home may not be properly grounded—required to test safely that electricity to a specific circuit is shut off. Unless you can confirm proper grounding of the electrical system, shut off the entire electrical system *(page 10)* before undertaking a repair. Consult an electrician about proper grounding of the electrical system.

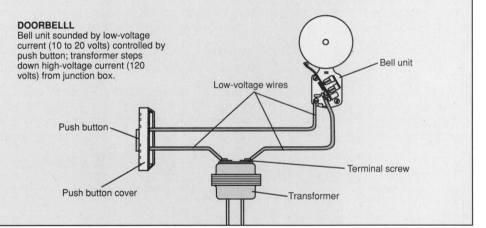

DOORBELLL
Bell unit sounded by low-voltage current (10 to 20 volts) controlled by push button; transformer steps down high-voltage current (120 volts) from junction box.

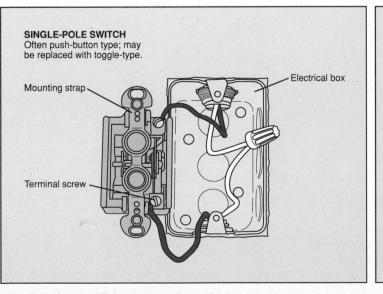

SINGLE-POLE SWITCH
Often push-button type; may be replaced with toggle-type.

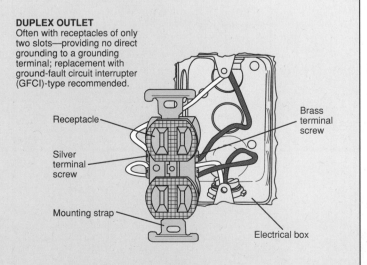

DUPLEX OUTLET
Often with receptacles of only two slots—providing no direct grounding to a grounding terminal; replacement with ground-fault circuit interrupter (GFCI)-type recommended.

ASSESSING THE ELECTRICAL SYSTEM

Evaluating the electrical system.
Before undertaking a repair, assess the system following the guidelines below:

• Confirm that the system is properly grounded by consulting an electrician, if necessary; otherwise, shut off electricity to the system *(page 10)* to undertake a repair.

• Check the amperage rating for the system marked on the service panel. If the rating is less than 100 amps, consult an electrician about upgrading the system.

• Thoroughly inspect the service panel; there may be more than one if the system has been upgraded. Consult an electrician if there is a broken or cracked cable, a black mark or other sign of possible scorching, a burning odor or a buzzing noise.

• For a fuse-type service panel, check each plug fuse for its amperage rating; finding one of 30 amps or two of 20 amps may indicate overfusing. To confirm overfusing, consult an electrician; otherwise, replace each plug fuse of a rating higher than needed *(step below)*.

• Check for knob-and-tube wiring and test it *(step right)*. Having an electrician replace the wiring is advised; local building codes no longer permit its installation or repair.

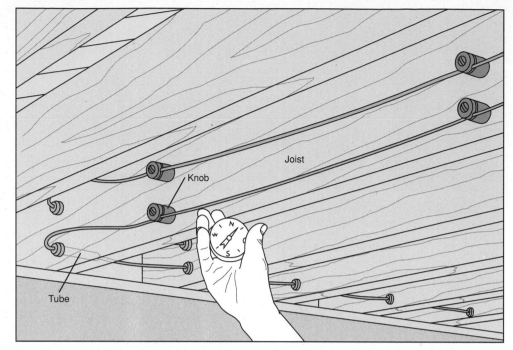

Locating and testing knob-and-tube wiring. Work in an unfinished area such as the basement or attic to check for knob-and-tube wiring—identified by the porcelain knobs used to secure it along joists and the porcelain tubes used to run it through joists. Hold a compass near the wiring to test it *(above)*. If the needle of the compass deflects, the wiring is connected and carries electricity; have an electrician inspect it before undertaking a repair. If the needle of the compass does not deflect, the wiring does not carry electricity and may be disconnected.

CHECKING A FUSE-TYPE SERVICE PANEL

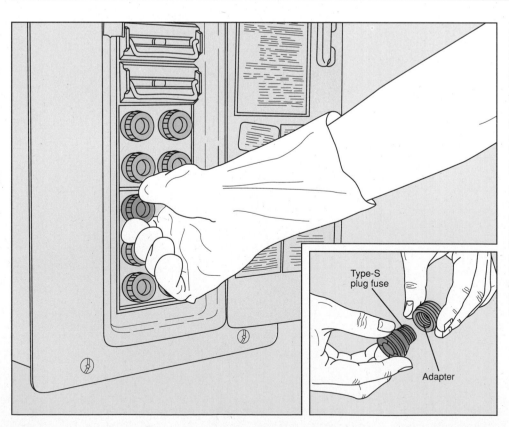

Replacing a plug fuse. Caution: Work only in dry conditions; if the area at the service panel is damp, stand on a dry board and wear rubber boots. Wear rubber gloves, work only with one hand and avoid touching any metal. To prevent overfusing and the risk of an electrical fire, no plug fuse should be of an amperage rating higher than needed: usually, 15 amps to protect a circuit for lights; 20 amps to protect a circuit for kitchen appliances. Check for the amperage rating of a plug fuse on its base or insulated rim. To remove a plug fuse, grasp it only by its insulated rim and unscrew it *(left)*. Buy a replacement type-S plug fuse with an adapter of the correct amperage rating for the circuit at an electrical supply center. Screw the type-S plug fuse into the adapter *(inset)*, then screw the adapter into the service panel; the adapter prevents accidental overfusing, accepting only a replacement type-S fuse of the same amperage rating. If there is regular or repeated blowing of a plug fuse, consult an electrician.

SERVICING AN ELECTRICAL BOX

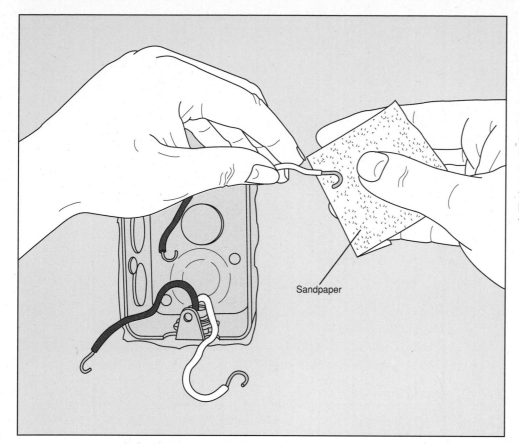

Sandpaper

1 **Burnishing wires.** Vacuum particles and dust out of the electrical box, then inspect the wires of each cable; damaged or missing insulation or dirty, corroded, blackened or otherwise damaged ends can cause intermittent functioning—and sparks or shocks. The insulation of each wire should be sound; the exposed end of the wire should be no longer than 3/4 inch. If the insulation of a wire is cracked or stripped beyond 3/4 inch from the end, cut back the wire and strip the end *(step 2)*. If the end of a wire is dirty, burnish it with fine sandpaper *(left)* and wipe particles off it. If the end of a wire is corroded, blackened or otherwise damaged, cut back the wire and strip the end.

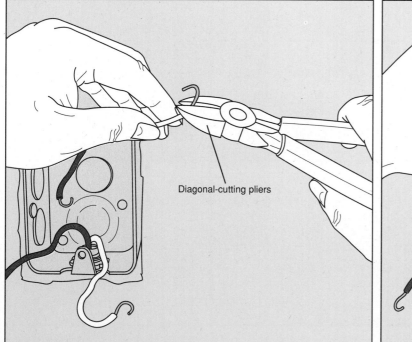

Diagonal-cutting pliers

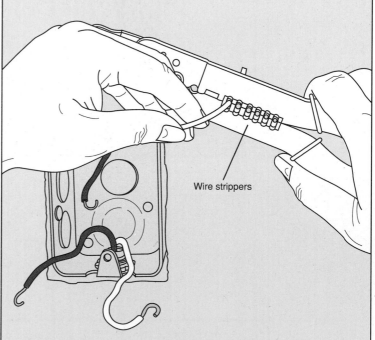

Wire strippers

2 **Cutting back and stripping wires.** Cut back and strip each wire with insulation that is cracked or stripped beyond 3/4 inch from the end or with an end that is corroded, blackened or otherwise damaged. If a wire is too short to cut back, strip and reconnect, consult an electrician. Otherwise, cut back a wire using diagonal-cutting pliers, snipping cleanly as far along it as needed to remove the damaged end *(above, left)* or insulation. Strip 3/4 inch of insulation off the end of the wire using wire strippers, inserting the wire into the appropriate-gauged slot and closing the jaws *(above, right)*. Apply gentle pressure on the handles of the wire strippers to sever the insulation, then pull it off the end of the wire. To reconnect the end of each wire, make the appropriate connection: to a switch, an outlet or the push button or bell unit of a doorbell with a terminal connection; to a fixture or the transformer of a doorbell with a wire cap connection *(page 137)*.

SERVICING A SWITCH

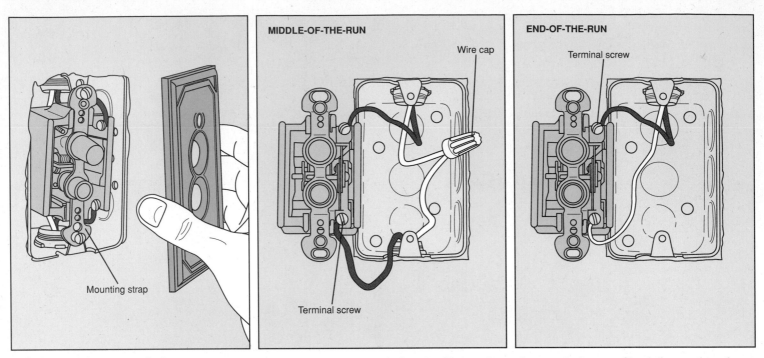

MIDDLE-OF-THE-RUN

Wire cap

END-OF-THE-RUN

Terminal screw

Mounting strap

Terminal screw

1 **Identifying the switch.** Assess the system to ensure that repairs can be done safely *(page 104)*. Turn off the switch and shut off electricity to it *(page 10)*. Run a utility knife along the edges of the cover plate to break any paint bond, then unscrew and remove it *(above, left)*. Carefully unscrew the mounting strap and pull the switch out of the electrical box. **Caution:** Test for voltage *(step 2)* before touching a wire end or terminal screw. Check the number of cables entering the electrical box to identify the switch: a middle-of-the-run *(above, center)* with two cables, each black wire connected to a terminal screw and the white wires connected together with a wire cap; an end-of-the-run *(above, right)* with one cable, the black wire and the white wire each connected to a terminal screw.

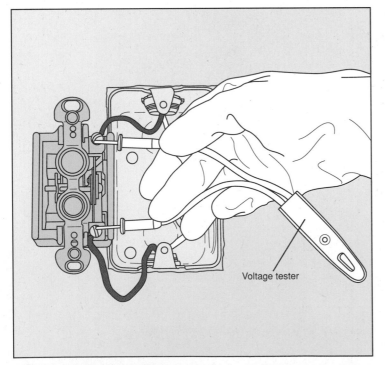

Voltage tester

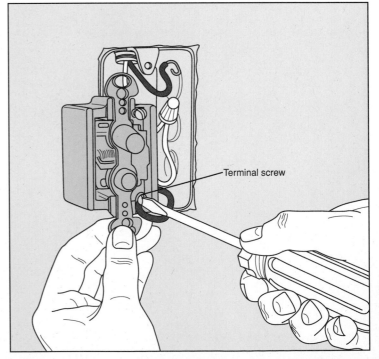

Terminal screw

2 **Checking for voltage.** To confirm that electricity to the switch is shut off, test for voltage using a voltage tester. Wearing a rubber glove, hold the probes by the insulated handles with only one hand. Touch a probe to each terminal screw *(above)*, then touch one probe to the electrical box and the other probe in turn to each terminal screw. If the tester glows, electricity to the switch is not shut off; shut off the correct circuit and test again.

3 **Removing the switch.** Make a sketch of the wire connections or tag the wires, then disconnect each wire from the switch by loosening its terminal screw *(above)*. If the switch is an end-of-the-run *(step 1)*, recode the white wire as black by marking the insulation with electrical tape or paint. Service the electrical box to inspect the wires of each cable *(page 105)* and test the switch *(step 4)*.

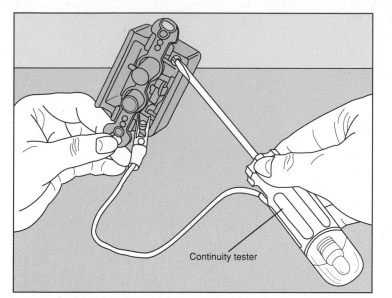

Continuity tester

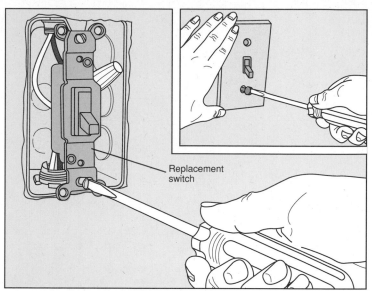

Replacement switch

4 **Testing the switch.** Test the switch with a continuity tester. Connect the clip to one terminal screw and touch the probe to the other terminal screw *(above)*, then set the switch in turn to ON and OFF. The tester should glow when the switch is set to ON and not glow when it is set to OFF. If the switch does not pass the test, buy a replacement switch with a cover plate at an electrical supply center and install them; otherwise, reinstall the original switch with its cover plate the same way *(step 5)*.

5 **Replacing the switch.** Using the sketch of the connections or the tags, connect each wire to the switch by wrapping it clockwise around its terminal screw and tightening the connection with a screwdriver. If the switch is a middle-of-the-run, reconnect the white wires with a wire cap *(page 137)*. Carefully fold the wires to position the switch, then screw the mounting strap to the electrical box *(above)*. Install the cover plate *(inset)* and restore electricity to the switch.

SERVICING A LIGHT FIXTURE

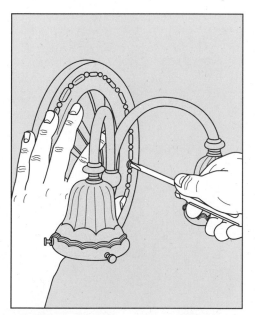

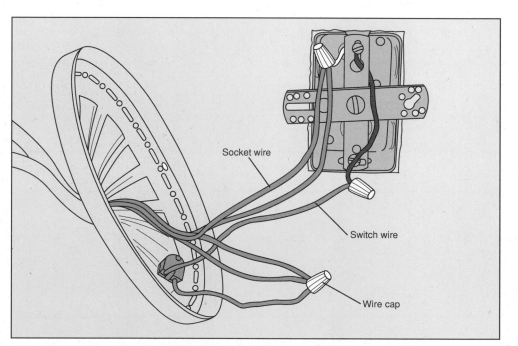

Socket wire

Switch wire

Wire cap

1 **Removing the canopy.** Assess the system to ensure that repairs can be done safely *(page 104)*. Turn off the fixture and shut off electricity to it *(page 10)*, then remove each bulb and globe. Run a utility knife along the edges of the canopy to break any paint bond, then unscrew it *(above)* and carefully remove it. **Caution:** Test for voltage *(step 3)* before touching a wire end.

2 **Identifying the wires.** Make a sketch of the wire connections or tag the wires. A fixture with its own switch *(above)* has a set of two wires for the switch and for each socket: one wire for the switch connected to the black wire of the cable entering the electrical box; one wire for each socket connected to the white wire of the cable entering the electrical box. The other wire for the switch and the other wire for each socket are connected together; code the wire for each socket as black by marking the insulation with electrical tape or paint.

SERVICING A LIGHT FIXTURE (continued)

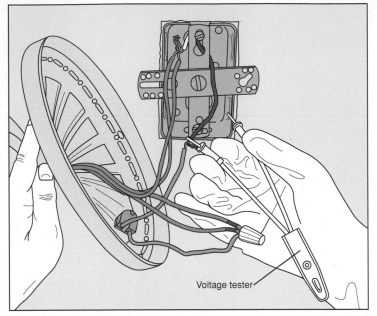

Voltage tester

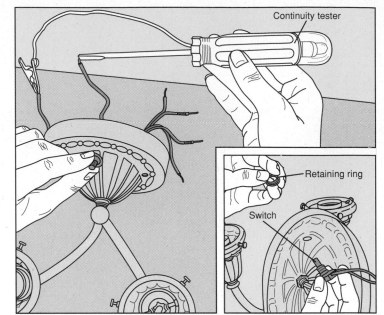

Continuity tester

Retaining ring

Switch

3 **Checking for voltage.** To confirm that electricity to the fixture is shut off, test for voltage using a voltage tester. Wearing a rubber glove, hold the probes by the insulated handles with only one hand. Carefully remove the wire caps from the black wire and the white wire of the cable entering the electrical box and touch a probe to each set of twisted wire ends, then touch one probe to the electrical box and the other probe in turn to each set of twisted wire ends *(above)*. If the tester glows, electricity to the fixture is not shut off; shut off the correct circuit and test again.

4 **Testing and replacing the switch.** Disconnect the wires, then test the switch and its wires with a continuity tester. Connect the clip to one wire end of the switch and touch the probe to the other wire end of the switch *(above)*, then set the switch in turn to ON and OFF. The tester should glow only when the switch is set to ON. If the switch and its wires pass the test, test each socket *(step 5)*. Otherwise, buy a replacement switch with wires at an electrical supply center and install it *(inset)*, then service the electrical box to connect the wires *(page 105)* and reinstall the fixture *(step 9)*.

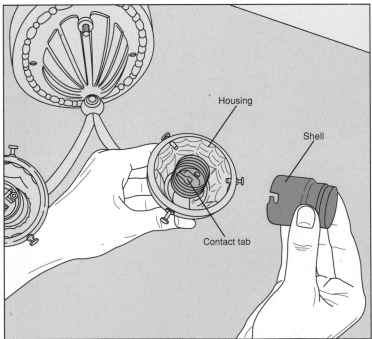

Housing

Shell

Contact tab

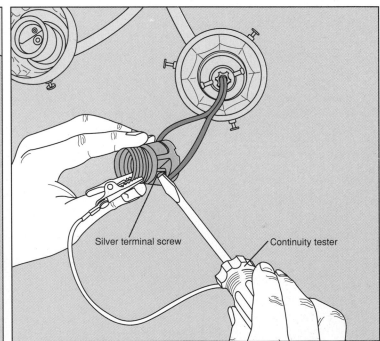

Silver terminal screw

Continuity tester

5 **Testing a socket.** To provide enough slack at the socket, unscrew the cap from the housing and loosen the locknut on the threaded nipple of the canopy. Pull the socket out of the housing far enough to remove any screws from the cap, then twist the shell and pull it off *(above, left)*. Check the insulating sleeve of the socket; if it is missing or damaged, replace the socket *(step 6)*. Otherwise, burnish the contact tab of the socket and pry it up slightly with an old screw-

driver, then test the socket using a continuity tester. Connect the clip to the threaded tube and touch the probe to the silver terminal screw *(above, right)*, then connect the clip to the brass terminal screw and touch the probe to the contact tab. The tester should glow for both tests. If the socket passes the test, test its wires *(step 7)*; otherwise, tag its wires, then disconnect them to replace it.

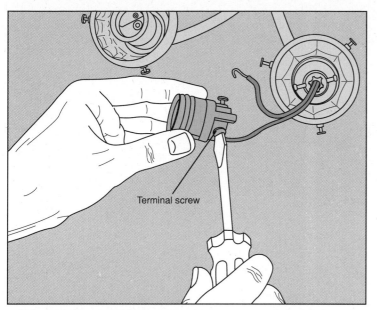

Terminal screw

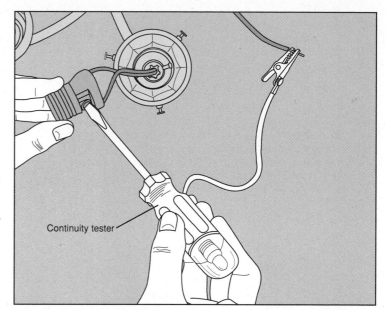

Continuity tester

6 **Replacing a socket.** Buy a replacement socket at an electrical supply center. To install the socket, twist the shell and pull it off the cap, then remove the insulating sleeve. Reconnect each wire of the socket, wrapping it clockwise around its terminal screw and tightening the connection with a screwdriver *(above)*. Slip the insulating sleeve onto the socket and snap the shell back onto the cap. Screw the cap into the housing and tighten the locknut on the threaded nipple of the canopy. Then, service the electrical box to connect the wires *(page 105)* and reinstall the fixture *(step 9)*.

7 **Testing the socket wires.** Test each wire of the socket in turn with a continuity tester. Connect the clip to the untwisted end of the wire and touch the probe to the end of the wire at the terminal screw *(above)*. The tester should glow. If the wires do not pass the test, replace them *(step 8)*. Otherwise, slip the insulating sleeve onto the socket and put the shell back onto the cap. Screw the cap into the housing and tighten the locknut on the threaded nipple of the canopy. Then, service the electrical box to connect the wires *(page 105)* and reinstall the fixture *(step 9)*.

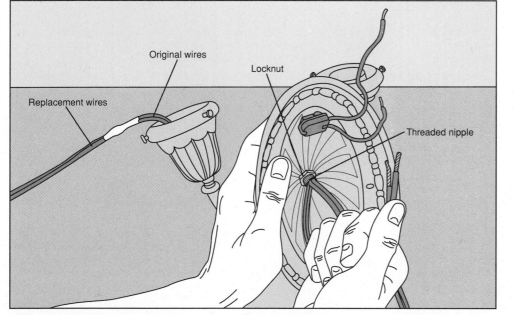

Original wires

Locknut

Replacement wires

Threaded nipple

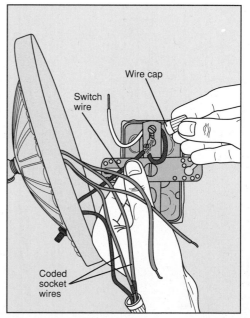

Wire cap

Switch wire

Coded socket wires

8 **Replacing the socket wires.** Buy replacement wires of the same gauge as the original wires at an electrical supply center. Loosen the terminal screws to remove the socket and wrap the original wires around the replacement wires, then secure them with electrical tape. Pull the original wires out of the canopy *(above)*, bringing in the replacement wires. Code the replacement wires, then cut back and strip the ends to connect them to the socket *(page 105)*. Slip the insulating sleeve onto the socket and put the shell back onto the cap. Screw the cap into the housing and tighten the locknut on the threaded nipple of the canopy. Remove the original wires, then service the electrical box to connect the replacement wires *(page 105)* and reinstall the fixture *(step 9)*.

9 **Installing the fixture.** Using the sketch of the connections or the tags, use wire caps *(page 137)* to connect one switch wire with the coded socket wires, the other switch wire to the black wire entering the electrical box *(above)*, and the other socket wires to the white wire entering the electrical box. Carefully fold the wires and reinstall the canopy, put back the globes and bulbs, then restore electricity to the fixture.

SERVICING AN OUTLET

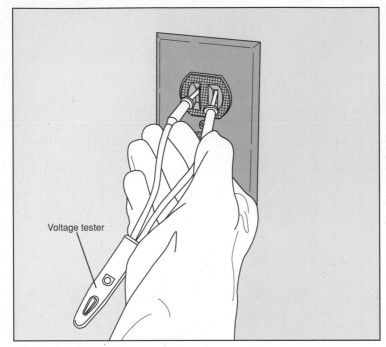

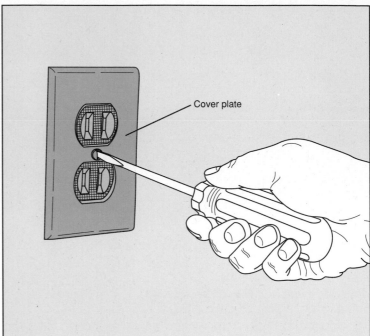

Cover plate

1 **Reaching the wires.** Assess the system to ensure that repairs can be done safely *(page 104).* Shut off electricity to the outlet *(page 10);* if its circuit is protected by two fuses or a double breaker, have it serviced by an electrician. To check that electricity to the outlet is shut off, test each receptacle in turn for voltage using a voltage tester. Wearing a rubber glove, hold the probes by the insulated han-

dles with only one hand and insert a probe as far as possible into each slot of the receptacle *(above, left).* If the tester glows, electricity to the outlet is not shut off; shut off the correct circuit and test again. Otherwise, run a utility knife along the edges of the cover plate to break any paint bond, then unscrew and remove it *(above, right).*

Voltage tester

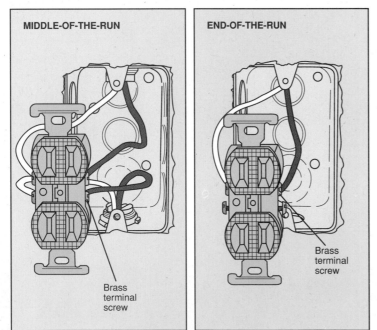

MIDDLE-OF-THE-RUN

END-OF-THE-RUN

Brass terminal screw

Brass terminal screw

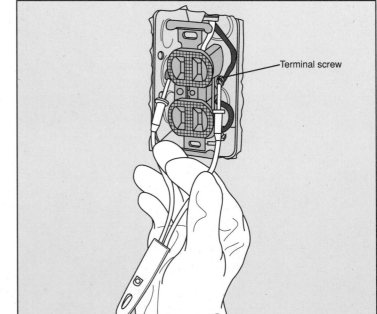

Terminal screw

2 **Identifying the outlet.** Carefully unscrew the mounting strap and pull out the outlet. **Caution:** Test again for voltage *(step 3)* before touching a wire end or terminal screw. Check the number of cables entering the electrical box to identify the outlet: a middle-of-the-run *(above, left)* with two cables, each black wire connected to a brass terminal screw and each white wire connected to a silver terminal screw; an end-of-the-run *(above, right)* with one cable, the black wire connected to a brass terminal screw and the white wire connected to a silver terminal screw.

3 **Checking for voltage.** To confirm that electricity to the outlet is shut off, test each receptacle in turn again for voltage using a voltage tester. Wearing a rubber glove, hold the probes by the insulated handles with only one hand. Touch a probe to each terminal screw of the receptacle *(above),* then touch one probe to the electrical box and the other probe in turn to each terminal screw. If the tester glows, electricity to the outlet is not shut off; shut off the correct circuit and test again for voltage.

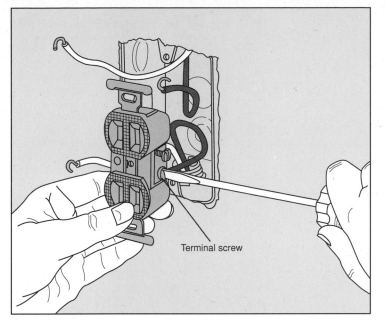

Terminal screw

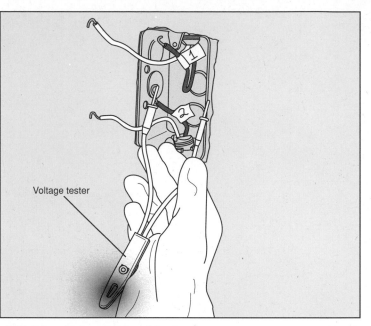

Voltage tester

4 **Removing the outlet.** Make a sketch of the wire connections or tag the wires, then disconnect each wire from the outlet by loosening its terminal screw *(above)*. Service the electrical box to inspect the wires of each cable *(page 105)*. Reinstall the outlet and its cover plate, then restore electricity to it. If the problem persists, reach the wires *(step 1)* and check for voltage *(step 3)*, then remove the outlet and install a replacement outlet; or, identify the hot black wire *(step 5)* and install a GFCI (ground-fault circuit interrupter) outlet *(step 6)*.

5 **Identifying the hot black wire.** The one black wire of an end-of-the-run outlet is hot—brings current to the electrical box. For a middle-of-the-run outlet, label the black wires with masking tape and isolate the ends. **Caution:** Restore electricity to the outlet to test with a voltage tester. Wear a rubber glove and hold the insulated handles with only one hand, then touch one probe to the electrical box and the other probe in turn to each black wire *(above)*. The tester will glow when the hot black wire is touched. Note the hot black wire, then shut off electricity to the outlet.

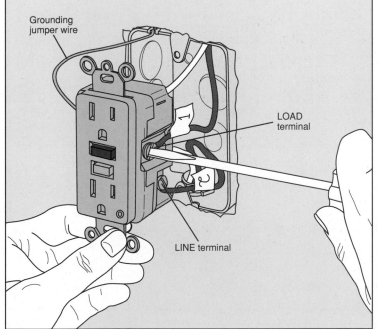

Grounding jumper wire

LOAD terminal

LINE terminal

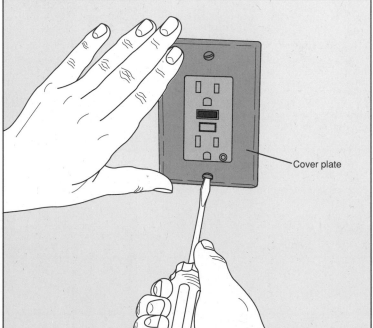

Cover plate

6 **Installing a GFCI outlet.** Buy a receptacle-type GFCI outlet at an electrical supply center. Install a grounding jumper wire in the electrical box *(page 136)*, then connect the outlet. Wrap the hot black wire clockwise around the brass terminal screw marked LINE and tighten the connection using a screwdriver, then connect the white wire of the cable to the corresponding silver terminal screw the same way. For a middle-of-the-run outlet, use the same procedure to connect

the wires of the other cable: the black wire to the brass terminal screw marked LOAD *(above, left)*; the white wire to the corresponding silver terminal screw. Connect the grounding jumper wire to the grounding terminal screw, then carefully fold the wires to position the outlet and screw the mounting strap to the electrical box. Install the cover plate *(above, right)* and restore electricity to the outlet. Test the outlet following the manufacturer's instructions.

SERVICING A DOORBELL

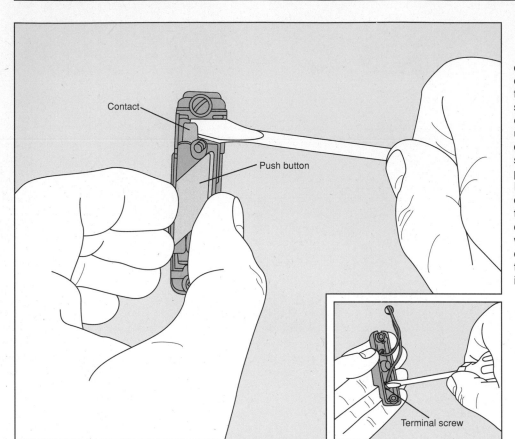

Contact

Push button

Terminal screw

1 **Servicing the push button.** Assess the system to ensure that repairs can be done safely *(page 104)*. Shut off electricity to the doorbell *(page 10)* and take the cover off the push button. Burnish each contact using fine sandpaper and pry it up slightly with an old screwdriver *(left)*. Reinstall the cover and restore electricity to the doorbell; if it sounds constantly, use the same procedure to bend each contact down slightly. If the doorbell does not sound, shut off its electricity and take the cover off the push button, then unscrew it to check the wires. If a section of wire is damaged, cut it out with diagonal-cutting pliers and replace it with wire of the same gauge, connecting the ends with wire caps *(page 137)*. If a wire is loose, wrap it clockwise around its terminal screw and tighten the connection *(inset)*. Reinstall the push button and the cover, then restore electricity to the doorbell; if it does not sound, test the push button *(step 2)*.

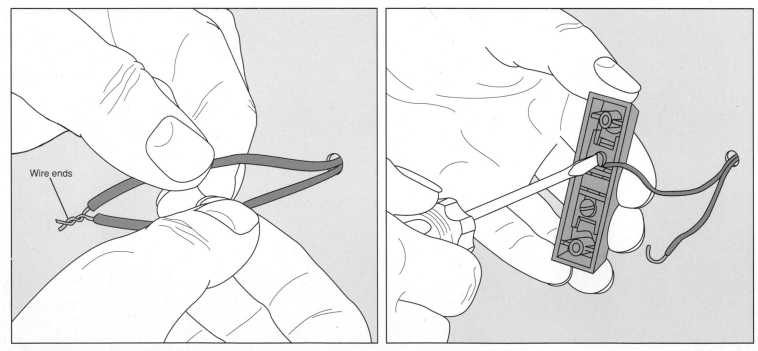

Wire ends

2 **Testing and replacing the push button.** Shut off electricity to the doorbell *(page 10)*, take the cover off the push button to unscrew and disconnect it, then twist the wire ends together *(above, left)* and restore electricity to the doorbell. If the doorbell does not sound, shut off its electricity to reinstall the push button and the cover, then test at the transformer *(step 3)*. If the doorbell sounds constantly, shut off its electricity and replace the push button. Buy a replacement push button at an electrical supply center and connect it, wrapping each wire in turn clockwise around a terminal screw and tightening the connection *(above, right)*. Screw the push button into place and install the cover, then restore electricity to the doorbell.

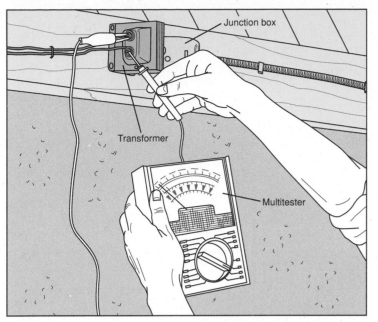

Junction box

Transformer

Multitester

3 **Testing at the transformer.** Locate the transformer at a junction box, usually in the basement or attic. If a wire is loose, wrap it clockwise around its terminal screw and tighten the connection. To test at the transformer, use a multitester. Set the multitester to the ACV scale and 50-volt range, then clip or touch a probe to each terminal screw *(above)*. If the multitester registers no voltage, test at the junction box *(step 4)*; if it registers the 10 to 20 volts stamped on the transformer, test the bell unit *(step 6)*.

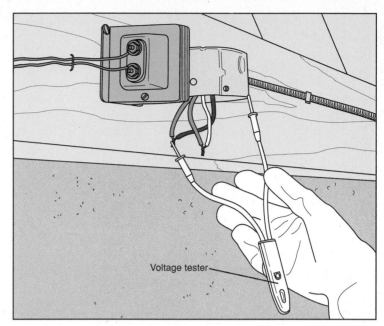

Voltage tester

4 **Testing at the junction box.** Carefully unscrew the cover of the junction box. **Caution:** Test for voltage using a voltage tester before touching a wire end. Wearing a rubber glove, hold the insulated handles with only one hand and remove the wire caps. Touch a probe to each set of twisted wire ends, then touch one probe to the junction box and the other probe in turn to each set of twisted wire ends *(above)*. If the tester glows, electricity to the doorbell is not shut off; shut off the correct circuit and test again.

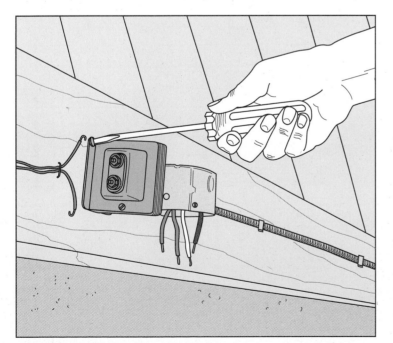

5 **Replacing the transformer.** Service the junction box *(page 105)*, then screw on the cover and restore electricity to the doorbell to test it. If the doorbell does not sound, shut off its electricity *(page 10)* and test at the junction box *(step 4)*, then disconnect the transformer and remove it *(above)*. Buy a replacement transformer at an electrical supply store, install it and connect the wires *(page 137)*, then screw the cover on the junction box and restore electricity to the doorbell to test it. If the doorbell does not sound, shut off its electricity and test the bell unit *(step 6)*.

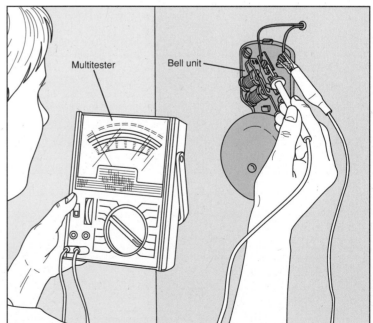

Multitester

Bell unit

6 **Testing and replacing the bell unit.** Remove the cover of the bell unit. If a wire is loose, wrap it clockwise around its terminal screw and tighten the connection. Set a multitester to the ACV scale and 50-volt range, then touch a probe to each terminal screw *(above)*; if no voltage is registered, consult an electrician. If the multitester registers within 2 volts of the 10 to 20 volts stamped on the transformer, disconnect the bell unit and remove it. Buy a replacement bell unit at an electrical supply store, install it and connect the wires *(page 137)*, then restore electricity to the doorbell.

RADIATORS AND FIREPLACES

Radiators of cast iron and the fireplace are typically decorative as well as functional features of an older home; refer to page 115 for illustrations on their common construction. Although seldom beset with a major problem, the heating system and the fireplace require proper, routine maintenance to keep them operating at peak efficiency—and safely. At least once each year, have the boiler of the heating system serviced; have the chimney cleaned. For help in undertaking a minor repair to a radiator or the fireplace or chimney, use the Troubleshooting Guide below.

Most repairs to a radiator or the fireplace or chimney of an older home are easily undertaken with only a few basic tools; the materials and supplies needed are usually readily available at a building supply center. Refer to Tools & Techniques (*page 124*) for instructions on using tools properly and on working safely on the roof; a cut-off saw for replacing the chimney pot can be obtained at a tool rental center. Before starting any repair to a radiator or the fireplace or chimney, familiarize yourself with the information presented in the Emergency Guide (*page 8*).

TROUBLESHOOTING GUIDE

SYMPTOM	POSSIBLE CAUSE	PROCEDURE
WATER RADIATOR		
Radiator cool; too little heat	Thermostat set too low	Reset thermostat
	Air trapped in radiator	Bleed radiator (*p. 117*) □ ○
	Floor sags; radiator slopes away from bleed valve, preventing trapped air from being bled	Slope radiator (*p. 118*) □ ○
Radiator or pipe emits gurgling sound; hammering noise	Air trapped in radiator	Bleed radiator (*p. 117*) □ ○
	Floor sags; radiator slopes away from bleed valve, preventing trapped air from being bled	Slope radiator (*p. 118*) □ ○
Bleed valve leaks	Bleed valve loose	Tighten bleed valve
	Bleed valve faulty	Replace bleed valve (*p. 117*) ◨ ●
Bleed valve stuck	Bleed valve painted shut; lacks lubricant	Scrape paint off bleed valve; apply penetrating oil and wait 1 hour to open
	Bleed valve faulty	Replace bleed valve (*p. 117*) ◨ ●
Inlet valve leaks	Packing nut loose	Tighten packing nut
	Packing worn	Repack inlet valve (*p. 119*) ◨ ◓
	Inlet valve faulty	Replace inlet valve
STEAM RADIATOR		
Radiator cool; too little heat	Thermostat set too low	Reset thermostat
	Floor sags; radiator slopes away from return pipe, preventing condensate from escaping	Slope radiator (*p. 118*) □ ○
	Air vent faulty	Replace air vent (*p. 118*) □ ◓
Radiator or pipe emits gurgling sound; hammering noise	Floor sags; radiator slopes away from return pipe, preventing condensate from escaping	Slope radiator (*p. 118*) □ ○
	Air vent faulty	Replace air vent (*p. 118*) □ ◓
Air vent leaks	Air vent faulty	Replace air vent (*p. 118*) □ ◓
FIREPLACE AND CHIMNEY		
Firebox emits smoke; sparks	Firebox open; chimney draw inadequate	Install fireplace glass doors (*p. 120*) ◨ ◓
Firebrick mortar joint loose, cracked or crumbling	Settlement; prolonged exposure to heat	Repoint firebricks (*p. 120*) □ ◓
Firebrick loose, cracked or crumbling	Settlement; prolonged exposure to heat	Replace firebrick (*p. 121*) ◨ ◓
Chimney pot cracked	Aging; temperature and humidity changes; accidental blow or impact	Replace chimney pot (*p. 122*) ◨ ◓
Chimney crown cracked	Aging; temperature and humidity changes; accidental blow or impact	Repair chimney crown (*p. 123*) ◨ ◓

DEGREE OF DIFFICULTY: □ Easy ◨ Moderate ■ Complex
ESTIMATED TIME: ○ Less than 1 hour ◓ 1 to 3 hours ● Over 3 hours

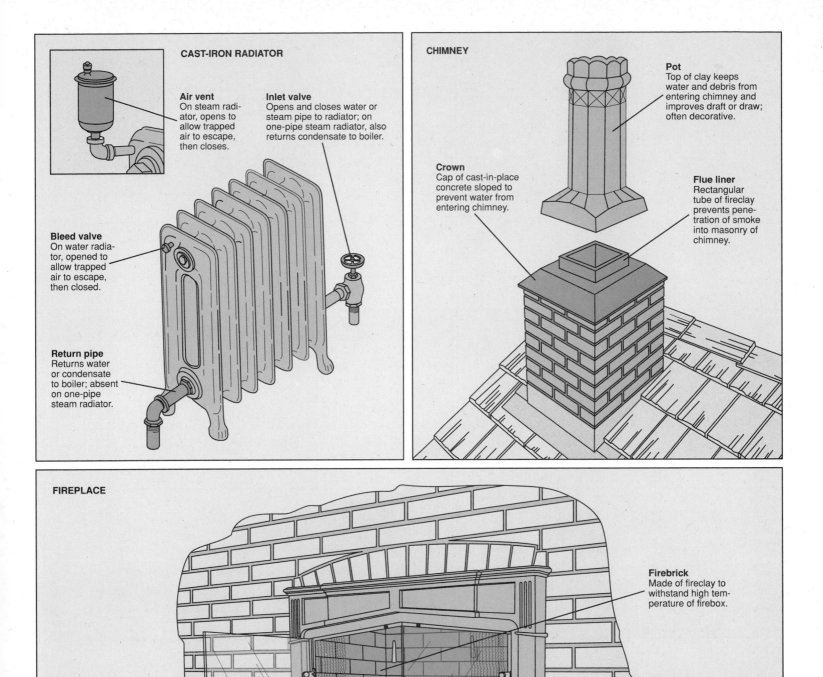

CAST-IRON RADIATOR

Air vent
On steam radiator, opens to allow trapped air to escape, then closes.

Inlet valve
Opens and closes water or steam pipe to radiator; on one-pipe steam radiator, also returns condensate to boiler.

Bleed valve
On water radiator, opened to allow trapped air to escape, then closed.

Return pipe
Returns water or condensate to boiler; absent on one-pipe steam radiator.

CHIMNEY

Pot
Top of clay keeps water and debris from entering chimney and improves draft or draw; often decorative.

Crown
Cap of cast-in-place concrete sloped to prevent water from entering chimney.

Flue liner
Rectangular tube of fireclay prevents penetration of smoke into masonry of chimney.

FIREPLACE

Firebrick
Made of fireclay to withstand high temperature of firebox.

Glass doors
Prevent smoke and sparks from entering living area; stop heat from escaping living area when fireplace not in use.

Mortar joint
Fireplace mortar usually 3/8-inch thick fills joints between firebricks; may be less than 1/8-inch thick.

SHUTTING OFF ELECTRICITY TO THE BOILER

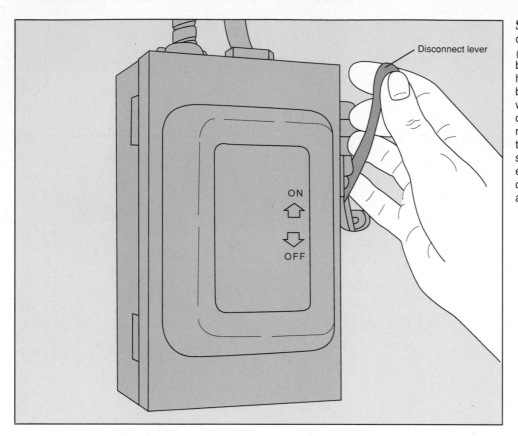

Disconnect lever

ON

OFF

Shutting off the disconnect unit. Shut off electricity to the boiler at the service panel *(page 10)*. Locate the disconnect unit for the boiler, usually found indoors near it; for an older home, there may be no disconnect unit for the boiler. **Caution:** To shut off the disconnect unit, work only in dry conditions; if the area at the disconnect unit is damp, wear rubber boots and rubber gloves. Working only with one hand, shift the lever of the disconnect unit to OFF *(left)*, shutting off electricity to the boiler. To restore electricity to the boiler, shift the lever of the disconnect unit to ON, then restore electricity to it at the service panel.

DRAINING AND REFILLING RADIATORS (WATER SYSTEM)

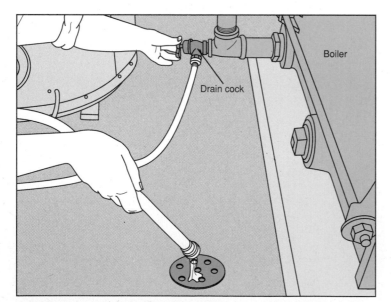

Boiler

Drain cock

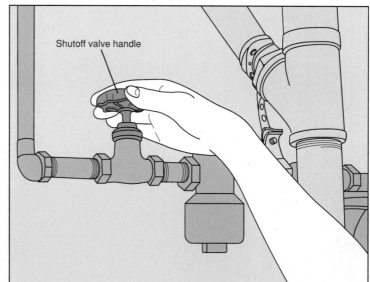

Shutoff valve handle

1 Draining the system. Shut off electricity to the boiler *(step above)* and locate its shutoff valve on the supply pipe, usually just above it. Turn the handle fully clockwise to shut off the water supply, then let the boiler cool for about 1 hour. Run a garden hose from the drain cock to the nearest drain, then open the drain cock *(above)* and the bleed valve of a radiator on the top story *(page 117)*. When the water slows to a trickle, open the bleed valve of each radiator on the first story. When the water stops, close the bleed valves and the drain cock, then remove the garden hose.

2 Refilling the system. To restore the water supply to the boiler, turn the handle of its shutoff valve fully counterclockwise *(above)*—slowly to avoid a pressure surge. Watch the reading of the pressure gauge for the boiler, usually mounted on the top of it. When the pressure of the boiler reaches about 5 pounds per square inch (psi), work upward from the first story to bleed each radiator *(page 117)*. When the pressure of the boiler reaches 15 to 20 psi, turn on its disconnect unit and restore electricity to it at the service panel. When the radiators are warm to the touch, bleed them again.

BLEEDING A RADIATOR (WATER SYSTEM)

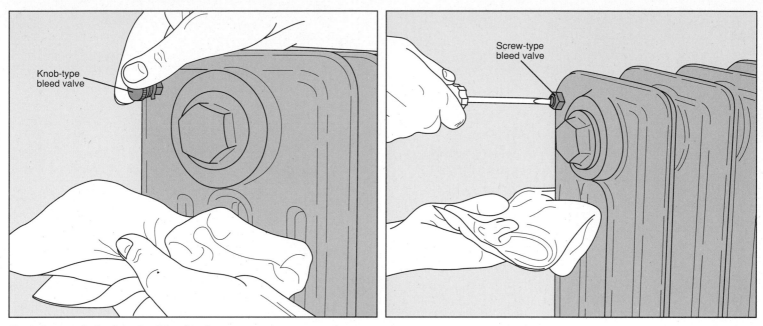

Opening and closing the bleed valve. Turn the thermostat below its normal setting to help cool the radiators, then work upward from the first story to bleed them. To bleed each radiator, hold an absorbent cloth under the bleed valve to catch escaping water and open it by turning it fully counterclockwise: for a knob-type valve, by hand *(above, left)*; for a screw-type valve, with a screwdriver *(above, right)*; for a nut-type valve, using a radiator key or a socket wrench. When water begins to escape from the bleed valve in a steady stream, close it by turning it fully clockwise. After bleeding each radiator, turn the thermostat back to its normal setting.

REPLACING A BLEED VALVE (WATER SYSTEM)

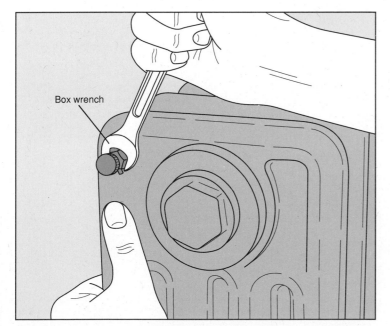

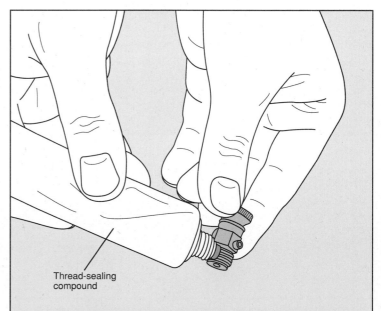

1 Removing the bleed valve. Shut off electricity to the boiler *(page 116)*; if water leaks from the bleed valve, drain the system just enough to stop it *(page 116)*. Loosen the bleed valve using a box *(above)* or adjustable wrench; if it is stuck, apply penetrating oil and wait 1 hour to loosen it. If water begins to leak from the bleed valve, drain the system just enough to stop it. Otherwise, unscrew the bleed valve from its fitting by hand.

2 Installing the replacement bleed valve. Buy a replacement bleed valve at a heating supply center. To prepare the bleed valve, coat the threads with thread-sealing compound *(above)* or wrap them tightly clockwise with 1 1/2 turns of pipe tape. Screw the valve into the fitting on the radiator by hand and tighten it using a box or adjustable wrench. Refill the system and restore electricity to the boiler *(page 116)*.

REPLACING AN AIR VENT (STEAM SYSTEM)

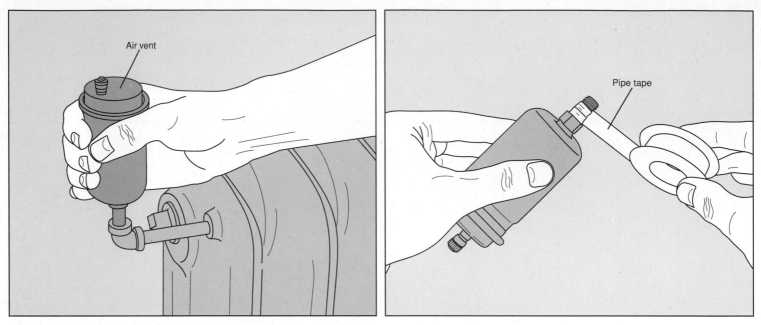

Removing and installing an air vent. Turn the thermostat below its normal setting to help cool the radiator. Loosen the air vent using a box or adjustable wrench; if it is stuck, apply penetrating oil and wait 1 hour to loosen it. Otherwise, unscrew the air vent from its fitting on the radiator by hand *(above, left)*. Buy a replacement air vent at a heating supply center. To prepare the air vent, wrap 1 1/2 turns of pipe tape tightly clockwise around its threads *(above, right)*. Screw the air vent into the fitting on the radiator by hand and tighten it using a box or adjustable wrench. Turn the thermostat back to its normal setting.

SLOPING A RADIATOR

Wood shim

Shimming a radiator. Adjust the slope of a radiator by installing a wood shim no more than 1/2 inch thick under each leg on one side of it. For a water distribution system, raise the radiator on the side with the bleed valve, helping air to rise toward it for releasing; for a steam distribution system, raise the radiator on the side opposite the return pipe, helping condensate to flow toward and drain into it. Work with a helper to lift the side of the radiator only enough to slip a shim under each leg *(left)*; adjust the shims as necessary to ensure that the radiator remains level from front to back.

REPACKING A RADIATOR INLET VALVE

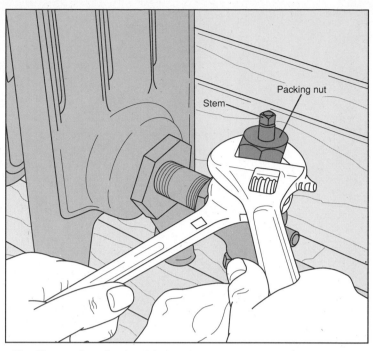

1 **Taking off the handle.** Shut off electricity to the boiler *(page 116)*; if water leaks from the inlet valve, drain the system just enough to stop it *(page 116)*. Wrap old towels around the pipe below the inlet valve, then unscrew the handle *(above)* and pull it off the stem; if the screw or the handle is stuck, apply penetrating oil and wait 1 hour to remove it. If water begins to leak from the inlet valve, drain the system just enough to stop it.

2 **Removing the packing nut.** Loosen the packing nut using a double-wrench technique, turning it counterclockwise with one wrench and steadying the fitting under it with another wrench *(above)*; if it is stuck, apply penetrating oil and wait 1 hour to loosen it. If water begins to leak from the inlet valve, tighten the packing nut and drain the system just enough to stop it *(page 116)*. Otherwise, remove the packing nut from the stem.

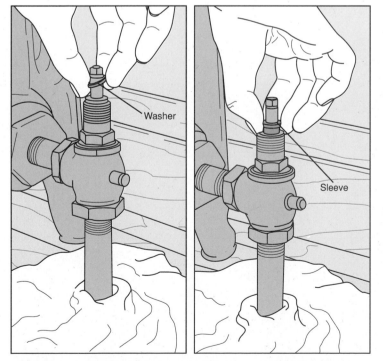

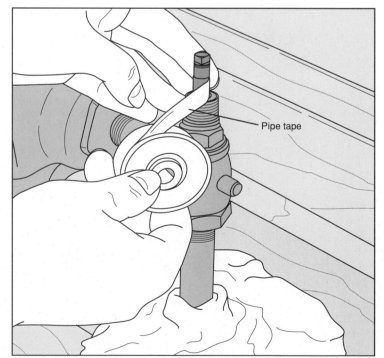

3 **Removing the old stem packing.** To reach the stem packing, pry up the washer using an old screwdriver and slide it off the stem *(above, left)*. If there is a sleeve, pry it up and slide it off the stem the same way *(above, right)*. Check the packing at the base of the stem; if it is deteriorated, use a sharp knife to scrape it out. Scrub encrusted deposits off the stem using fine steel wool.

4 **Replacing the stem packing.** Buy pipe tape or graphite-impregnated packing string at a plumbing supply center and wrap 2 or 3 turns of it tightly clockwise around the base of the stem *(above)*. Put back any sleeve and the washer, then reinstall the packing nut and handle, reversing the procedure used to remove them. Refill the system and restore electricity to the boiler *(page 116)*.

INSTALLING FIREPLACE GLASS DOORS

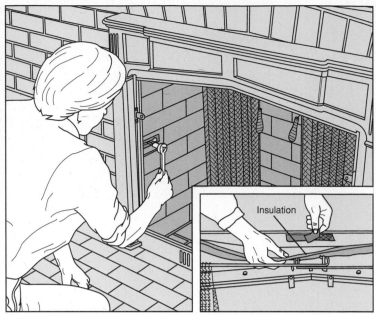

Fitting the fireplace with glass doors. Buy glass doors to fit the opening of the fireplace at a building supply center and install them following the manufacturer's instructions. For the doors shown, remove the glass panels and install a mounting bracket at the top, center and bottom on each side of the frame. Position the frame in the opening of the fireplace and mark the bolt holes on the firebricks *(above, left)*; if necessary, reposition a mounting bracket to center its bolt holes on firebricks rather than the mortar joints. Remove the frame and install any insulation provided for it *(inset)*. Wearing safety goggles, drill a hole for a lead shield at each marked hole on the firebricks using an electric drill fitted with a masonry bit. Tap a lead shield into each hole with a ball-peen hammer, then reposition the frame and drive in the lag bolts using a socket wrench *(above, right)*. Reinstall the glass panels on the doors.

REPOINTING FIREBRICKS

1 Removing the damaged mortar. Wearing work gloves and safety goggles, cut back each damaged joint as far as necessary to reach sound mortar using a cold or plugging chisel and a ball-peen hammer *(above)*; if it is narrower than 1/8 inch, use an old screwdriver or a utility knife. Work carefully to avoid damaging the firebricks. Brush loose mortar pieces out of the joint, then vacuum particles and dust. Buy fireplace mortar at a building supply center; to help bonding of the mortar, dampen each joint with water before filling it.

2 Filling the joints. Wearing work gloves, use a caulking gun to apply a continuous bead of mortar along each joint, working first along any vertical joint, then along any horizontal joint *(above)*. Overfill each joint slightly with mortar, then clean off excess with a damp sponge. Let the mortar set until it is just hard enough to hold a thumbprint—usually about 30 minutes. Then, draw the wet blade of a putty knife along each joint to smooth it. Tape plastic over the joints to help keep the mortar moist until it cures for 3 days.

REPLACING A FIREBRICK

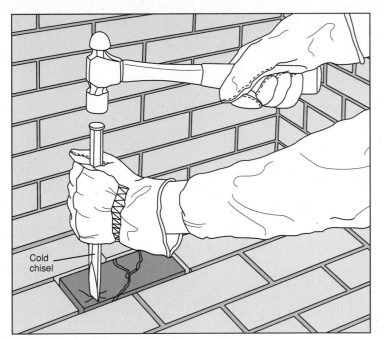

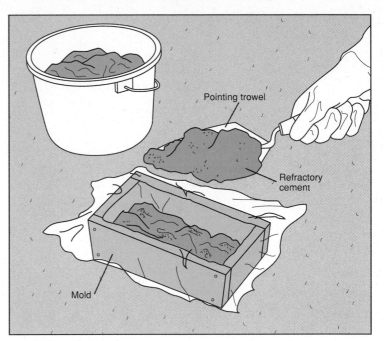

1 **Removing the damaged firebrick.** Wearing work gloves and safety goggles, chip out the mortar and break the firebrick into pieces using a cold chisel and a ball-peen hammer *(above)*; work carefully to avoid damaging adjacent firebricks. Remove the firebrick pieces and chip enough mortar from the cavity to fit in a replacement firebrick, then vacuum mortar particles and dust. Buy a replacement firebrick to fit the cavity at a building supply center or brick distributor and install it *(step 3)*; otherwise, buy refractory cement powder and cast a replacement firebrick *(step 2)*.

2 **Casting a replacement firebrick.** Build a mold out of wood with the same internal dimensions as the cavity, allowing enough space for mortar joints. Line the interior of the mold with plastic and wear work gloves to prepare enough cement to fill it. Pack cement into the mold with a pointing trowel *(above)* until it is half full, then gently agitate it to eliminate air pockets and finish filling it. Scrape off excess cement and smooth it flush with the top of the mold using the trowel, then cover it with plastic until it cures. Pry apart the mold and remove the plastic from the firebrick.

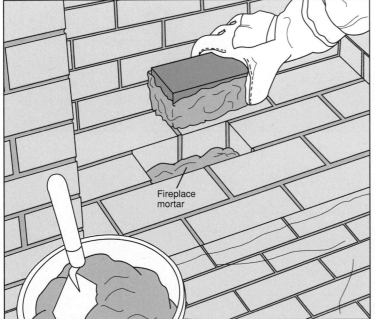

3 **Installing the replacement firebrick.** Buy fireplace mortar at a building supply center; to help bonding of the mortar, dampen the cavity with water. Using a pointing trowel, apply a 3/4-inch layer of mortar on the sides and bottom of the cavity and the firebrick. Fit the firebrick into the cavity *(above, left)*, aligning it with the adjacent firebricks; if necessary, tap it flush with the handle of the trowel. If mortar is not forced out of the joints, they are too thin; remove the firebrick

to add mortar. Draw the trowel along the joints to scrape off excess mortar, then clean mortar off the firebricks with a damp sponge. Let the mortar set until it is just hard enough to hold a thumbprint—usually about 30 minutes. Then, draw the wet blade of a putty knife along each joint to smooth it *(above, right)*. Tape plastic over the joints to help keep the mortar moist until it cures for 3 days.

REPLACING THE CHIMNEY POT

1 **Removing the damaged chimney pot.** Working safely on the roof *(page 128)*, wear work gloves and safety goggles to remove the pot. If the pot is small, chip it off the crown using a cold chisel and a small sledgehammer. Otherwise, rent a cut-off saw fitted with a masonry-cutting blade at a tool rental center and have its use demonstrated. Working in turn along each side of the pot, align the blade with the mortar joint between the pot and the crown *(above)*, then cut through it and the flue liner behind it. Work with a helper to take the pot off the crown, then tie a rope around it and lower it to the ground. Buy a replacement pot to fit the flue at a building supply center.

2 **Preparing the crown.** Brush mortar particles and dust off the crown. Buy premixed mortar at a building supply center and follow the manufacturer's instructions to prepare it; to help bonding of the mortar, dampen the crown with water. Wearing work gloves, use a pointing trowel to apply a 1 1/2-inch layer of mortar evenly along the top of the crown *(above)*.

3 **Installing the replacement chimney pot.** If required by local building code, fit the pot with a spark arrester—wire mesh fastened to the interior with fireplace mortar. Wearing work gloves, work with a helper to set the pot into the mortar on the crown *(left)*. Use a pointing trowel to scrape off excess mortar along each joint, then clean mortar off the crown with a damp sponge. Let the mortar set until it is just hard enough to hold a thumbprint—usually about 30 minutes. Then, strike each joint using a wet convex jointer, applying firm, steady pressure to draw along it *(inset)*. Tape plastic over the joints to help keep the mortar moist until it cures for 3 days. To create a watertight seal, use a caulking gun to apply a continuous bead of exterior-grade caulk along each joint.

REPAIRING THE CHIMNEY CROWN

1 **Preparing the damaged surface.** Work safely on the roof *(page 128)* to repair the crown; if it is crumbling or extensively damaged, consult a professional about replacing it. Otherwise, wear work gloves and safety goggles to cut back the edges of the damaged section as far as necessary to reach a solid surface. Use a cold chisel and a ball-peen hammer to work along a crack and undercut its edges, widening it to about 1/4 inch and deepening it to about 1/2 inch *(above, left)*. Brush off loose particles and dust using a whisk broom *(above, right)* or an old paintbrush.

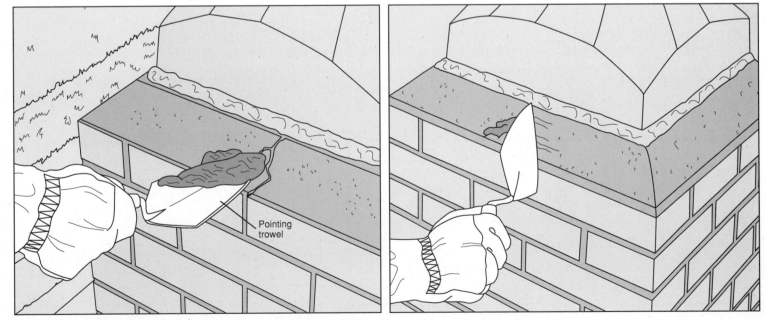

2 **Patching the damaged surface.** Wearing work gloves, prepare a mortar mix of 1 part portland cement, 1 part lime and 6 parts sand; to help bonding of the mortar, dampen the damaged surface with water. Use a pointing trowel to work mortar into the damaged surface, overfilling it slightly *(above, left)*. Scrape off excess mortar with the trowel *(above, right)* and clean off stray mortar using a damp sponge. Let the mortar set until it is just hard enough to hold a thumbprint—usually about 30 minutes. Then, smooth the patch flush with the surrounding surface using the trowel. Tape plastic over the patch to help keep the mortar moist until it cures for 3 days.

TOOLS & TECHNIQUES

This section introduces the tools and techniques that are basic to repairing an older house—from using handsaws *(page 133)* and an electric drill *(page 134)* to working safely from a ladder *(page 127)*, on the roof *(page 128)* or with electricity *(page 136)*. Charts on fasteners *(page 135)*, patching products *(page 138)* and finishes *(page 140)* are presented for easy reference. Also included is information on finding replacement materials in keeping with the character of an older house *(page 127)*.

Most repairs to an older house can be handled with the basic kit of tools and equipment shown below. Special tools that may be needed can be obtained at a tool rental center—a safety harness, rope grab and lanyard, a drum sander, floor edger and commercial floor polisher, a slate ripper or a cut-off saw, for example *(page 126)*. For the best repair results, always use the right tool for the job—and use it correctly. When shopping around for tools, buy or rent the highest-quality ones you can afford.

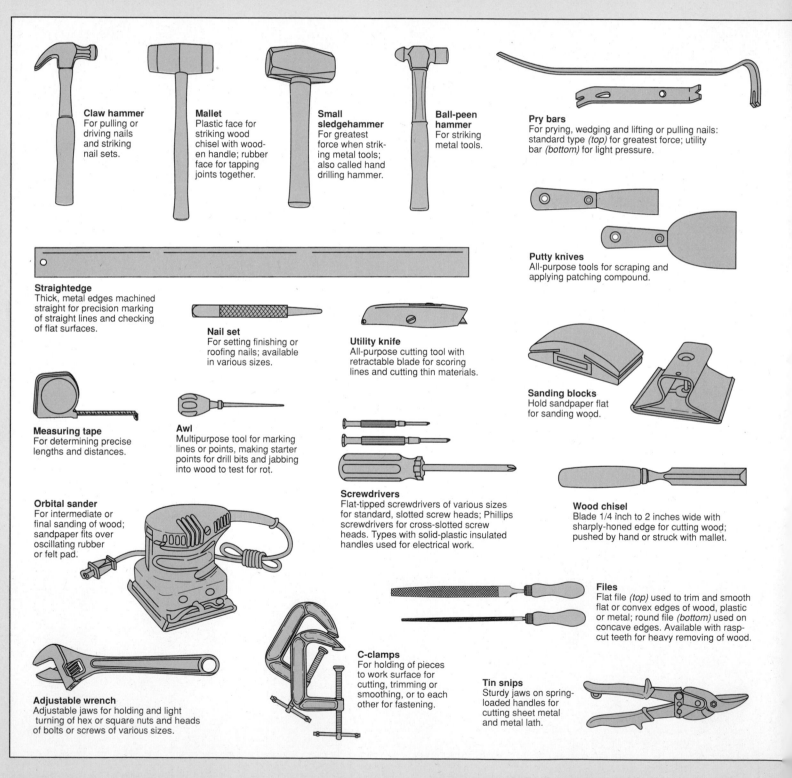

Claw hammer
For pulling or driving nails and striking nail sets.

Mallet
Plastic face for striking wood chisel with wooden handle; rubber face for tapping joints together.

Small sledgehammer
For greatest force when striking metal tools; also called hand drilling hammer.

Ball-peen hammer
For striking metal tools.

Pry bars
For prying, wedging and lifting or pulling nails: standard type *(top)* for greatest force; utility bar *(bottom)* for light pressure.

Putty knives
All-purpose tools for scraping and applying patching compound.

Straightedge
Thick, metal edges machined straight for precision marking of straight lines and checking of flat surfaces.

Nail set
For setting finishing or roofing nails; available in various sizes.

Utility knife
All-purpose cutting tool with retractable blade for scoring lines and cutting thin materials.

Sanding blocks
Hold sandpaper flat for sanding wood.

Measuring tape
For determining precise lengths and distances.

Awl
Multipurpose tool for marking lines or points, making starter points for drill bits and jabbing into wood to test for rot.

Screwdrivers
Flat-tipped screwdrivers of various sizes for standard, slotted screw heads; Phillips screwdrivers for cross-slotted screw heads. Types with solid-plastic insulated handles used for electrical work.

Wood chisel
Blade 1/4 inch to 2 inches wide with sharply-honed edge for cutting wood; pushed by hand or struck with mallet.

Orbital sander
For intermediate or final sanding of wood; sandpaper fits over oscillating rubber or felt pad.

Files
Flat file *(top)* used to trim and smooth flat or convex edges of wood, plastic or metal; round file *(bottom)* used on concave edges. Available with rasp-cut teeth for heavy removing of wood.

Adjustable wrench
Adjustable jaws for holding and light turning of hex or square nuts and heads of bolts or screws of various sizes.

C-clamps
For holding of pieces to work surface for cutting, trimming or smoothing, or to each other for fastening.

Tin snips
Sturdy jaws on spring-loaded handles for cutting sheet metal and metal lath.

Take the time to care for and store your tools properly. To avoid damaging a cutting tool, for example, check for hidden fasteners before starting to cut. When a blade becomes dull, replace it or have it sharpened by a professional. Keep a tool out of the way when it is not in use; set a handsaw or plane down carefully on its side. Check a tool thoroughly before each use of it; tighten a loose handle or screw and replace a damaged part. Service a power tool according to the manufacturer's instructions.

Always wear the appropriate protective clothing and recommended safety gear for a repair. The paint stripper, patching compound, adhesive, finish or other product needed for a job may contain chemicals that can release toxic or flammable vapors into the air; follow the safety precautions printed on the label. Before starting a repair, familiarize yourself with the information presented in the Emergency Guide (page 8); while working, keep children and pets away from the job site.

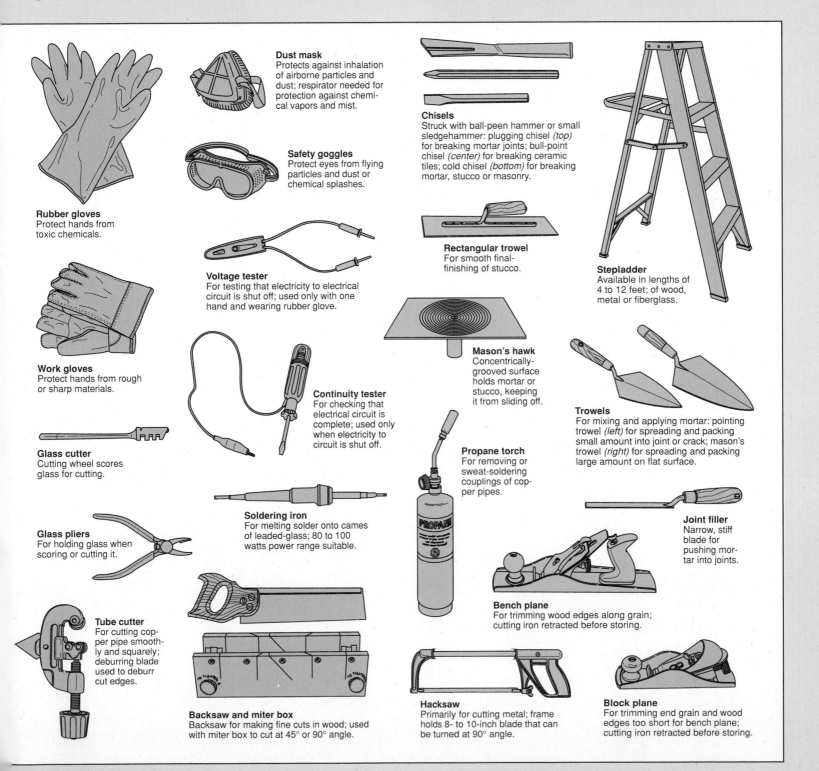

Rubber gloves
Protect hands from toxic chemicals.

Work gloves
Protect hands from rough or sharp materials.

Glass cutter
Cutting wheel scores glass for cutting.

Glass pliers
For holding glass when scoring or cutting it.

Tube cutter
For cutting copper pipe smoothly and squarely; deburring blade used to deburr cut edges.

Dust mask
Protects against inhalation of airborne particles and dust; respirator needed for protection against chemical vapors and mist.

Safety goggles
Protect eyes from flying particles and dust or chemical splashes.

Voltage tester
For testing that electricity to electrical circuit is shut off; used only with one hand and wearing rubber glove.

Continuity tester
For checking that electrical circuit is complete; used only when electricity to circuit is shut off.

Soldering iron
For melting solder onto cames of leaded-glass; 80 to 100 watts power range suitable.

Backsaw and miter box
Backsaw for making fine cuts in wood; used with miter box to cut at 45° or 90° angle.

Chisels
Struck with ball-peen hammer or small sledgehammer: plugging chisel (top) for breaking mortar joints; bull-point chisel (center) for breaking ceramic tiles; cold chisel (bottom) for breaking mortar, stucco or masonry.

Rectangular trowel
For smooth final-finishing of stucco.

Mason's hawk
Concentrically-grooved surface holds mortar or stucco, keeping it from sliding off.

Propane torch
For removing or sweat-soldering couplings of copper pipes.

Hacksaw
Primarily for cutting metal; frame holds 8- to 10-inch blade that can be turned at 90° angle.

Stepladder
Available in lengths of 4 to 12 feet; of wood, metal or fiberglass.

Trowels
For mixing and applying mortar: pointing trowel (left) for spreading and packing small amount into joint or crack; mason's trowel (right) for spreading and packing large amount on flat surface.

Joint filler
Narrow, stiff blade for pushing mortar into joints.

Bench plane
For trimming wood edges along grain; cutting iron retracted before storing.

Block plane
For trimming end grain and wood edges too short for bench plane; cutting iron retracted before storing.

WORKING WITH RENTAL TOOLS

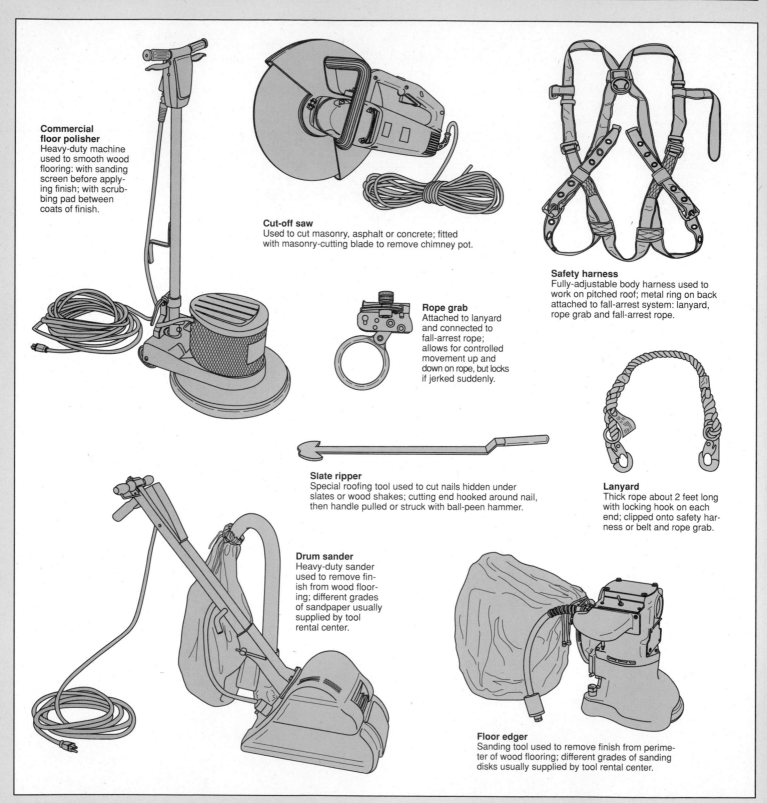

Commercial floor polisher
Heavy-duty machine used to smooth wood flooring: with sanding screen before applying finish; with scrubbing pad between coats of finish.

Cut-off saw
Used to cut masonry, asphalt or concrete; fitted with masonry-cutting blade to remove chimney pot.

Safety harness
Fully-adjustable body harness used to work on pitched roof; metal ring on back attached to fall-arrest system: lanyard, rope grab and fall-arrest rope.

Rope grab
Attached to lanyard and connected to fall-arrest rope; allows for controlled movement up and down on rope, but locks if jerked suddenly.

Lanyard
Thick rope about 2 feet long with locking hook on each end; clipped onto safety harness or belt and rope grab.

Slate ripper
Special roofing tool used to cut nails hidden under slates or wood shakes; cutting end hooked around nail, then handle pulled or struck with ball-peen hammer.

Drum sander
Heavy-duty sander used to remove finish from wood flooring; different grades of sandpaper usually supplied by tool rental center.

Floor edger
Sanding tool used to remove finish from perimeter of wood flooring; different grades of sanding disks usually supplied by tool rental center.

Renting special tools. Shop around to a number of tool rental centers when looking for tools—prices and terms often vary. Tools usually can be rented at different rates by the hour or by the day. To refinish the wood flooring of an average-sized room, for example, rent a drum sander, floor edger and floor polisher for at least one day; inquire about the full range of accessories, attachments and supplies needed for each tool. Ask about the policy for returning unused supplies; many tool rental centers accept their return and apply a credit to the final bill.

Review the manufacturer's instructions for using each tool; ask for a demonstration before taking it home, if possible. In most cases, insurance coverage is included in the rental price of a tool, but sometimes it is not; ask about liability in the event of damage to a tool. A tool rental center may include delivery and pick-up charges in the rental price of a tool; others may deliver and pick up a tool for an additional fee. Always inquire about the conditions for returning a tool; there may be an extra charge if it is returned uncleaned.

MAINTAINING THE CHARACTER OF AN OLDER HOUSE

Finding replacement materials. Repairs to an older house can call for resourcefulness and ingenuity in hunting down replacement materials. Finding fasteners, patching compounds and other materials that are out-of-sight once installed is rarely a problem; modern types can usually be used without affecting the character of an older house and are readily available at a building supply center. But finding a piece of wood for the interior trim or the flooring, a part for a light or plumbing fixture, or other material for an original feature is often an arduous task; without a proper matching of materials, the character of an older house can be spoiled. For help in finding replacement materials in keeping with the character of an older house, refer to the list of resources below:

• **Architectural salvage and residential demolition yards.** Companies that specialize in architectural salvage or residential demolition usually can be relied on for a wide range of different materials—from doors, windows, and siding to hardware, wood trim, and electrical and plumbing fixtures. Most of these companies update their stock on a regular, ongoing basis, obtaining additional materials from houses undergoing demolition or renovation.

• **Antique stores.** Dealers of antiques often can be helpful in finding materials to repair an original electrical or plumbing fixture or in locating a suitable replacement; they may offer to look for you and keep you informed of their progress.

• **Lumber yards.** Wood siding, trim and flooring usually can be custom-milled at a reasonable cost at a lumber yard. Take a piece of the original wood with you; for an exact match, a replacement piece may need to be specially stained or otherwise treated.

• **Publications.** A public library typically subscribes to journals and magazines on subjects related to older house restoration—many of which offer catalogs of their inventories, selling materials on a mail-order basis. Refer to the yellow pages of your local telephone directory for the names of restoration companies and building preservation organizations in your local area that may be able to provide or help locate needed materials.

• **Your own older house.** One of the best sources of replacement materials usually is the older house itself. Often, the simple taking of a replacement material from an inconspicuous spot is the solution—the taking of wood trim or flooring from a closet, for example. Sometimes, imaginative replacement and relocating of materials is the answer—the replacing of a working light fixture of one room and the relocation of it in another room, for instance. Whenever an original feature cannot be matched and must be replaced, keep it for use as a possible replacement material elsewhere.

WORKING SAFELY FROM A LADDER

Spreader brace

Siderail

Using a stepladder. To work up to 10 feet off the ground, use a stepladder at least 2 feet longer than the height at which you need to stand. Do not use the stepladder if a foot, step or spreader brace is damaged. Set up the stepladder on a firm, level surface, opening its legs fully and locking its spreader braces. Indoors, set up away from stairs and overhead obstructions *(above, left)*; if the feet slip, place a non-slip mat under them. Outdoors, if the ground is soft or uneven, place boards under the feet *(above, right)*; dig up the soil to level them, if necessary. Climb the stepladder using both hands to grasp the steps—not the siderails. Lean into the stepladder to work from it, keeping your hips between the siderails; do not stand higher than the third step from the top. Never overreach or straddle the space between the stepladder and another surface; instead, climb down and move the stepladder.

WORKING SAFELY FROM A LADDER (continued)

Setting up an extension ladder. To work more than 10 feet off the ground, use an extension ladder that can extend 3 feet above the height at which you need to stand. Do not use the ladder if a shoe, rung or rung lock is damaged. Set the ladder unextended on the ground perpendicular to the wall, its fly section on the bottom and its feet out from the wall 1/4 of the height to which it is to be raised. With a helper bracing the bottom of the ladder, raise the top of it and walk along under it, using your hands to push it upright. Bracing the ladder with your foot, pull the rope to release and raise the fly section *(left)*, then lock it; if the ground is soft or uneven, place a board under the feet. Drive a stake into the ground between the ladder and the wall, then tie each rail to it. Climb the ladder using both hands to grasp the rungs, keeping your hips between the rails. To work on or at the edge of the roof, use a 2-by-4 to keep the gutter from crushing, then install an eye screw in the fascia and tie each rail to it *(inset)*.

WORKING SAFELY ON THE ROOF

Getting onto the roof. Consult a professional for work on a roof of slates or tiles or with a pitch greater than 6 in 12—a slope of 6 inches vertically every 12 inches horizontally. For work on a roof with a pitch of 4 to 6 in 12, rent a safety harness or belt at a tool rental center and have its use demonstrated. Set up an extension ladder *(step above)* on the side of the house opposite the work area; if using a safety harness or belt, tie the fall-arrest rope to it and a sturdy, fixed object on the same side of the house. Climb the ladder until your feet are on the rung just below the edge of the roof; if using a safety harness or belt, tie the fall-arrest rope to the left rail. Holding the top of the rails with your hands, step onto the roof with your right foot *(above, left)*. Grasp the right rail with your left hand, then remove your right hand from it and step onto the roof with your left foot *(above, right)*. When both feet are on the roof, let go of the ladder; if using a safety harness or belt, tie the fall-arrest rope back to it.

WORKING SAFELY ON THE ROOF (continued)

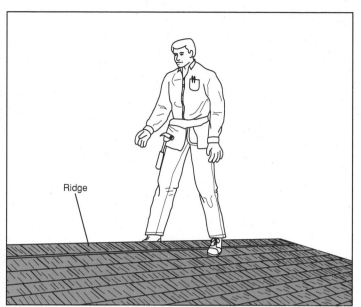

Working on the roof. To raise tools and supplies to the roof, have a helper place them in a bucket and tie one end of a rope to the handle. Have your helper tie the other end of the rope to his belt loop and climb the ladder to pass it to you. Sitting on the roof with your feet planted firmly, pull the rope *(above, left)* to raise the bucket. When the bucket reaches the edge of the roof, carefully pull it over the gutter or overhang and onto the roof. If a tool or supply does not fit into the bucket, have your helper tie the rope around it, then raise it to the roof the same way. To reach your work area, walk straight up the slope of the roof to the ridge, keeping your knees bent slightly. Walk along the ridge straddling it *(above, right)*, then walk straight down the slope of the roof to the work area. Reverse the procedure to walk back to the ladder and to lower tools and supplies to the ground.

Getting off the roof. If using a safety harness or belt, untie the fall-arrest rope and drop it to the ground. Standing to the left of the ladder and facing it, grasp the top of the rail closest to you with your right hand *(above, left)*. Then, swing your left foot onto the center of the rung just below the edge of the roof and grasp the top of the other rail with your left hand *(above, center)*, pivoting on your right foot. Swing your right foot onto the center of the rung below your left foot, still grasping the rails *(above, right)*. Step down one rung with your left foot and spread your legs slightly, keeping your feet against the rails. Have a helper on the ground brace the bottom of the ladder, then remove the rope and eye screw used to stabilize the top of it and the wood block used to protect the gutter. Climb down the ladder one rung at a time.

REPLICATING TEXTURED SURFACES

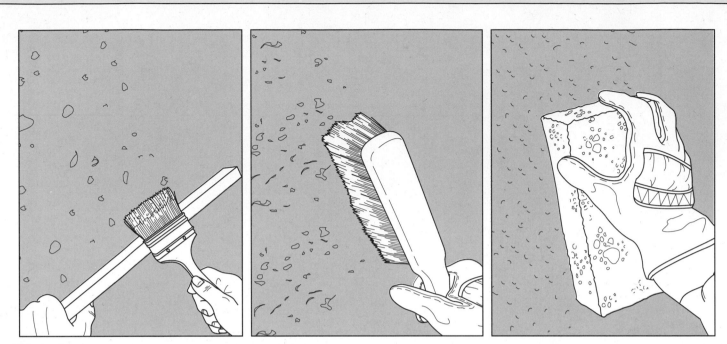

Texturing stucco. Practice replicating the texture on plywood or thick cardboard, then texture the patch when you are satisfied with your technique. For a dash or spatter texture, prepare a batch of stucco for a finish coat *(page 21)* and dilute it slightly by adding extra water. Load a large paintbrush with stucco and strike the handle against a board, spattering stucco onto the surface *(above, left)*.

For a stipple texture, let the patch begin to set, then gently press the tips of a stiff-bristled fiber brush against the surface *(above, center)* without sweeping or overlapping passes. Wipe off stucco that accumulates on the tips using a damp cloth. For a sponge texture, let the patch begin to set, then press a damp sponge against the surface *(above, right)* without sweeping or overlapping passes.

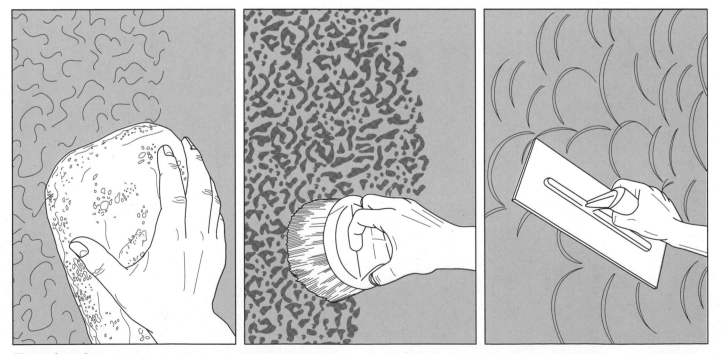

Texturing plaster. Practice replicating the texture on plywood or thick cardboard, then texture the patch when you are satisfied with your technique. For an orange-peel type of texture, let the patch begin to set, then lightly press a dry sponge against the surface *(above, left)* without sweeping or overlapping passes. For a stipple texture, let the patch begin to set, then gently press the tips of a stippling brush *(above, center)*, whisk broom or wire brush against the surface without sweeping or overlapping passes. For a ridged-adobe texture, let the patch begin to set, then sweep a trowel in semicircular passes across the surface *(above, right)*; when the patch sets, use fine sandpaper on a sanding block to soften sharp peaks or ridges, if necessary.

PREPARING STUCCO

Mixing stucco ingredients. Choose a stucco recipe *(page 21)* and buy the dry ingredients at a building supply center; use sand of a color, size and texture that matches the test sample. Wear work gloves to measure each dry ingredient by volume in a graduated container, then mix the stucco in a mortar box, filling it no more than 3/4 full. Pour in the sand *(above, left)* and portland cement, mix them with a mason's hoe, then pour in and mix the lime. Form a well in the center of the ingredients and add clean water (prefer-

ably with low mineral content to prevent efflorescing) a little at a time, mixing thoroughly *(above, right)*. Test the consistency of the mix when it begins to thicken, using a pointing trowel to place a small mound of it on a mason's hawk and slice it in half *(inset)*; it should hold its shape and separate firmly without collapsing or crumbling. If the mound collapses, add dry ingredients in the correct proportions. If the mound crumbles or is too stiff to flow slightly, add water a little at a time.

MATCHING MORTAR COLOR

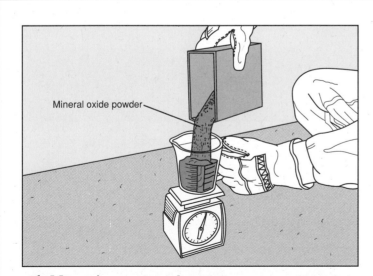

1 Measuring mortar colorant. Buy a mortar colorant such as mineral oxide powder at a building supply center. Wearing work gloves, weigh the dry ingredients for a small test batch of mortar on a kitchen scale in a preweighed container. Weigh *(above)* and add mortar colorant to the dry ingredients following the manufacturer's instructions, using no more than 10% of the weight of the dry ingredients. Record the weight of the proportion of mortar colorant used.

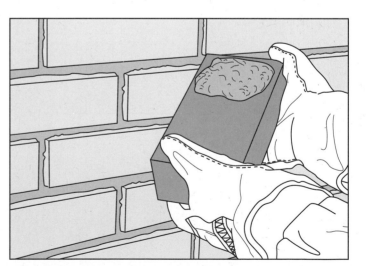

2 Comparing mortar colors. Mix the test batch of mortar until its color is even and without streaks, then apply it to a brick using a pointing trowel. Allow the test batch of mortar to cure for 3 days and compare it with existing mortar *(above)*. If the colors of the mortar match, mix mortar for the repair using the proportion of mortar colorant recorded *(step 1)*. Otherwise, make another test batch of mortar: with less mortar colorant for a lighter color; with more mortar colorant for a darker color.

USING A PLANE

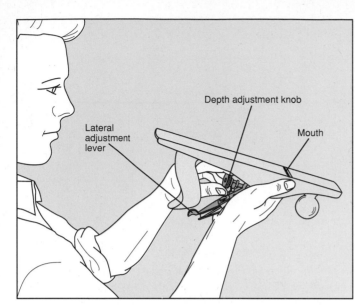

1 Adjusting the cutting iron. To trim an edge of wood using a plane, adjust the cutting iron. For the bench plane shown, turn the depth adjustment knob *(above)* until the cutting edge of the cutting iron projects slightly from the mouth; it should be just barely visible. Move the lateral adjustment lever until the cutting edge of the cutting iron is aligned squarely with the mouth. Test the plane on a scrap board and readjust the cutting iron, if necessary.

2 Trimming an edge. To trim an edge of wood, position the toe of the plane flat on it—without the cutting iron touching it. Pressing down firmly with the hand in front to keep the plane flat, use the hand in back to push it smoothly forward. Apply only forward pressure on the handle of the plane to start, then apply equal downward pressure with both hands to keep the plane flat. Move with the plane along the edge *(above)* rather than trying to overextend your reach.

USING A FILE

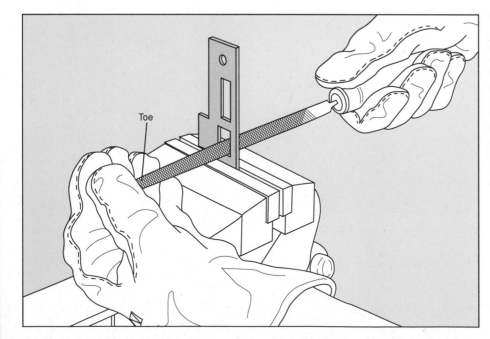

Trimming an edge. Trim an edge of metal or wood using a file: a flat type for a flat or convex edge; a half-round type for a flat, convex or concave edge; or, a round type for a tight concave edge. To trim a curved edge, use a half-round or round file that matches its shape as closely as possible. To trim a flat edge of metal, position the toe of a flat file level on it and push straight across it *(left)*, applying enough pressure to cut. At the end of the stroke, lift the file off the edge smoothly and without stopping. Continue filing the same way, overlapping each stroke slightly.

USING A HANDSAW

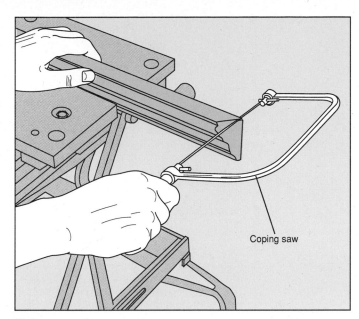

Using a coping saw. For fine curved cuts in wood, use a coping saw with a suitable blade. To cut a coped end in a piece of wood trim, as shown, align the blade with the waste side of the cutting line. Start the cut with short, smooth push and pull strokes. Gradually lengthen the strokes to continue the cut, pushing away firmly and pulling back lightly *(above)*. Angle the frame of the saw to follow the cutting line; do not twist the blade.

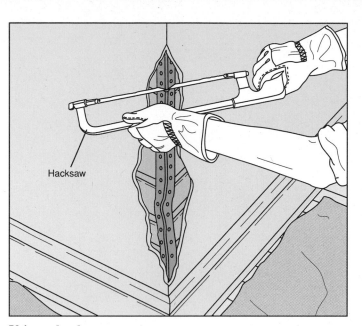

Using a hacksaw. For standard cuts in metal, use a hacksaw with a suitable blade; wear work gloves and safety goggles. To cut through a section of corner bead, as shown, align the blade on it and notch it by making several short push strokes across it, lifting the blade on the pull strokes. Continue the cut with short, smooth push and pull strokes, then gradually lengthen them *(above)*, pushing away firmly and pulling back lightly.

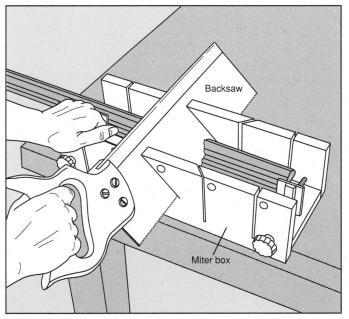

Using a backsaw and miter box. For fine straight cuts in wood, use a backsaw; with a miter box, as shown, for a 45° or 90° angle. Set the piece in the miter box and align the waste side of the cutting line with the appropriate slots, then clamp it and fit the backsaw into the slots. Notch the piece by making several short push strokes across it, lifting the blade on the pull strokes. Continue the cut with smooth push and pull strokes *(above)*, pushing away firmly and pulling back lightly.

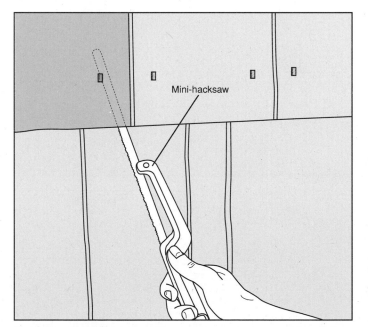

Using a mini-hacksaw. Work with a mini-hacksaw fitted with a suitable blade to make cuts in metal that are impractical to perform with a hacksaw—the piece is small or access to it is obstructed, for example. To cut off a nail from behind a wood shingle, as shown, grip the handle of the saw firmly and butt the blade against the shank of the nail. Make the cut with short, smooth strokes *(above)*; if necessary, apply pressure to bend the blade slightly.

WORKING WITH AN ELECTRIC DRILL

Using a drill. An electric drill is sized by the largest diameter bit its chuck can hold; for most drilling purposes, use a 3/8-inch variable-speed drill. Always use the drill with the proper bit or attachment for the material: a twist bit or spade bit for wood; a carbide-tipped masonry bit for masonry or ceramic tile. The type and size of bit to use depends on the hole you are making *(step below, right)*. To install a bit, use the chuck key of the drill to open the chuck jaws enough to insert its shank. Tighten the chuck jaws securely around the bit with the chuck key, fitting it in turn into each chuck hole and turning it clockwise. If necessary, mark the bit to a specified drilling depth *(step below, left)*. Wearing safety goggles, grip the drill firmly with both hands to position the bit. To bore into wood, apply light pressure to depress the trigger switch *(left)*, then gradually increase pressure. Withdraw the bit from the hole before releasing the trigger switch.

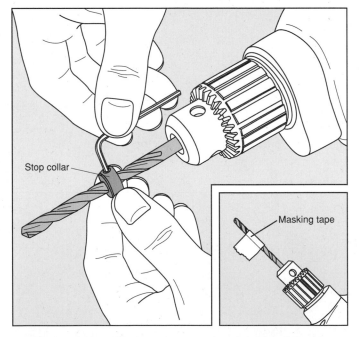

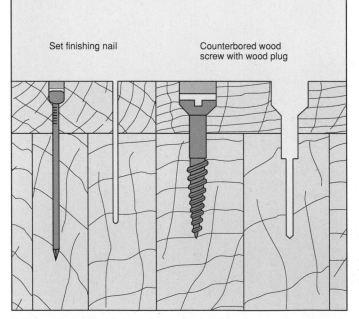

Drilling to a specified depth. Measure the drilling depth from the tip of the bit. To mark the drilling depth on the bit, slide a stop collar into position on the bit and tighten it using its hex wrench *(above)*. Or, wrap a strip of masking tape around the bit to create a short flag *(inset)* that can be seen when the drill is running. When drilling, withdraw the bit when the stop collar or masking tape just touches the surface.

Boring holes for fasteners. To bore a pilot hole for a nail, use a twist bit slightly smaller than the shank and bore to a depth equal to 2/3 its length *(above, left)*; shown is a set finishing nail. To counterbore a hole for a wood screw and a wood plug, use a combination bit equal to 2/3 the diameter of the screw shank and bore to a depth equal to the length of the screw shank and thickness of the plug *(above, right)*.

WORKING WITH FASTENERS

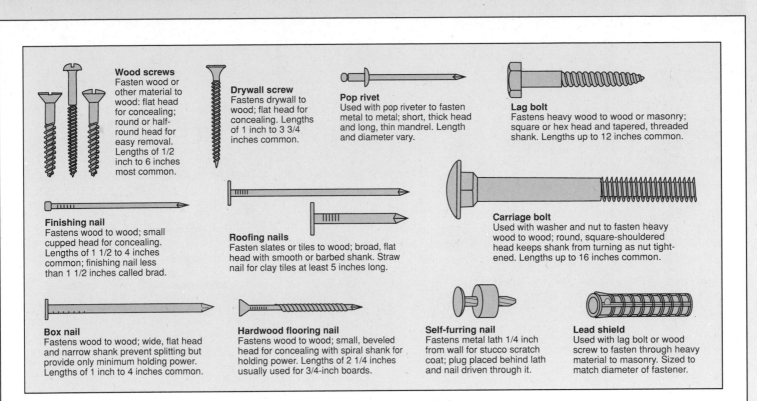

Wood screws
Fasten wood or other material to wood: flat head for concealing; round or half-round head for easy removal. Lengths of 1/2 inch to 6 inches most common.

Drywall screw
Fastens drywall to wood; flat head for concealing. Lengths of 1 inch to 3 3/4 inches common.

Pop rivet
Used with pop riveter to fasten metal to metal; short, thick head and long, thin mandrel. Length and diameter vary.

Lag bolt
Fastens heavy wood to wood or masonry; square or hex head and tapered, threaded shank. Lengths up to 12 inches common.

Finishing nail
Fastens wood to wood; small cupped head for concealing. Lengths of 1 1/2 to 4 inches common; finishing nail less than 1 1/2 inches called brad.

Roofing nails
Fasten slates or tiles to wood; broad, flat head with smooth or barbed shank. Straw nail for clay tiles at least 5 inches long.

Carriage bolt
Used with washer and nut to fasten heavy wood to wood; round, square-shouldered head keeps shank from turning as nut tightened. Lengths up to 16 inches common.

Box nail
Fastens wood to wood; wide, flat head and narrow shank prevent splitting but provide only minimum holding power. Lengths of 1 inch to 4 inches common.

Hardwood flooring nail
Fastens wood to wood; small, beveled head for concealing with spiral shank for holding power. Lengths of 2 1/4 inches usually used for 3/4-inch boards.

Self-furring nail
Fastens metal lath 1/4 inch from wall for stucco scratch coat; plug placed behind lath and nail driven through it.

Lead shield
Used with lag bolt or wood screw to fasten through heavy material to masonry. Sized to match diameter of fastener.

Choosing a fastener. Building supply centers stock fasteners of many types and sizes; the nails, screws and bolts typically used for repairs to an older house are shown above. Buy a fastener compatible with the material and dimensions of the pieces being joined. As a rule of thumb, use a nail or screw three times as long as the thickness of the piece being fastened; use a carriage bolt at least 3/4 inch longer than the combined thickness of the pieces being fastened.

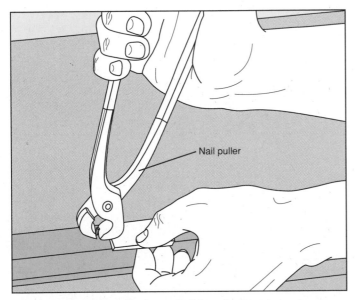

Nail puller

Removing nails with concealed heads. Wearing safety goggles, pull nails with concealed heads out of the back of the piece using a pliers-type nail puller. Grip as far along the shank of the nail as possible with the jaws, squeezing the handles enough to bite into it without severing it. Holding the base of the handle firmly, pull back on it to remove the nail *(above)*; for better leverage, set a wood shim under the jaws.

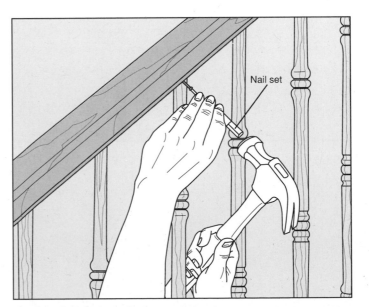

Nail set

Setting finishing nails. Drive finishing nails into pilot holes with a hammer until they are almost flush with the surface. To set the heads of the finishing nails, use a nail set with a tip slightly smaller than them. Place the tip of the nail set on the center of the nail head and tap sharply on the top of it with the hammer *(above)*, driving the head about 1/8 inch below the surface. Cover the nail head using a wax stick.

WORKING SAFELY WITH ELECTRICITY

Working with your electrical system. Carefully follow all standard safety procedures when undertaking a repair that involves working with the electrical system—replacing a switch, light fixture or outlet, for example. While repairs to an element of the electrical system are not complicated or dangerous if you work logically and observe safety precautions, accidents can happen if your work is rushed, improper tools are used or shortcuts are taken. Refer to the guidelines below to undertake repairs:

• Assess the electrical system to ensure that work can be done safely *(page 104)*. If proper grounding of the electrical system cannot be confirmed, consult an electrician; otherwise, shut off the entire electrical system *(page 10)* to undertake a repair.

• Never work on the electrical system in damp or wet conditions.

• Always shut off electricity *(page 10)* to the circuit controlling the switch, light fixture, outlet or other unit being repaired—before starting the job. Leave a note on the service panel warning others not to restore the electricity.

• Use a voltage tester to confirm that electricity to the circuit controlling the switch, light fixture, outlet or other unit being repaired is shut off—before touching a terminal screw or wire end.

• If the circuit controlling the switch, light fixture, outlet or other unit being repaired cannot be located or electricity to it cannot be shut off, shut off the entire electrical system *(page 10)* before starting the job.

• Take the time to set up properly for work on the electrical system. Light the work area well, and keep children and pets safely away from it. Take off your watch and jewelry before starting the job.

• Never work on the cables or wiring of the service panel. Entrance wires to the house may remain live even when electricity to the entire electrical system is shut off.

• Do not touch metal or any other material that may act as a ground when working on the electrical system; if a ladder is needed, use only a type made of wood or fiberglass—not of metal.

• Use only electrical units that bear a recognized seal of approval; look for the UL (Underwriters Laboratories) or CSA (Canadian Standards Association) stamp on the unit.

• Use only electrical units that conform to national and local electrical codes; if necessary, check with your authorities before starting the job. After working on the electrical system, have the job checked by a certified electrical inspector.

PROVIDING GROUNDING FOR AN OUTLET

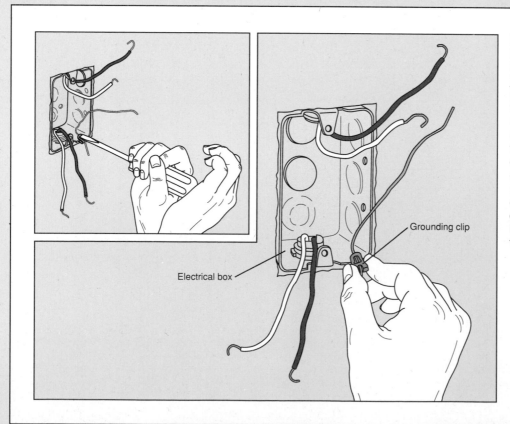

Electrical box

Grounding clip

Installing a grounding jumper wire. If there is no grounding wire in the electrical box of an outlet, install a grounding jumper wire. Buy a grounding clip and copper wire of the same gauge as the wires of the cable entering the electrical box at an electrical supply center. Cut a jumper wire about 6 inches long with wire cutters and thread one end of it through the grounding clip, then snap the grounding clip onto an exposed metal edge of the electrical box *(left)*. To secure the grounding clip to the electrical box, fit the tip of an old screwdriver in its notch *(inset)* and gently press it until the edge of the electrical box bottoms out against it.

MAKING TERMINAL CONNECTIONS

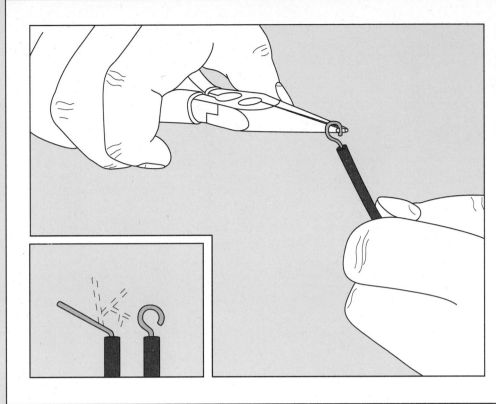

Connecting a wire to a terminal screw.
To connect a wire end to the terminal screw of a switch, light fixture, outlet or other electrical unit, grip it with long-nose pliers and bend it at a 45° angle to the length of the wire. Then, using the pliers to grip the wire end at the insulation, make a slight upward bend in it. Continue the same way, moving the pliers along the wire end to make one bend after another *(inset)*, until you form an open hook *(left)*. Wrap the wire end clockwise around the terminal screw, then use a screwdriver to tighten the connection.

MAKING A WIRE CAP CONNECTION

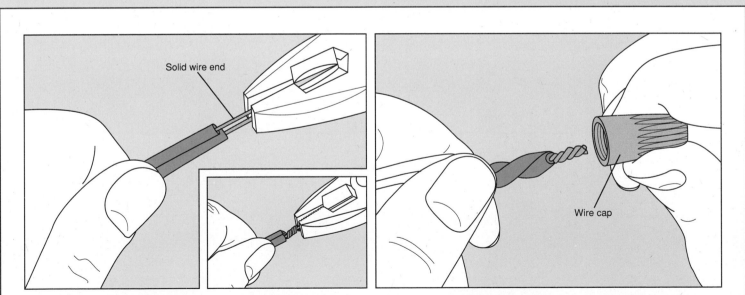

Solid wire end

Wire cap

Connecting wires with a wire cap. To connect solid wire ends, hold them side by side and twist them together clockwise with pliers *(above, left)*, then trim the twisted wire ends to a length of 5/8 inch using cutting pliers. For stranded wire ends, twist the strands of each wire end clockwise between your thumb and forefinger, then connect the wire ends the same way. To connect a stranded wire end and a solid wire end, use pliers to wrap the stranded wire end in a spiral clockwise around the solid wire end *(inset)*, then bend the solid wire end over it. Fit a wire cap of the appropriate size on the connected wire ends *(above, right)* and screw it on tightly; there should be no uninsulated wire exposed. Test the connection with a slight tug; if it is loose, remove the wire cap to reconnect the wires.

PATCHING SURFACES

PATCHING PRODUCT	CHARACTERISTICS AND USES
Wax stick	Available in wide range of colors to match most wood types Applied to small interior wood crack, nick or hole or set nail Can be sanded; accepts finish
Wood filler	Available in wide range of colors to match most wood types Applied with putty knife to large interior wood dent or gouge Can be sanded; accepts finish
Joint compound	Available in various formulations with different drying times Applied with putty knife to interior plaster crack or hole Can be sanded; requires primer before paint
Epoxy patching compound	Available in interior or exterior grade as resin and hardener that must be mixed together Applied with putty knife: interior grade to porcelain crack or nick; exterior grade to exterior wood crack, dent, gouge or hole
Roofing cement	Available in plastic-fiber formulation for metal roofing Applied with putty knife to exterior metal pinhole, crack or hole Can be sanded; requires primer before paint
Exterior-grade caulk/sealant	Available in silicone-rubber formulation in wide range of colors; in acrylic-latex formulation for painting Applied with caulking gun to exterior crack or joint

Choosing a patching product. Building supply centers stock patching products of many types and formulations; refer to the chart at left for ones typically used for repairs to an older house. Buy a patching product that is compatible with the material; for an exterior surface, make sure that it is marked for exterior use. If appearance is important, choose a patching product of an appropriate color and test it on an inconspicuous spot; or, choose a patching product that can be painted. Prepare the surface and apply the patching product following the manufacturer's instructions, observing safety precautions on its label; wear any safety gear recommened. Keep the label of the patching product for reference when another repair is needed.

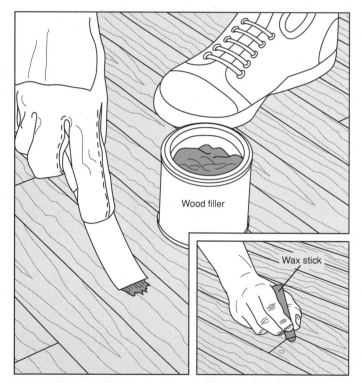

Wood filler

Wax stick

Patching interior wood. Choose a wax stick or wood filler of a color that matches the wood *(step above)*. Trim damaged fibers with a utility knife, then wipe the surface using a soft cloth dampened with mineral spirits and blot it dry. For a small crack, nick or hole, rub the tip of a wax stick back and forth across it *(inset)*, filling it level with the surrounding surface. For a large dent or gouge, use a putty knife to work wood filler into it and overfill it slightly *(above)*, then scrape off excess to level it with the surrounding surface. Sand the patch using fine sandpaper and brush or wipe off particles before applying a finish.

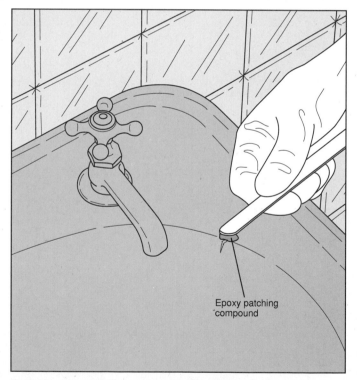

Epoxy patching compound

Patching porcelain. Choose an interior-grade epoxy patching compound of a color that matches the porcelain *(step above)*. Wear rubber gloves and work in a well-ventilated area to prepare the compound and test it. To patch a small crack, nick or gouge, work compound into it using a stick *(above)* or putty knife and overfill it slightly, then immediately scrape off excess to level it with the surrounding surface. Wipe up stray compound using a soft cloth dampened with mineral spirits and blot the surface dry. Sand the patch using fine sandpaper, if necessary.

REPAIRING MINOR ROT AND INSECT DAMAGE

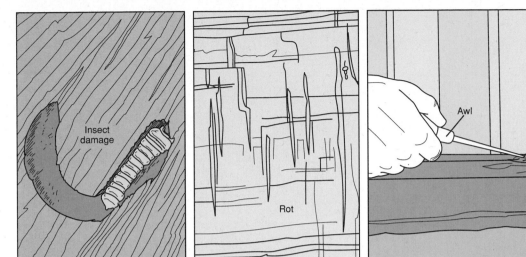

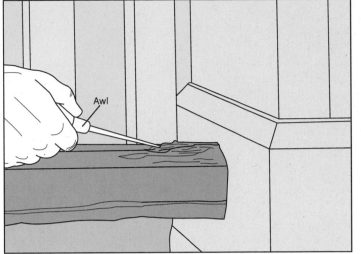

Identifying wood damage. To check for rot and insect damage, closely inspect wood exposed to moisture and wood near the ground; siding and roofing, exterior trim around windows and doors, and flooring around plumbing fixtures are especially vulnerable. Peeling or lifting finish, spongy or crumbling fibers and gray or dark discoloration are telltale signs of damage. If the wood is pitted or powdery, riddled with tiny holes or tunnels *(above, left)*

or supporting long, gray tubes, suspect insect damage and consult a pest control professional. Wood suffering from rot may be split or cracked *(above, center)* or show no visible sign. To test for rot, press an awl into the wood *(above, right)* and pry up the fibers. If the wood is soft and gives way, crumbling instead of splintering, it is weakened by rot. To repair a small area of rot, remove damaged fibers using a paint scraper and apply an epoxy patching compound.

REMOVING A WOOD FINISH

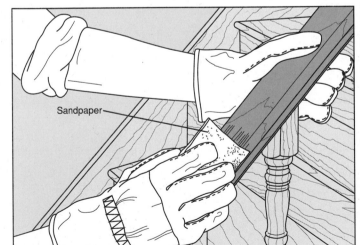

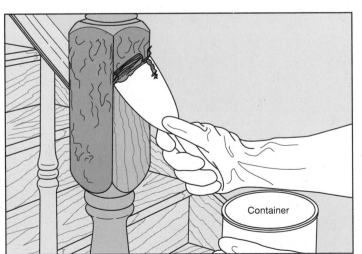

Removing old finish. To remove a finish from wood, sand or apply a chemical stripper. To sand a curved or contoured surface, wear work gloves and work along the grain using a folded sheet of sandpaper *(above, left)*; on a flat surface, work along the grain with a sanding block to ensure even sanding. Wipe or brush off particles before applying a new finish. Apply a stripper only in a well-ventilated area, wearing rubber gloves and safety goggles; use a gel type on a vertical surface to avoid drips. Apply stripper

along the grain with a paintbrush. When the finish starts softening and lifting, scrape it off: using a putty knife on a flat surface *(above, right)*; using fine steel wool on a curved or contoured surface. Collect finish and stripper scraped off in a metal container for disposal. Wash stripper residue off the surface using the solvent recommended and let it dry, then sand with fine sandpaper and brush or wipe off particles before applying a new finish.

IDENTIFYING A WOOD FINISH

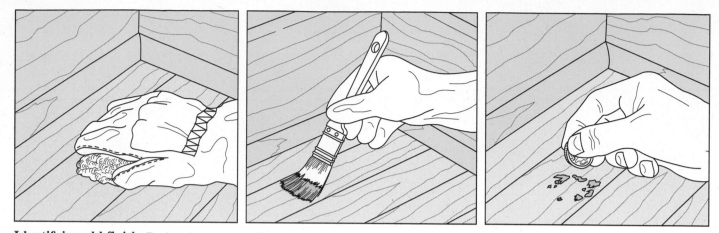

Identifying old finish. For interior wood, test for wax by scraping a low-traffic spot with a fingernail; if there is wax, the surface may be cleaned with a solvent-based wood floor cleaner. Otherwise, test for a penetrating finish by scraping with the edge of a coin; if there is no mark, a penetrating finish may be applied to the surface. If there is a white, powdery mark, test for a finish of shellac, lacquer, varnish or polyurethane. If finish dissolves when the surface is rubbed using a cloth dipped in denatured alcohol, it is shellac; if not and it dissolves when the surface is rubbed using a cloth dipped in lacquer thinner, it is lacquer. Otherwise, test for compatibility with a test finish of varnish or polyurethane. Roughen the surface slightly with fine steel wool *(above, left)*, then wipe off particles and apply a thin layer of test finish using a paintbrush *(above, center)*. Let the test finish dry, then scrape it with the edge of a coin *(above, right)*; if it flakes off, it is not compatible. If the test finish is compatible, it may be applied to the surface.

APPLYING A FINISH

FINISH	CHARACTERISTICS AND USES
Penetrating finish	Available in liquid; produces soft, deep finish Good durability if waxed; dries slowly Applied to interior wood
Shellac	Available in liquid; produces clear, gloss finish Low durability; dries quickly Applied to interior wood (trim, balustrades)
Lacquer	Available in liquid or spray; produces clear, gloss finish High durability; dries very quickly and difficult to apply Applied to interior wood (trim, balustrades)
Varnish	Available in liquid; produces clear, gloss finish High durability; dries slowly Applied to interior wood
Polyurethane	Available in liquid; produces clear, satin or gloss finish Very high durability; dries quickly Applied to interior wood
Wood stain	Available in liquid; produces semi-transparent or opaque finish Good durability; dries quickly Applied to interior or exterior wood
Wood preservative	Available in liquid; provides protection from moisture Very high durability; dries quickly Applied to exterior wood
Latex paint	Available in liquid; produces flat or semi-gloss finish Good durability; dries quickly Applied to interior wood, plaster or drywall
Alkyd paint	Available in liquid; produces flat, semi-gloss or gloss finish Very high durability; dries slowly Applied to interior or exterior wood or stucco; plaster or drywall
Aluminum paint	Available in liquid; provides protection from moisture Good durability; dries quickly Applied to exterior metal

Choosing a finish. Building supply centers stock finishes of many types and formulations; refer to the chart at left for ones typically used for repairs to an older house. Buy a finish that is appropriate for the material; identify an interior wood finish to match it *(step above)*. For an exterior surface, make sure that the finish is marked for exterior use. If appearance is important, choose a finish of an appropriate color and test it on an inconspicuous spot. Prepare the surface and apply the finish following the manufacturer's instructions, observing safety precautions on its label; wear any safety gear recommended. Keep the label of the finish for reference when another repair is needed.

APPLYING A FINISH (continued)

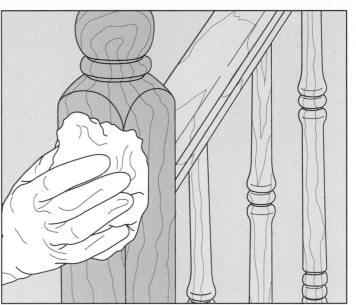

Using a paintbrush. Apply a finish with a paintbrush to a small surface—a stair tread or newel post, for example. For a water-based finish, use a paintbrush with synthetic bristles; for a solvent-based finish, use a paintbrush with natural bristles. To load the paintbrush, dip the bristles into the finish: for a penetrating finish or stain, coating half the length; for a surface finish, coating one third the length. Position the brush at the edge of the surface to be coated; on a vertical surface, at the top. Brush along the grain with a light, even stroke *(above, left)*, lapping back slightly at the end of it over the surface just coated. When the paintbrush starts to apply finish spottily, lift it gently to avoid creating air bubbles and reload it. Continue applying the finish the same way, overlapping parallel strokes slightly and smoothing any unevenness immediately. For a penetrating stain or finish, let it soak into the surface for the time specified, then wipe the surface almost dry with a clean, lint-free cloth *(above, right)*.

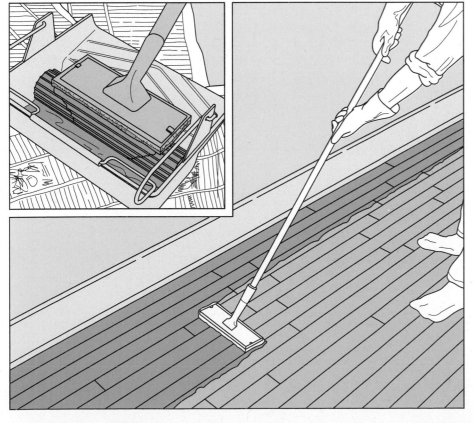

Using a paint pad. Work in stockinged feet to apply a finish with a paint pad to a large, flat surface—a floor, for example. To load the paint pad, fill the well of a paint pad tray halfway with finish and pull it across the roller *(inset)*: for a penetrating stain or finish, soaking it thoroughly; for a surface finish, wetting it. Position the paint pad at the edge of the section to be coated, then draw it lightly in one direction along the surface, parallel to the grain *(left)*. When the paint pad starts to apply finish spottily, lift it gently to avoid creating air bubbles and reload it. Continue applying the finish the same way, overlapping parallel strokes slightly and smoothing any unevenness immediately. For a penetrating stain or finish, let it soak into the surface for the time specified, then wipe the surface almost dry with a clean, lint-free cloth.

INDEX

Page references in *italics* indicate an illustration of the subject mentioned, Page references in **bold** indicate a Troubleshooting Guide for the subject mentioned.

Mortar, *131*
    Repointing, *24-25, 120*
Nails, *134, 135*
Newel posts, *88*

O-P

Outlets, *110-111*
Paints. *See* Finishes
Parquetry, *86*
Patching compounds, *138*
Pipes, **92**, *93*
    Cast iron, *94, 97-98*
    Copper, *100-101*
    Galvanized steel, *99*
Planes (tools), *132*
Plaster:
    Decorative trim, *73-75*
    Interior walls, *68-72*
    Textures, *130*
Plumbing systems, **92**, *93*
    Faucets, *93, 94-96*
    See also Pipes
Pocket doors, *43, 48-51*
Porcelain:
    Patching, *138*
Power tools:
    Drills, *134*
    Rental, *126*
Professional services, 14
    Electrical systems, 102
    Exterior walls, 16, 27
    Heating systems, 114
    Pest control, *139*
    Plumbing systems, 92
    Roofing, 29

R

Radiators, **114**, *115, 118*
    Bleeding, *117*
    Valves, *117, 119*
Rental tools, *126*
Replacement materials, 127
Repointing, *24-25, 120*
Rolling doors, *43, 48-51*
Roofing, **30**
    Cap and pan tiles, *29, 38-40*
    Interlocking tiles, *28, 36-37*
    Metal, *28, 31-33*
    Safety precautions, *128-129*
    Shakes, *29, 40-41*
    Slate, *28, 34-35*
    S-shaped tiles, *29, 37-38*

S

Safety precautions, 8
    Chemicals, 125
    Electrical systems, *10*, 104, *116*, 136
    Ladders, *127*
    Roofs, *128-129*
Salvaged materials, 127
Saws, *133*
Screws, *134, 135*
Service panels, *10, 104*
Shakes, *29, 40-41*
    See also Shingles
Shingles, *17, 20-21*
    See also Shakes
Shutoff valves, *94*
Skylights, *53, 64-65*
Slates, *28, 34-35*
Soldering, *101*
S-shaped tiles, *29, 37-38*
Stairs, **78**, *79*
    Balusters, *87*
    Handrails, *88*
    Newel posts, *88*
    Treads, *89*
Strike plates, *46-47*
Stucco, *17, 21-24*
    Mixing, *21, 131*
    Textures, *130*

T

Tiles:
    Ceramic floors, *90-91*
    Roofing
        cap and pan, *29, 38-40*
        interlocking, *28, 36-37*
        S-shaped, *29, 37-38*
    See also Slates
Tools, *124-125*
    Door jacks, *51*
    Drills, *134*
    Files, *132*
    Handsaws, *133*
    Miter boxes, *133*
    Molding jigs, *73*
    Planes, *132*
    Rental, *126*
Trims:
    Plaster, *71-75*
    Wood, *26, 76-77*
Troubleshooting Guides:
    Doors, 42
    Electrical Fixtures, 102
    Emergency Guide, 9

Exterior Walls and Trim, 16
Faucets and Pipes, 92
Floors and Stairs, 78
Interior Walls and Trim, 66
Radiators and Fireplaces, 114
Roofing, 30
Windows, 52
Trouble spots, *14-15*
Type-S fuses, *104*

W

Walls. *See* Exterior walls; Interior walls
Windows, **52**
    Leaded glass, *53, 61-64*
    Skylights, *53, 64-65*
    See also Casement windows; Double-
        hung windows
Wiring:
    Connections, *137*
    Disconnect units, *116*
    Electrical boxes, *105*
    Grounding jumper wires, *136*
    Knob-and-tube, *104*
    Light fixtures, *107, 109*
    Outlets, *111*
    See also Electrical systems
Wood:
    Clapboards, *17, 18-19*
    Finishes, *139-140*
    Floors, 78, *80-86*
    Patching, *138*
    Rot and insect damage, *139*
    Shakes, *29, 40-41*
    Shingles, *17, 20-21*
    Trims, *27, 76-77*

ACKNOWLEDGMENTS

The editors wish to thank the following:
B & S Electrical Supplies, Montreal, Que.; Bakelite Thermosets Limited, Building Materials Division, Ville St. Pierre, Que.; Mark Barrett, Montreal, Que.; Terry Birck, Reed Illinois Corp., Chicago, Ill.; John Boland, Chicago Plastering Institute, Chicago, Ill.; John Bonar, Follansbee Steel, Follansbee, W.Va.; Canadian Plumbing & Heating Supplies, Montreal, Que.; Marsha Caporaso, Abatron, Inc., Gilberts, Ill.; Cumberland Woodcraft Co., Inc., Carlisle, Pa.; Tony Dovell, Bangkok Floors, Philadelphia, Pa.; Marzolo Federico, Studio du Verre, Montreal, Que.; Brent Gabby, Brick Institute of America, Reston, Va.; Grant Hardware Company, West Nyack, N.Y.; Ashok Hingorany, Minuteman International, Fitchburg, Mass.; Donald Hooper, Vintage Plumbing, Northridge, Ca.; JGR Enterprises, Inc., Littleton, Pa.; Leonard A. Juliani Jr., Stewart Electric, Inc., Philadelphia, Pa.; John and Rusty Kent, Roofing Tools & Equipment Co., Inc., Wilson, N.C.; Ken Larsen, C. Howard Simpkin, Ltd., Montreal, Que.; Elliott Levine, Levine Brothers Plumbing, Montreal, Que.; Ludowici-Celadon, New Lexington, Ohio; M & S Equities and Fontana Developments, Montreal, Que.; Karl Marcuse, Montreal, Que.; Tom Martin, Rutland Fire Clay, Rutland, Vt.; Dante J. Martini, Superior Clay Corporation, Uhrichsville, Ohio; Donald Miller, Donald M. Miller Co., Uniontown, Pa.; Locations d'Outillages ERA, Montreal, Que.; NMC Decoration, Inc., Zebulon, N.C.; Bernard Pepi, Les Ardoises BDL, Montreal, Que.; Portland Cement Association, Chicago, Ill.; Quincaillerie Notre Dame, Montreal, Que.; Manon Ramaciere, Ramca Tiles, Montreal, Que.; Cedar Shake & Shingle Bureau, Bellevue, Wa.; Julie Reynolds, National Fire Protection Association, Quincy, Mass.; W. Creighton Schwann, Hayward, Ca.; Serendipity Antiques, Montreal, Que.; Solger Products, Montreal, Que.; Claude Taylor, Memphis Hardwood Flooring, Memphis, Tenn.; George Taylor Specialities, New York, N.Y.; Steve Tillotson, Great American Salvage Company, Montpelier, Vt.; Vintage Plumbing, Northridge, Ca.; Gilbert Wolf, National Plastering Industries, Washington, D.C.

The following persons also assisted in the preparation of this book:

Lousnak Abdalian, Philippe Arnoldi, Kent J. Farrell, Graphor Consultation, Shirley Grynspan, Jennifer Meltzer, Shirley Sylvain